CHEERS FOR
GREG MITCHELL'S
SPIRITED LITTLE LEAGUE® MEMOIR
JOY IN MUDVILLE

"Mitchell writes with wit and humanity. . . . He treats readers to an exciting glimpse of the psychological, emotional, and strategic considerations inherent in running a team."
—*Publishers Weekly*

"Part memoir, part sociology . . . funny, insightful . . . there's much for readers to like, whether they have kids in Little League or played it themselves [or even if they didn't]."
—*Baseball America*

"A wonderful, fatherly account. . . . Anyone who has coached or played Little League will smile with memories similar to those that Mitchell shares. And anyone who has watched a Little League game even while just driving past will be taken by this book."
—*The News & Record* (Greensboro, NC)

"Fascinating and delightful. . . . Thoughtful. . . . Well worth reading."
—*Winston-Salem Journal* (NC)

"[A] thoughtful account."
—*San Jose Mercury News*

"Fun reading by a talented writer who can analyze his role as a parent without losing touch with his inner child."
—*Booklist*

"A winning change-up . . . fine humor, genuine depth."
—*Seattle Post-Intelligencer*

Also by Greg Mitchell

Who Owns Death? (with Robert Jay Lifton)

Tricky Dick and the Pink Lady:
Richard Nixon vs. Helen Gahagan Douglas

Hiroshima in America (with Robert Jay Lifton)

The Campaign of the Century: Upton Sinclair's
Race for Governor of California and the Birth of Media Politics

Acceptable Risks

Truth and Consequences: Seven Who Would Not Be Silenced

Joy in Mudville

A Little League® Memoir

GREG MITCHELL

WASHINGTON SQUARE PRESS

New York   London   Toronto   Sydney   Singapore

This book has not been authorized or approved by Little League® Baseball, Incorporated. LITTLE LEAGUE is a registered trademark of Little League Baseball, Incorporated.

Copyright © 2000 by Greg Mitchell

Originally published in hardcover in 2000 by Pocket Books

All rights reserved, including the right to reproduce this book or portions thereof in any form whatsoever. For information address Washington Square Press, 1230 Avenue of the Americas, New York, NY 10020

ISBN: 0-671-03532-0

First Washington Square Press trade paperback printing June 2002

10 9 8 7 6 5 4 3 2 1

WASHINGTON SQUARE PRESS and colophon are registered trademarks of Simon & Schuster, Inc.

For information regarding special discounts for bulk purchases, please contact Simon & Schuster Special Sales at 1-800-456-6798 or business@simonandschuster.com

Cover design by Rod Hernandez; photo credit: © Tom and Dee Ann McCarthy/corbisstockmarket.com

Printed in the U.S.A.

For Jon Albert,
who was "one of the good guys"

ACKNOWLEDGMENTS

First, I'd like to thank the little people—Bobby Shantz, Freddie Patek, Joe Morgan, John Cangelosi.

I'd also like to thank everyone who made this book possible. First and foremost, all of the Aliens and their parents, not only for their performance (and good humor) on and around the field, but also for agreeing to be interviewed for this book. As Casey Stengel said, "I couldn't have done it without any players."

Thanks to my friends John Demeter, John Doble, and Peter Knobler—and my lovely daughter, Jeni Mitchell—for sharing their memories (of me). Thanks, too, to my sister, Susan, and my brother, Brian, for tolerating the baseball obsessions of my youth. Fortunately for them, they're at a safe distance today.

My wife is not so fortunate. I acknowledge that she is long-suffering but supportive and that she made some key additions (and deletions) in the final manuscript. And, of course, extra special thanks to Andy Mitchell, the real All-Star in our family, who usually comes through in the clutch. But Andy, beware—next time I'm making you pitch to Rocco.

I'd like to acknowledge many other local Little Leaguers who shared their views and life stories with me, including board members Rich and Joanne Apostle, Stu Baltimore and Brian Thomas; fellow managers Tom Gannon, Glenn Meyerson, John Miller, Dennis O'Neill, and Marty Schupak; and longtime Nyack base-ballers Pat D'Auria (father and son), Bob Giacobbe, Jimmy Kane, Dave Siegriest, Mike Witte, and the great Bob Wolff.

I'd also like to acknowledge that maybe Eddie Badger just had a bad year.

Thanks to Verne Becker for his helpful read of the manuscript. Others who've been involved with youth baseball, and somehow lived to tell the tale in books that informed or inspired me, include Jeff Burroughs, Vincent M. Fortanasce, Harvey Frommer, Bill Geist, Pete Gent, Dick Wimmer, and Rick Wolff.

My agent, Sarah Lazin, admits she knows little about baseball but despite that—or perhaps because of that—encouraged me to write this book. Paul Schnee, my editor at Pocket, guided the manuscript with a sharp mind and creative hand when he wasn't running off to Dylan concerts.

As it turns out, Casey Stengel was right—the trick is to "grow up without getting older." May we all stay forever young.

Everything in the following pages *actually* happened. The characters are real. You can't make this stuff up. Only a couple of names have been changed.

Baseball is fathers and sons playing catch, lazy and murderous,
wild and controlled, the profound, archaic song of birth, growth,
age, and death. This diamond encloses what we are.

—Donald Hall

1

It's opening night at Memorial Park in Nyack, New York, hard by the Hudson River, and already the Little League season is looking bleak. My Red Sox are trailing, my ace pitcher is getting bombed, and my son has already booted one ball and struck out in his only at bat. Even worse, our uniforms haven't arrived yet, so we are not Red Sox, but Braves, wearing faded, mismatched shirts from a distant decade. We do not look good out there, in any sense. In fact, we don't even look like we belong on this level. We seem young and small and inept, and appearances, in this case, do not lie. Our outfielders can't field. Our catcher can't catch and cannot peg the ball to second base, or even get it back to the pitcher half the time. Our only offensive weapon is the base on balls. Our only hit was a hit batter. We are, in short, the Better Dead Than Red Sox.

And the parents, all potential Steinbrenners, are already getting restless.

It didn't get much better the rest of the year for the team or its manager. We ended up winning two games and losing twelve, and got knocked out of the playoffs in the opening round. My son, Andy, age nine, barely lifted the bat off his shoulder the entire year and finished with a .155 batting average, which is bad, even for a pitcher. Comically, the only one who got injured was me—completing the 1997 season with a serious arm ailment from stabbing for wild throws.

A year later, however, it was baseball like it ought to be. Renamed the Athletics, we were surely the only Little League team in the nation with an extraterrestrial for a mascot—hence our nickname, the Aliens. We staged one impossible comeback after another; our battle cry was "Alien Resurrection!" This time Andy would play a pivotal role in the team's thrilling drive to the playoffs, and his manager/father, at a key moment, would deliver a stroke of genius that came to be called the Walk on the Wild Side.

This, then, is a tale of two seasons, the ridiculous and the sublime. It stars my "cardiac kids"—Matt the Bat, RBI Keiser, Little Stevie Wonder, Cool Taddy Bell, and all the rest. It explores the intersection of two baseball lives, manager and son, and how this produces both profound conflict and ineffable joy. More than that, it is a saga of all fathers and all sons, and baseball in our time, as America's Game enters its third century.

Andy is tall for his age, lanky, brown-eyed, brown-haired, good-looking. He adores his mom. Born in Manhattan, he now prefers Nyack. He's a typical pre-teen American kid, into Game Boy and *X-Files,* Old Navy and MTV, *The Simpsons* and *Austin Powers,* and hiking around our local megalo-mall. We don't let him watch *South Park,* but he knows every character, gag, and plot line through schoolyard osmosis. Yet his favorite book is *To Kill a Mockingbird,* his favorite film *Saving Private Ryan.* He's a talented cartoonist, and a movie maven. He plays electric guitar in a rock band called We Don't Suck.

I tell him, "Andy, if you say you don't suck, all the kids will shout out, 'Yes, you do!' Even if you don't."

"So we'll change our name to We Suck, then they'll yell, 'No, you don't!'"

"Don't bet on it." Little League and rock 'n' roll—this is how Bruce Springsteen started?

He's our only child, the male baseball heir of his father. That's
a lot of pressure, real or imagined. Not long ago the New York
Mets' top minor league prospect, Ryan Jaroncyk, quit baseball
entirely because he was sick and tired of getting advice from his
father—ever since Little League—and had come to hate the game.
He claimed, in fact, that he had *never* liked playing ball and had
only kept at it to please his dad, a former University of Southern
California defensive back. His mother, who had complained about
this for years, packed up and left, too, so Dad lost wife and son
within the same week.

Obviously there's a lesson there. I think of that story almost
every day during the baseball season, and my wife, Barbara
Bedway, also a writer, often points out similar ones. Barbara sup-
ports Andy playing Little League but sometimes feels his father
should not be so involved. She once cited the case of the Little
League coach in Illinois who got beat up by another coach after a
game, sustaining several broken bones, a lacerated kidney, and a
scratched retina. "Hey," I reminded her, "didn't he get $750,000
in a settlement?"

Fortunately our little family remains intact and Andy is still
playing ball, happily (for the most part). Sometimes, however,
Little League drives us apart—when it isn't bringing us
together.

The American Psychiatric Association recently sponsored a sym-
posium entitled "Youth Sports: Character Building or Child
Abuse?" During the rollicking 1998 season I would be accused of
both—in the same game. Youth baseball takes place in a cultural
milieu where fistfights between adults can break out on a ball field
filled with children. It's the kind of world where an umpire kicks a
twelve-year-old catcher out of a playoff game for not wearing a
"cup." The catcher was a *girl*. Coaches, parents, and league officials
argued about it for a week. Then the lawyers got involved. Only in
America.

• • •

Our disastrous 1997 season actually ended on something of a high note. In his first year of pitching, Andy had progressed nicely after recovering from a mid-season wrist sprain, an injury he'd earned sliding off a porch chasing a girl in a game of tag. My wife felt that, as injuries go, this one was almost worth it; until then, he had displayed an almost pathological aversion to the opposite sex. I pointed out that Andy had years to get involved with girls but would never have another rookie season in Little League.

Luckily, his interest in girls faded before his fastball, and he pitched well in the two games we did manage to win that year. At age nine he was holding his own against kids two or three years older. After he hurled his first win in Little League we retrieved the dirt-smudged ball, signed and dated it, stuck it in a plastic globe, and put it on a shelf, joking that one day we'd donate it to Cooperstown (or sell it at auction).

By the end of the year, as we headed into the playoffs, Andy was clearly our best pitcher. How did a 2 and 10 team qualify for the playoffs? Everyone makes the playoffs in our league. But Andy was no prodigy. He was still a below-average hitter and it was uncertain how far he would advance as a pitcher, since he's not especially fond of practicing. For better or worse, he's not one of those kids who *live* to play ball. When he grows up he wants to be Fox Mulder, not Nellie Fox.

Most games at this level are played down by the Hudson at Nyack's Memorial Park. Nyack is a community of about twelve thousand, counting Upper Nyack and South Nyack—the three adjacent villages known collectively as "the Nyacks." We're located twenty miles up the river from Manhattan on the west bank of the river across from Tarrytown, the historic Westchester town. From Memorial Park, you can gaze across three miles of spectacular river and admire Washington Irving's Sunnyside estate. He set his most famous story, "The Legend of Sleepy Hollow," nearby.

Nyack dates back three centuries to Indian camps and then Dutch settlements. Today it's a funky river town with a Main Street lined by fine restaurants, antique shops, and a new Starbucks. Some people refer to racially diverse Nyack as the Upper Upper West Side of Manhattan or, getting carried away, "Greenwich Village-on-Hudson." The boyhood home of artist Edward Hopper, it is still favored by slightly offbeat freelance types with moderate incomes—writers, jazz musicians, and movie and theater people who trek to New York City at odd hours or not at all. It stages one of the wackiest Halloween parades this side of, yes, Greenwich Village.

Decades ago, the town was perhaps best known from the song lyric about taking "a kayak to Nyack." It hit the headlines in 1981 when radical fugitives, including ex-Weatherman Kathy Boudin, robbed a Brinks truck at the nearby Nanuet Mall, then killed a guard and two Nyack cops. One of the getaway cars sped east down Sixth Avenue in Nyack and crashed into a high brick wall surrounding a fine Victorian home on the Hudson.

The house belonged to actress Helen Hayes. Now Rosie O'Donnell lives there.

Among others who call Nyack home are controversial performance artist Karen Finley; movie directors Nancy Savoca and Jonathan Demme; actors Ellen Burstyn, Dennis Boutsikaris, and Deborah Hedwall; AIDs activist Mary Fisher; authors James McBride, Lynn Lauber, and E. Jean Carroll—and Hall of Fame baseball announcer Bob Wolff. Susanna Styron, daughter of William Styron and director of the film *Shadrach,* recently arrived in town. It's the kind of place where a kid can go from headlining the middle school play to starring in an NBC television series six months later.

As it happens, one of my neighbors starred as Grizabella in the Broadway production of *Cats*. My neighbor on the other side is a graphic artist and first cousin of a famous pop singer. She bought the house from a fellow who made Broadway props. When he was working on *Titanic* he asked Andy (a *Titanic* buff, pre-Leonardo) to lend him some of his books and models. Walking up the hill in back of our house my wife often runs into an elegant, gray-haired woman who was Carson McCullers's psychiatrist in Nyack.

Karen Finley probably speaks for most when she says she moved to Nyack because she felt it was "integrated and progressive and had a sense of history and identity. It's not a bedroom community." The writer Toni Morrison has a house nearby and co-owns a soul food restaurant in Nyack. When a New Orleans eatery opened on Main Street it felt only right that the owner once played in the Neville Brothers band. Most of these people have raised one or more children in this area, and some of them have played baseball down there at Memorial Park.

Our local Little League, however, reaches beyond Nyack. If anything, it is dominated by players and parents from Valley Cottage, a distinctly different hamlet just up the road, populated by many fine people who are more conventionally suburban, and like it that way.

As the 1997 playoffs began, on a lovely June evening along the river, we sent Andy out to the mound for game one, and all he did was pitch a no-hitter for three innings. We were down one player because we had suspended our part-time catcher Victor for nearly coming to blows with an opposing batter in the previous game. Apparently Victor was still high from sniffing helium at a balloon booth at the school carnival that afternoon. He was the kind of kid who'd ask you for the score of the game, and when you told him 14–1, he'd inquire, "Who's winning?"

So, with his favorite catcher, Enrique, behind the plate, Andy was getting nearly everyone out, albeit with a few walks and errors mixed in. His mechanics still left a lot to be desired, but when he threw hard they couldn't hit him and when he didn't they stared at strikes on the outside corner. Just as miraculously, our team had managed to scratch out some runs and we led 3–0 going to the bottom of the fourth, which began like most of the previous frames: out, error, walk, out. Two outs, two on, and only two innings to go after this one. And then the next batter hit a little pop-up back to the mound. Maybe we were destined to win the playoffs, a Cinderella story in the making, the Red Sox riding the strong right arm of Andy "Kid" Mitchell! But while there was nothing wrong with his arm, his glove apparently still needed some work, for that infield fly fell from the evening sky and landed gently in his mitt—and just as lazily dropped out. Bases loaded, and still one out to go.

Fighting to keep his composure, Andy walked in a run, then gave up a hard grounder booted by our second baseman. Now it was 3–2 and it seemed prudent to get him out of there with a lead—and no-hitter—intact. Andy never shed a tear, perhaps the most remarkable thing of all. In came a new pitcher, who promptly walked a couple and gave up a hit, and we never recovered.

One more loss and we'd be out of the playoffs, and we started game two with Andy back at shortstop. It was a 95-degree day in late June, so hot we banished our kids from our uncovered bench and sent them off to sit in the shade under some trees. One kid took a nap between innings. Our pitcher hit two batters in the first inning, started hyperventilating in the second, and we lost badly. Well, it could have been worse. Andy might have hurled that last game and allowed ten runs, and then we'd have to think about *that* all summer, fall, and winter. Instead, he still had a no-hit string going—sure to last, now, for another nine months, at least.

• • •

Although our season had ended early, the playoffs rolled on, climaxing in a typical Little League altercation.

The Giants and Rockies would meet in a three-game series to decide the champion. The Giants, coached by a burly Valley Cottage fellow, were heavily favored over the Rockies, managed by a Nyack photographer. It was another hot day at Memorial Park. Starting in the first inning, from near the Giants' bench, the father of one of their players started heckling the veteran umpire on every close call. The ump called time and warned the father to cut it out, but the tall, muscular man said, essentially, "You and what army?" The Giants' manager claimed he couldn't control this guy.

So the ump threw the father out of the game (that is, out of the spectators' section). Easier said than done, without the aforementioned army. Finally, under threat of forfeit, the heckler promised to not say another word to the umpire—and spent the remainder of the game taunting *opposing players,* reducing some of them to tears. After all that, the Giants ground out a 10–5 win. When the Rockies' manager said he'd play the next day only if the league sent a board member to ump the game, one of the Giants' parents called him a "wimp."

The issue of adult violence in youth sports becomes scarier every year. Parents assault coaches with far more than words, and "Kill the ump!" no longer is an idle threat. In Riverdale, Georgia, a coach shot a father in the arm after the dad complained that his son was not pitching enough. A T-ball coach in Wagoner, Oklahoma, was sentenced to twelve days in jail for choking a fifteen-year-old umpire during a game. T-ball, incidentally, is a game played by five- and six-year-olds.

The majority of managers control their emotions—and a lifetime of sports frustrations—fairly well, but some believe in winning at all costs, leading to what is known as Little League Rage. In a recent article on this subject, *The New York Times* reported, "Adult misbehavior is becoming a familiar blight on children's games in all sports. . . . Fathers yell at coaches. Mothers belittle players. And umpires are attacked. Game officials have long taken verbal abuse, of course. But now they are shoved and spat on, even stabbed and shot."

The national umpires' association plans to offer members a new benefit: assault insurance. Still, it's getting harder to find umps to absorb threats and abuse for $15 to $25 a game. Youth leagues in Houston, Texas, now require background checks on all coaches. Some leagues have stopped keeping score to dampen competitive flame-outs. A league in Jupiter, Florida, recently became the first to *require* all parents to take a one-hour "ethics" course.

"Parents and coaches have lost perspective on what sports is about," an official with the umpires' association observes. Consider the following incident: A youth baseball manager in Boca Raton, Florida, was recently charged with disorderly conduct for "mooning" players and fans from the pitcher's mound after his team lost a tournament game. Witnesses said he stood on the mound, yelled at the opposing team, pulled down his pants, and exposed his back side. Then he turned around and did it again. He later told police he was simply bending down to pick up some caps and gloves. "I know my pants are constantly falling down," he explained. "My wife calls it plumber's butt." Good line, but it sounds like his upstairs pipes are leaking.

A couple of years ago, ABC News documented the climax of a typical Little League season in Hagerstown, Maryland, for a two-hour Peter Jennings special. Jennings wanted to find out "what makes Little League so exciting and occasionally terrifying." He certainly got his wish. The league's all-stars—one of them a very talented girl—advanced far along the road to a state title. Their manager admitted, however, that he was a "sexist" and didn't believe girls should be on the team or allowed to play Little League at all. "Girls should be cheerleaders," he affirmed. Another manager got thrown out of a game for arguing with umpires, then verbally attacked a league official, leading to a one-year suspension.

The ABC microphones overheard a parent tell his boy, after he struck out in a big game: "When you get home I'm going to get you tonight, because you let me down . . . I'll get you, buddy." Confronted with this evidence, the father told Jennings that sometimes his son gets lazy and he has to hit him. His wife, sitting next to him, looked forlorn, and told Jennings that she didn't agree with this philosophy. A viewer had to worry about what happened to *her* when she got home.

One player in the league, a talented catcher, gained a reputation as a troublemaker, harassing opposing players, umpires, and even his own coaches. "He's bad," his father told Jennings, "but not all bad." When the kid got passed over for the all-stars, Dad ambushed the manager, knocked him down and kicked him, then told ABC he was "glad" he did it.

And this all happened at the end of one season in one league.

Looking ahead to another season, I worried about violence, even in our relatively sane league, for I'd heard stories about local coaches and fathers going Duke City out in the parking lot after a game. Still, I could understand the attraction of winning. For me, the past Little League season could charitably be chalked up as a "learning experience." Mainly what I learned was that it is no fun to lose— all the time. Now what was I going to do? Tryouts, and coaching assignments, for the following year would be arriving soon.

For five years, stretching back to T-ball, I had coached with a man named Bob Giacobbe. Like me, he grew up as a Boston Red Sox fan, but *he* has not outgrown it. Bob attended Ted Williams's final game at Fenway in 1960. As everyone knows, Ted hit a home run in his last at bat, at age forty-two, dashed around the bases, and disappeared in the dugout without tipping his hat or otherwise acknowledging the cheers of the crowd. This seemed ungracious, but as John Updike points out, one can admire it as perfectly fitting, for Ted had long had a rotten relationship with the local fans and sportswriters. On a previous occasion, he had spit in their direction, so maybe on his final day they were getting off easy.

Anyway, Bob recalls that he and his father had cheered the final round-tripper with gusto, then turned gloomy when Ted failed to wave good-bye. "Why, that rotten son of a bitch," Mr. Giacobbe said. It was the first time Bob had ever heard his old man curse.

Perhaps that's why we always taught our Little League teams to have fun and not worry about hitting home runs. Most coaches say they don't care about winning, and all of us lie, but we rarely pushed the competitive buttons. This led to a mixed record over the years: finishing last in Rookies (when Andy was seven), nearly unbeaten our second year at that level, then last again with the Red Sox during our first year in Little League minors.

Winning is nice—for one thing, it helps get parents off your back—but I'd gladly settle for breaking even every year. I'd never had a chance to test that principle, however, for our teams had never been mediocre. So which would it be next season—all or nothing?

Co-managing a team seemed to suit me. I liked sharing the responsibility and felt I didn't have time to take my own team. Also, I questioned my teaching skills. I'd played a lot of ball in my life, including a few years in Central Park softball leagues, but frankly hadn't learned much from playing against Meat Loaf, Jodie Foster, or even Bruce Springsteen. I'd never instructed anyone, except my son, and didn't know much beyond the basics, such as putting the glove on the hand you *don't* throw with—that kind of stuff. My limits, as they say, were limitless.

Still, I enjoyed being back on a ball field and helping a few kids, while making sure that my son had fun and avoided playing for an evil manager. These are typical reasons dads coach Little League. (Even the lunatics don't want their kid playing for *another* lunatic.) Honestly, I did not fantasize about Andy going on to play college or professional ball—or his father piloting a Little League team to a national title.

Others, obviously, are a bit more intense about youth sports. No one carries it further than Bill Ingraham, who gained national attention recently when he built a ball field with major league dimensions in his backyard in Tewksbury, New Jersey. Ingraham had complained that his kid wouldn't go to the sandlots to practice fundamentals, like he did in his day. So he built a three-acre ball-park in his backyard at a cost of $75,000. Frankly, most Little League fathers would do this if we could.

If he had just let his son and a few friends fool around on the field—like in those good old days—Ingraham might have gotten away with it, but he couldn't resist inviting noisy adults to play there, too. When neighbors complained, and then brought legal action, he claimed that baseball, like puberty, is part of every boy's childhood and, therefore, unpreventable. A lot of locals sympathized with that, but then Ingraham stopped sounding like Dr. Spock, and started calling his critics "white trash" and homo-sexuals. Finally, a local judge ruled that he could stage full-scale games no more than once a month.

Up here, on our quarter-acre spread on the outskirts of Nyack, we don't even have a backyard big enough to practice a throw from short to first. Our yard slopes downhill in the rear, then snakes around one side, almost pathlike. We do our ball playing, such as it is, in the front yard, which is only about fifty feet across: barely enough room to throw some pitches and hit a few Wiffle balls or tennis balls into our neighbor's garden. Strips of dirt usurp the lawn around the "batter's box" and pitching rubber, which my lovely wife is not too thrilled about.

When it rains, puddles quickly form out front, then small ponds, and the exposed dirt turns to brown mush. "Mudville," we call it. Every year I assure my wife that I'll hire someone to re-sod the lawn when the season ends, knowing that midsummer is a terrible time to plant grass, so it never gets done. The dirt patches are now perennial—like our hopes and fears at the start of every Little League season.

2

Look at me
I can be . . . center field
—John Fogerty

It was a splendid Indian summer October afternoon as we arrived at Liberty Field in Valley Cottage to find it already teeming with anxious kids and parents. Bob Giacobbe, in a Red Sox cap, stood off to the side with the rest of the coaching brigade. As Mary Karr, author of *The Liar's Club,* said in a recent interview, "Coach Little League with a hat and a clipboard—you might as well be eight years old!" Since she's coached baseball herself, I presume she meant that approvingly.

Unlike Memorial Park, Liberty is considered a "real" Little League field. It was built in the early 1970s after the Village of Nyack refused to upgrade Memorial Park with bleachers, a concession stand, and lights for night play. The focus of local Little League shifted north to Valley Cottage, where it remains today. This seems unfair, since most Valley Cottage kids attend middle school and high school in Nyack. Yet it's fitting, since Valley Cottagers are more rabid about baseball. With a population just under ten thousand, Valley Cottage has fewer kids than Nyack but provides the league with most of its players, officials, and coaches.

A manager from Valley Cottage once told me that he never drafted anyone from Nyack because the kid's father "probably plays flute with the New York Philharmonic and won't take him to practice." He has Nyack pegged all wrong. More likely the kid's father is working on a screenplay.

The two Little League fields reflect baseball's standing in each community. Liberty has bleachers, enclosed dugouts, a snack bar, state-of-the-art lights, an electronic scoreboard, a public address system, and an outfield fence adorned with advertising signs, like the classic old stadiums. It's safe and quiet and tucked away from the suburban community.

Nyack's field sits in the middle of a busy village park. It's a lovely setting, overlooking sailboats on the Hudson, but leaves much to be desired as a baseball site. In fact, it lacks nearly everything found at Liberty Field. Advertising signs on the outfield fence? There *is* no outfield fence. Concession stand? A Good Humor truck will have to do. Spectators must stand or bring their own chairs. Dogs roam free in the outfield, dropping markers on the lawn. Games sometimes clash with band concerts emanating from the gazebo in deep center field. Foul balls threaten to bash toddlers romping in an adjoining playground. With no lights, umpires routinely halt play on account of darkness. Street people, partying above the field just behind home plate, sometimes add a certain . . . flavor to the proceedings, as boom boxes pound out rhythms and the scent of marijuana wafts toward home plate. Perhaps this explains some of the umpires' dubious ball and strike calls.

Memorial Park can amuse, it can aggravate, but it's also thoroughly *Nyack*.

As the tryouts began, some waited in line to get a number, others walked around, worried, squeezing a bat or ball in their hands. Their sons were nervous, too. They pounded their mitts or asked their fathers when they'd get to run on the field, tension so thick it made your head hurt.

This tryout was for both majors and minors, since their age range, nine to twelve, overlaps. I'd already decided to keep Andy in minors, no matter how well he did today, since he had three years of eligibility remaining. If Bob wanted to manage another year, Andy and I would sign on with him again. The alternative was to try to get a team of my own. Either way I'd still be in the dugout. Sometimes, however, I felt that Andy should finally go off on his own. It had to happen someday, and in my heart I knew that Bob and I were not the best coaches around.

Since I'd be coaching again next year, Andy didn't take the try-out seriously, knowing he'd make the cut. Still, we'd spent a couple of afternoons getting him back into playing shape after a long spell away from the diamond. In truth, Andy's never practiced all that much. At his age, I'd be out in the alley throwing a rubber ball against the side of the garage for hours every week. Andy doesn't even like to play baseball video games.

Back in my youth, as the son of an Eisenhower-era accountant and a housewife, I needed every bit of what novelist Philip Roth calls "the mythic and aesthetic dimension" that baseball gives to every boy's life. Andy needs that, too, but either he does not want it or baseball can no longer provide it. He loves baseball but, unlike me, then and now, he is not consumed by it. He rarely listens to a game on the radio and he'd rather watch *The Simpsons* than a Yankees or Mets game (unless they're in a hot pennant race). He's already bored with baseball cards. He can recite every movie Matt Damon has ever made but can't tell you which team Matt Williams currently plays for.

Willie Morris, the writer, once recalled the many afternoons his father hit fly balls to him back in Yazoo, Mississippi, before his dad would finally cry out, "I'm whupped!" With us, it's often the junior partner who calls a halt to practice. While I never force Andy to do anything, it annoys me when he's sprawled on the couch aimlessly watching women in their underwear on MTV, yet still resists taking a few swings in the front yard.

"You've got nothing better to do," I inform him, "and I'd swear you told me yesterday that you wanted to make the all-star team this year."

"Okay, ten swings, TEN." He really does want to make the all-star team, so he listens to reason, eventually.

Most kids today do not associate baseball with spontaneous fun. They mainly play in the spring at *organized* practices and in *scheduled* games. It's a long way from the days when a kid might put in a forty-hour week at the ball field while simultaneously holding down a full-time job as a student at the local grammar school (as Philip Roth once recalled). Nowadays, once the Little League season ends, kids have little interest in pickup games. Hardly anyone slips on a mitt and rushes to a nearby field to choose up sides; they'd rather jump in the pool, head to the mall, or play Nintendo. Deep down, their feelings about baseball are shallow. What this means is—when the kids do play baseball, *adults are always around*. It's a lot like going to school, or out on a date with a chaperone along. It stifles creativity, and produces players with little flair.

Long ago, my hero Will Rogers warned that one day kids might not go for baseball, "for it takes too long to learn it, and learn it good. It's a skilled game." Today, few neighborhood baseball diamonds endure—they've paved paradise and put up a Stop & Shop. Like a hero in the movies, the so-called baseball revival arrived in the late 1990s just in the nick of time—to save the sport itself.

Some of the kids at our tryout showed a lot of talent, but those skills would probably only take them so far. Not a single big league player has ever emerged from the Nyack/Valley Cottage Little League. Roughly 80 percent of today's pros played Little League somewhere, however. Braves outfielder Andruw Jones graduated from Little League in tiny Curaçao. Some things are universal. Sandy Alomar Jr. claims that Little League parents "are even worse in Puerto Rico than they are in the States. They will scream at the kids for whole games."

Mark McGwire hit a homer in his first Little League at bat. His parents were on a cruise to Mexico and missed it, but they'd have plenty of other opportunities. Cal Ripken Jr. shined his cleats after every game and sometimes wore his uniform to bed. Randy Johnson played *catcher*. "You just had fun," recalls Derek Jeter. "You didn't worry about making an error or striking out." (But then, *he* was Derek Jeter.) Chipper Jones recalls that there were only two teams in his hometown in Florida and the kids felt tremendous pressure—they all wanted to play for the Lions because they had snazzier uniforms. Hey, Chipper, it could have been worse. When writer George Will entered Little League in Champaign, Illinois, in 1949, he joined the Panthers, the Mittendorf Funeral Home team— wearing a uniform that was all black.

"I still remember it like it was yesterday," says Paul O'Neill. "I pitched the championship game and struck out a kid named Darren Waugh to end it. I remember every detail. The games then meant as much to you as these games do now. And you got to go to Dairy Queen afterward." Nolan Ryan recalls Little League fondly, as the first opportunity for kids in little Alvin, Texas, to get involved in any organized activity. Decades later, in his forties, still in Alvin, he had a chance to coach his own sons, but there was just one problem— "My career lasted a little longer than I thought it would." So his wife had to do it.

Although I never played Little League myself, I've always felt profoundly linked to it. You might say it's even in my blood. My mother was born and raised in Lock Haven, a central Pennsylvania coal town just forty miles west of Williamsport, the cradle of Little League. We often visited my grandmother there. The year I was born, Lock Haven sent a team to the first Little League World Series—this was 1947—and captured the title the following season.

A Williamsport native named Carl Stotz thought up the idea for Little League when he was still a boy. Playing right field, he grew bored one day listening to the other players constantly argue over close plays. He dreamed—so the story goes—of organizing a league one day, run by adults, where kindly umpires would make all the calls. Then he forgot about it.

Years later, his two nephews, Harold and Jimmy Gehron, ages eight and six, came to him complaining about being excluded from pickup games, or suffering the humiliation of being chosen last when they did play. Stotz, who worked at a sandpaper plant in Williamsport, recalled his earlier fantasy, a league in which any-one could sign up, learn the sport from grown-ups, and play on a real team. Adult supervision would, theoretically, reduce the number of arguments and bullying on the ball field. Now he added the concept of uniforms, well-kept fields, and parents in the bleachers. It was an ambitious idea in the Great Depression year of 1938. His nephews asked, "Who are we going to *play*?" And, "Who's going to pay for the uniforms and balls?"

The following year, a futuristic World's Fair opened in New York. *Gone With the Wind* and *The Wizard of Oz* premiered in movie theaters. The Baseball Hall of Fame inducted its first class in Cooperstown. And, with two brothers named Bebble, Carl Stotz organized a little league. He approached about sixty local compa-nies for sponsorship, and only three came through: Lycoming Dairy, Jumbo Pretzel, and Lundy Lumber. Carl managed one team, George and Bert Bebble the other two. The three teams would share eight fielder's gloves and a catcher's mitt. The bases: cloth stuffed with wood shavings. The scoreboard: a piece of slate and some chalk. Stotz kept fiddling with the size of the diamond, shrinking the dimensions to kid size, before arriving at sixty-foot bases and a pitcher's mound about forty-six feet from home plate.

Carl Stotz's fantasy evolved into Little League Inc. By 1950 there were more than eight hundred teams playing in twelve states, although it remained segregated in the South. Little League came to South Korea in 1951, then to Europe, and then much of the rest of the world. A team from Mexico caused a sensation in 1957 when it won the World Series, as an ambidextrous kid named Angel Macias hurled a perfect game. Starting in the late 1960s, teams from Asia, particularly Taiwan, came to dominate. Today, there are seven thousand leagues in more than fifty countries, and the Little League World Series takes place in Williamsport every August before a national television audience. Home base in Williamsport includes an office building, a museum, two stadiums, and five diamonds.

Carl Stotz is widely hailed as the father of Little League. Few know he was forced out as chairman of Little League Inc. in the mid-1950s after U.S. Rubber, which made Keds sneakers (and foresaw a lucrative new market in rubber baseball cleats), took over the franchise, replacing the father of Little League with one of their publicity men. Stotz considered starting a rival circuit and later lamented the commercialism that had come to Little League. He confessed that he felt a bit like Dr. Frankenstein. According to his biographer, he felt the league had become "so overly competitive that managers and even many parents had one objective—to win, no matter what the cost."

Little League keeps growing, with three million players and 750,000 coaches taking part today. Not everyone thinks that's something to celebrate. Baseball writer Murray Chass recently knocked the Little League World Series for giving Americans "the opportunity to watch the spectacle of twelve-year-old boys crying on national television" every August. Sports psychiatrist Ronald L. Kamm observes that Carl Stotz "changed youth sports forever" when he took a backyard game that had been played in splendid isolation by children, and burdened it with adults and "a miniaturized version of major league baseball." These adults, he adds, often "become so involved in their children's athletic lives that they take the fun out of youth sports." They forget that they are really only Carl Stotz's "invited hosts" in children's play.

As the tryouts continued, I realized it was going to be hard to judge the kids' overall skills because some of them hadn't picked up a ball in months. And due to the high turnout, they only had time to field five easy grounders, make five throws off the mound, swing at five pitches, and run around the bases. You can judge arm strength and batting power, but it comes down to: Do they *look* like ballplayers out there? Do they feel confident in their ability, or seem like strangers in their own skin?

As one kid followed another, the coaches stood along the foul line or sat in the dugout scribbling on pads like livestock judges. Some of the kids were just good enough to make you wish they were better. I graded them on a scale of one through five, and noticed other coaches doing the same, except most seemed to have multiple columns, perhaps judging everything from attitude to haircut (or was that the same thing?). I was just looking for kids who didn't flub balls hit right at them.

Baseball, you see, is like marriage: You have to "make the routine plays" if you want to earn more playing time.

After a scrawny kid kicked a couple of grounders, one of the coaches, a short, dark-haired guy, said, "Might take him anyway, his mother's awfully nice. . . ."

". . . Nicely built!" another coach chimed in. This woman, indeed, was in a league of her own, and this guy probably figured, *How much damage could her kid do playing right field?* Picking players based on their mother's looks, or marital status, is a youth sports tradition, even though I've never met a Little League manager who isn't married.

Then the first guy said, "I'll take Demme's kid, what's his name, Brooklyn? Great baseball name." Everyone chuckled. The director's son was only one year removed from T-ball.

You can observe a lot by watching, as Yogi Berra advised. Still, I felt uncomfortable standing there with the clipboard, judging kids like some sort of St. Peter of the sandlots. I told myself it was for their own good. Generous and wise, we would promote the worthy, and deny the unready rather than doom them to failure. Besides, I had to admit that I kind of liked the feeling of authority and control.

When a talented boy botched a couple of ground balls, my friend and fellow coach Mike Witte said, "Someone wants to pick him in the draft and asked him to miss a few on purpose so no one else would take him." A joke. Or was it? Considerable intrigue surrounds Little League tryouts and drafts. Mike had just mentioned one stratagem. In another, a manager asks a gifted kid, new to the area, to sign up but skip the tryout. So no one takes him in the draft—except for Manager Machiavelli.

Most of the black kids who tried out rated high marks, but it was shocking how few of them there were: about one in fifteen, although the district's profile is one-quarter African-American and Haitian. This seemed to confirm conventional wisdom that black kids today care mainly about basketball. Even the ones trying out for Little League wore basketball jerseys. So much has happened since the 1960s when black comedian Dick Gregory quipped that baseball was "very big with my people" because "it's the only time we get to shake a stick at the white man without starting a riot."

I had hoped to see a few more girls at the tryout, but only a couple showed up, and neither one earned more than a "2." Judging from this, one might conclude that girls haven't embraced baseball in the more than two decades since they've been permitted in Little League (after a prolonged court fight). Actually, girls *have* flocked to baseball, but they shun hardball in favor of girls-only softball. There are exceptions, of course, but Little League baseball remains nearly all-boy (past the lower levels).

High school softball continues to soar in popularity, with college scholarships there for the taking. Players, coaches, and parents nearly match the intensity of boys' leagues. In Virginia not long ago a father upset with a call threatened the ump with a handgun. This was in a softball league for girls ages eight to eleven.

As the tryouts rolled along, many of Andy's fifth-grade friends appeared shaky, heaving the ball to the backstop or flailing away at bat. They stood little chance of getting drafted (unless their moms looked like Madonna). Andy's old Red Sox teammate, Rocco, on the other hand, played very well, but anyone would be tempted to take him on the basis of his name alone. Bob Giacobbe's son, Russell, showcased a strong arm, which counts for a lot here, and slammed a couple of line drives.

Finally Andy's turn came. He fetched the first grounder—and promptly flipped it past the first baseman. Then he settled down and made the rest of his throws on the mark, if somewhat weakly. On the mound he showed more style than most, but didn't exactly pop the ball. At bat, he hit one liner, missed a couple, hit two hard grounders. He rated a "3" like so many others, but seemed satisfied, and so was I. He didn't embarrass himself out there (or was the whole point that he not embarrass *me?*).

A couple of managers had approached Bob Giacobbe after Russell's turn, presumably to find out if he wanted to play majors next year. After a wave of jealousy passed, I realized that with Bob out of the picture, I'd likely get a team of my own.

"Congratulations," Bob confirmed a few minutes later. "Looks like the team's all yours."

As we put our clipboards away, Bob suggested that I contact a father of one of the better players at the tryouts to see if he wanted to coach with me. This would secure his kid for my team—a typical Little League ploy. But I didn't know many of the top-rated players or their parents, and some of the kids might not even *have* fathers at home. Still, I vowed to make a few calls, come what may.

It was no longer "wait till next year." Next year had already arrived. And now I'd finally be able to say, like Alexander Haig, "I'm in charge here"—and probably get almost as many laughs.

But is that what I really wanted? Sparky Anderson once called baseball managers nothing more than a "necessary evil." Perhaps I should quit while I was ahead, as a father if not a coach. I'd quarreled with Andy from time to time on the ball field, but we'd avoided bad scenes and shouting matches. A chilling incident involving one of our local managers occurred when he coached his son, at age nine, in a lower league. They were squabbling over something in the middle of the diamond during a game, when the boy suddenly yelled at the top of his lungs, "You're a loser!" No one who witnessed this will ever forget it—certainly not the father, I'm sure.

Something else concerned me. From what I'd observed, I was just about the only manager in the upper levels of the league who never yelled at his players or the umpires. Could any team I managed win its share of games?

In the car on the way home I told Andy that it looked like we'd finally get our own team, if we wanted it. What did he think of the idea?

"It makes me a little nervous," he replied.

"Oh, being the coach's kid and all, I know that's hard."

"No, I don't mean that. I'm nervous about what *Mom* will say."

3

Once I knew for certain I'd be managing my own team I had to find a couple of assistants. I felt like a candidate for President at that awkward moment when he's won his party's nomination and has to pick a running mate. He hopes to select someone with experience—but not too much, or it will make *him* look inferior. He wants his partner to have an engaging personality—but not if it might make the number two guy more popular than him. Think JFK picking LBJ. Think Ronald Reagan choosing George Bush. Think about me trying to select a Little League coach.

Through the grapevine I'd heard that some of the other managers had already picked coaches and, big surprise, the fathers of most of the best players had already landed positions. In picking coaches you want someone who's good with kids and knows something about baseball, but just as important, you want someone whose son is an above-average ballplayer, if not a young Alex Rodriguez.

Most of the managers seemed to know this, although one of them, Eddie Badger, seemed lost in a fog. This was surprising since Eddie, by reputation, was very competitive coaching teams in the past. But now, every time I ran into him, he said he didn't have any idea who might coach for him, and didn't much care. "Just pick the teams out of a hat," he advised. Or, "Make all the teams equal some way." I was all for that, but this didn't sound like the Eddie I knew.

Since the other managers were already sewing up the talented players, I had to move quickly or start the season in a hole we'd never crawl out of. The Little League father I knew best was Bob Keiser, who'd helped out on the bench as a kind of bouncer the past two years, keeping the kids from hurting each other and batting more or less in order. Bob played some basketball at West Point (and has some good Bobby Knight stories). His wife, Arlene, often plays flute professionally with her father, the well-known jazz vibraphonist Dave Carey.

Their son, Robby, had emerged as a strong hitter near the end of the previous year, but the Keisers appeared ambivalent about his returning this season. An excellent student, and dedicated piano player, Robby had just taken up golf, and was not a huge baseball fan. That left Plan B. What was Plan B? I didn't have one. Or rather, it was Plan B from Outer Space: Go into the draft with no coaches lined up, and suffer the consequences.

At this possible turning point in my baseball career it seemed like the perfect time to visit the Hall of Fame in Cooperstown. If there is, indeed, a Church of Baseball, as Susan Sarandon declared in *Bull Durham,* then "the Hall" is surely its shrine. I'd long wanted to take Andy there, and now he'd played enough baseball to be ready for a little history, or so I thought. Cooperstown was suddenly hot, featured in two Pulitzer Prize–winning books: *William Cooper's Town* by Alan Taylor and Richard Ford's *Independence Day.*

Having read the Ford novel, I had some qualms. The book climaxes with the father, a former sportswriter, taking his moody teenage son to Cooperstown, attempting desperately to bond. They insult each other along the way and the trip ends in disaster right in back of the Hall of Fame: Father challenges son to a contest in a fast-pitch batting cage, and the kid, hitting without a helmet, gets smashed in the face by a ball and nearly loses an eye. They never do get around to visiting the Hall.

Andy was still reasonably sweet, but he was ten going on fifteen, if you know what I mean, so he might suddenly turn into a
sullen teenager somewhere on the road between Nyack and
Cooperstown. Still, we were primed for a pilgrimage. My family
took me there precisely at Andy's age, even though we spent most
of our time at the town's Farmer's Museum.

Of course, Cooperstown as the birthplace of baseball is a bit of
a crock. No one seriously believes that Abner Doubleday invented
the game there in 1839. George Will calls it a "sweet myth,"
pointing out that it would be more accurate to say Doubleday
invented the Civil War, since he was at Fort Sumter. One histo-
rian calls the birth of baseball at Cooperstown the "immaculate
conception." It makes a good, perhaps even necessary fable—
Richard Ford considers it "shorthand to keep you from getting all
bound up in unimportant details."

No one disputes the founding of the Hall of Fame, in the 1930s,
however. By the time I got there in the late 1950s, I was vaguely
disappointed in the place. From the outside, the brick Greek
Revival building looked more like a town hall than The Hall.
Inside it was growing as tattered and dusty as some of the balls,
gloves, and lockers entombed there. I didn't return for another
twenty-five years, on a one-day visit with my old college buddy
John Demeter, driving through a rainstorm to see the recently
refurbished Hall. Once again, it let me down. It was still mainly
about equipment and statistics, embellished with seats from
Ebbets Field. What was missing? I couldn't put my finger on it.
Maybe it was a son to share it with.

Now I'd take my third stab at it, this time with Andy—and,
once again, man/child John, who would drive in from Boston.
We'd spend a night and give ourselves plenty of time to soak in
the atmosphere.

Andy was pretty excited about it, mainly because it meant staying overnight in a motel far from home. And it was baseball with-

out the pressure to perform. He could just observe—although there was pressure in that, too. He probably feared he had to *appreciate* what he saw ("Yeah, Dad, Sandy Koufax was pretty awesome") and have a good time, too.

Not being an avid reader, Andy didn't know a lot of baseball history. He'd heard of Cy Young only because he has an award named after him. Eddie Mathews sounded like someone in Pearl Jam. Andy constructed a diorama for school recreating Lou Gehrig's farewell speech, complete with a tape recording of his actual words, but don't ask him about Mazeroski's Homer or Merkle's Boner. (I'd be afraid to even mention Merkle's Boner.) So he was a good candidate for instant boredom.

Look what happened when Mark McGwire first visited the Hall, and he was much older than Andy. It happened in 1984 when Mark was traveling with the U.S. Olympic squad. "I walked in the door," he recalled recently, "took a step or two, turned around, and walked out. I was a young kid, and I just didn't appreciate history at the time. I was more interested in getting something to eat in the pizza joint down the street." This sounded all too much like my son.

When we got there, after our five-hour, mainly bucolic, drive from Nyack, Andy seemed captivated by the small-town ambiance. He wanted to walk around for a while, and put the Hall on hold. (History, by definition, can wait.) Richard Ford had described the town's Main Street as rather soulless, but as recent inductee Phil Niekro put it: "There's a mystique about this town that I've never felt in any other little town I've ever been to. It's super-friendly. It's got the lake, it's got the hills, it's got the fresh air. It's got everything you want in a little town."

Not to mention the Hall. Ever wonder what Hall of Famers do when they visit? "I love coming back here, especially when your plaque's on the wall," Niekro explained. "And it's still there. I keep checking. You can't help it. When you walk in, you're going to go see if it's still there." Despite his three hundred wins, Phil's still not sure be belongs in the Hall, he *has to keep checking.*

Andy was amazed by the number of baseball-related shops, which sell everything from personalized bats to Cooperstown Cigars and Old Slugger Pale Ale. They even have baseball memorabilia at the local McDonald's. But he was most impressed by the fact that many of the "regular" businesses— drugstores, newsstands, bakeries—sold baseball stuff, old or new.

This almost proved hazardous to his health. One establishment, maybe a hardware store, sold unopened packs of Topps baseball cards from 1974, for $20. This seemed high, but one might score a Dave Winfield rookie card worth a hundred bucks, so my friend John splurged and bought the pack. We found no Winfields, nothing but Horace Clarkes. While moaning about that we noticed that Andy was chewing something. Sure enough, he'd palmed the petrified slab of pink chewing gum and put half of it in his mouth.

"Andy!" we screamed in unison. "Spit it out!" The pink shards flew out of his mouth as if someone had just done the Heimlich on him. Perhaps the gum was harmless, but we made him eject every last sliver, before we all collapsed in laughter.

I wanted to pick up an old baseball card or two myself, and where better to do it than Cooperstown? After scouting around, I spotted a '59 Willie Mays card I really wanted at a store called Mickey's Place. (I thought I was back at Disney World, but this store paid tribute to the *unwholesome* Mickey.) Well, I felt pretty satisfied with myself until I got out to the car and took the Mays card out of its plastic holder and saw that it had a slight crease near the bottom, making it worth about one-quarter its reputed value. I'd just gotten beat on a baseball card, in Cooperstown, no less! No wonder baseball was in trouble.

No way, after reading the Richard Ford book, was I going to suggest that Andy and I try the batting cages.

When we finally hit the Hall, Andy's spirits sank a bit. He admired the bronze plaques, and Ted Williams's bat, and Ty Cobb's cleats, and sat in Hank Aaron's locker, but never quite caught the spirit of the place, whatever it is. The museum now has something I'd craved on previous visits, a couple of machines that allow you to call up brief videos of Hall of Famers in action, and I spent a half hour checking out Bob Feller and Mel Ott, while Andy prowled the gift shop.

All in all, Andy liked the Hall okay and, unlike Mark McGwire, he did give it the old college try. But like most kids today he seems more comfortable in the commercial realm, and some of Cooperstown's baseball shops had historical displays that rivaled the Hall's. He had the most fun at a schlocky wax museum near the Hall. It was a hoot. Casey Stengel sat at a kitchen table staring into a crystal ball. Pete Rose flew overhead, suspended by wires, captured in a headfirst slide like a demonic Mighty Mouse. This, in fact, might be the closest Pete ever gets to the Hall of Fame. (Perhaps they should seat him at a *craps table* consulting a crystal ball.)

The next day on the way out of town we ignored a car museum that displays thirty-five Corvettes dating back to 1953, housed in a warehouse dedicated for some reason to Woody Guthrie. (I repeat—this is not a train museum.) We stopped instead at a strange roadside attraction with all sorts of rocks and minerals and reptiles. Andy bought a small red piranha preserved in Lucite. Well, I'll give him this, he got a better deal than I did on my Willie Mays card.

• • •

I failed to recruit a coach up in Cooperstown—John J. McGraw probably couldn't relate to today's kids anyway. Plan B, however, had finally materialized, but I'd have to move quickly if I was going to woo Richards Jarden to my crack coaching staff.

Through PTA at school we had met Richards and Pat Jarden, and they had become friends. Their son, Kipp, is a year ahead of Andy at school. We'd known Kipp as a swell kid, small and wiry but quick with a quip. He carried himself with confidence. But what kind of ballplayer was he? I didn't have a clue. He was one of the few twelve-year-olds who didn't make the majors, so how good could he be? Leaving nothing to chance, I called his former manager, who recommended him as a leadoff hitter who made contact, could take a walk, steal a base, and catch everything hit his way in center field. "But I hear he may not play," he added. This I didn't want to hear. Once past Richards, I didn't have another candidate for coach.

So I called Richards. I had no idea what kind of a baseball man he was. He's a soft-spoken fellow about my age, with a dry wit, and short blondish hair, who works as a restoration specialist (he's done projects for Ralph Lauren, among others) and designs embroidery. He belongs to the Nyack Boat Club and has the casual manner of a sailor, not a sports guy. Then again, who would peg *me* as a baseball nut?

Richards seemed flattered that I'd want him to coach, but he didn't know if his son would play. Friends were teasing Kipp about not making the majors. I assured his dad that I was going to try to draft a real "Nyack" team. And, by the way, Richards, what do you know about baseball?

He admitted he wasn't very baseball "literate." He'd played as a kid but not since, and didn't follow baseball much except at World Series time. But he'd always helped out with Kipp's teams in the vital role of "keeper of the book." This is the man or woman who keeps score and, more importantly, tracks the myriad comings and goings of players during the game. Well, every team needs a good scorekeeper, and Richards assured me that he'd help out in every way possible, although he admitted he no longer owned a baseball glove.

A few days later he called to say that Kipp had heard that some of his friends expected to ride the bench all year in the majors, so being a star in the minors didn't seem so bad. There was a Jarden house rule: No crying over homework—or baseball. Kipp should only play ball if he'd have fun and his mother told him she had a good feeling about this team. Finally, Kipp agreed.

Now things were looking up. I'd secured an ace scorekeeper, and I knew we had at least two good players on the team. Now all I had to do was find another competent coach (with a fairly talented son).

Andy's only baseball camp experience ever was a one-week summer program in a nearby town, and he didn't enjoy it. He didn't know any of the kids and most of them were older. Without my presence, he got stuck in right field, batted last, and often struck out. Despite this, I had signed him up for a mid-winter pitching clinic, a few Saturday morning sessions in a local gym—very low-key, lasting only an hour, with kids who were mainly a little younger. In January and February there was nothing much else to do and he'd at least get in shape for spring. It seemed like a compromise between doing too much and doing nothing.

Andy thought it was a fine idea, when it was months off, and my wife had agreed, with little enthusiasm. But now the first Saturday session had arrived and complaints filled our little cedar-shingled, 1920s Sears house on a hillside overlooking the river. My wife pointed out that it conflicted with an art class Andy had been taking. Andy also griped about the clinic, but he protests any new experience—such as, originally, the art class. Normally we handle it by insisting that Andy give it a try; inevitably he likes it and doesn't have to be pressured again. But this time Barbara objected, too, and accused me of pushing Andy into it.

"What's he going to get out of baseball right now that he can't get in March or April?" she asked, and this was a fair question. I should have answered, "Getting some exercise instead of sitting around the house watching coverage of the Lewinsky scandal on TV." (Andy was among the millions of American pre-teens who learned a few new X-rated words thanks to Bill and Monica.) Instead, I replied, "I want him to polish at least one skill." This, understandably, left her scratching her head.

"Andy has shown a certain knack for pitching," I explained, "and I don't have the slightest idea how to instruct him further. Pitchers are in demand because few kids master the mechanics and therefore can't throw strikes. And you don't have to be a great athlete. Who knows, maybe he'll find his niche. Pitching lets you be 'king of the day,' as Jack Kerouac put it."

Having lost his influence decades ago, Kerouac did not bail me out, and as our bickering intensified, Andy finally offered to go if I promised not to make him do it again if he hated it. Fine with me, but Barbara remained skeptical, suspecting that the laid-back guy she'd married was mutating into one of her worst nightmares, the obsessed father/coach. Little League now seemed insignificant next to a legal separation. Getting Andy to baseball practice would be so much harder if we weren't living under the same roof. And would his mom ever go out front and play catch with him?

After all that, we arrived at the gym only to discover that the first class had been canceled because the instructor broke his leg in a skiing accident. They'd have to find another coach, and weren't sure they could. Andy and I had a good laugh over that, both relieved, in a way, that pitching lessons could no longer fracture our family. A few days later we learned that the clinic would commence the following Saturday. We weren't out of the woods yet.

The first thing you must know about my wife is: She has never been a baseball fan. This may be the moral equivalent of Bill Gates's wife becoming a Luddite.

Now, we all know that baseball can be, well, a little *slow*. Philip Roth finds this something of a virtue, saluting baseball's "peculiarly hypnotic tedium." Red Barber, the great announcer, claimed that baseball is dull "only to dull minds." But my wife is fond of quoting someone else, namely her father, John Bedway, a former football star, who once likened baseball to "watching paint dry."

To which I usually respond, "Hey, have you ever *watched* paint dry? If you know what to look for, it can be fascinating. The streaks, the subtle shading, the way it catches the sun. . . ."

From the start, Barbara Bedway (or B.B. as I often call her) did little to hide her baseball apathy, and as it happened—as it was meant to happen—our first date took place on the opening night of the 1977 World Series, with my Yankees taking on the Dodgers. That first date had not come easily, so I did not take slender, raven-haired Barbara to a bar to watch the game, though it killed me. I had to catch the score on the streets of Greenwich Village as we walked, expectantly, to my studio apartment.

After we dated for a while, I paid her the supreme compliment: She was, I told her, a "better catch" than Willie Mays's famous grab in the '54 World Series. "What was *that?*" she replied. Poor Barbara. She would have to adjust to "the inescapable fact that baseball was going to loom very, very large in my life from now on," as she wrote years later in an essay entitled "Baseball and the Married Woman."

Barbara grew up in small-town Cadiz, Ohio (birthplace of Clark Gable), about an hour west of Pittsburgh. None of the males in her household—her father and two younger brothers—cared much about baseball. Her father had played football at the University of Cincinnati with his friend, future Cleveland Browns coach Nick Skorich. B.B. was a cheerleader in high school, but only performed at football and basketball games, never baseball, which suited her fine. She felt she "got" the other sports, but baseball baffled her.

As far as she can remember, Barbara never played baseball until she met me. Then she took part in one of my coed softball games in Central Park. First time up she hit a grounder to short and triumphantly slid into *first base*.

The highlight of our formative baseball years, however, came during the 1981 World Series, when we attended a game at Yankee Stadium on her thirtieth birthday. My friend Peter and his wife Jane smuggled a bottle of champagne and a cake to the upper deck in right field and, as we popped the cork, the row in back of us serenaded Barbara with "Happy Birthday." As years passed, in our retelling, that row became an entire section, the section became several sections, then the whole stadium, with the lyrics posted on the message board and her little cake somehow feeding half the upper deck.

Still, B.B. never really got into baseball, although she once interviewed Willie McCovey for a magazine article and found him charming. She loved to casually tell male friends, "Hey, I'm going to interview Willie McCovey," and then watch their jaws drop and hear them stammer something like, "YOU (of all people) are going to actually talk to . . . Stretch McCovey?!" She got a kick out of it, but then she'd ask me, "So what's the big deal with Willie McCovey, and why is he called Stretch?" I referred her to the *Baseball Encyclopedia,* the trunk-sized reference book recently given to us as a wedding present. ("Oh, thank you," Barbara had said politely, accepting that gift, "we don't *have* one.")

B.B. perked up again in the mid-1980s when, with some embarrassment, she followed the exciting Mets of that period, a team that featured the endearing "Nails," "Doc," "Mookie," and other Disney characters. She actually sat and watched entire innings on the tube, and sometimes even asked me, "Is there a game on tonight?" She was still awake and watching close to midnight when Billy Buckner let Mookie Wilson's ground ball scoot between his legs in game six of the '86 World Series. This behavior was so aberrant her mother suspected an *Invasion of the Body Snatchers* scenario, with me the alien who had turned her daughter into a pod-person.

"Barbara—YOU?" she asked.

"Look at what the game is really about, Mom," B.B. replied. "Endless variations on how to get home again."

Her mom thought it must be a passing illness, and she was right. For it was all over for B.B. when the dumb jocks started writing memoirs, and Lenny Dykstra bragged that he had never finished reading a book in his entire life, and Keith Hernandez started doing cartwheels naked in the locker room to scare away female reporters. Once the spell was broken, she became painfully aware of how long the games, and the season, last. My days of being able to listen to an entire game on the radio on a long road trip were over.

A few years later, however, B.B. blessed Andy playing Little League. At first, she often found herself at the mercy of moms who sat next to her at games and revealed more about the state of their marriage or the drugs their kids were taking than any near-stranger had a right to know. Now, when it's time to draft a new team, she requests that I choose a few kids based on the GHP (good humor potential) of their mothers, even if they're not terrific players. Sometimes I do just that.

Many times she has complained that there is too much of an emphasis on baseball in our house—me watching it and Andy (and me) playing it. Andy is a good student, but not especially diligent, so baseball can seem to be too high a priority. I understand this concern, but feel it's groundless, knowing that if he wasn't out front in "Mudville" batting a ball, he'd probably be watching TV, eating junk food, and getting on her nerves. And if I wasn't out there pitching to him, I'd probably be watching TV, eating junk food, and getting on her nerves, too.

With the winter draft rapidly approaching I had to find another coach, and Daniel Wolff came to mind. I'd ruled him out earlier because someone told me his son, Amos, didn't want to play minors again. Amos was only eleven but most of his friends were older and had made majors, so he figured he'd have no pals on his team next season. Also, I'd approached Dan the previous year with the same idea, and he'd said he didn't have time to commit to coaching.

Given my position, I figured Dan was worth another shot now. Amos was a big kid who was friendly with Kipp Jarden. Now that I'd recruited Kipp for the team, Amos might change his mind and play another year, especially with his dad as coach (unless, of course, that's exactly what he wanted to avoid). Dan was an interesting fellow. A few years back, he wrote the well-regarded biography of Sam Cooke, *You Send Me,* and I'm a big fan of Sam's gospel records. Long ago we both worked for antiestablishment music publications, *Crawdaddy* in my case, Dave Marsh's *Rock 'n' Roll Confidential* newsletter in his. But Dan has a movie credit—he had a cameo in neighbor Jonathan Demme's *Philadelphia*—and I do not.

Dan's wife, Marta Renzi, is a well-known dance teacher and choreographer. Her sister is movie producer Maggie Renzi, who is married to John Sayles, director of that fine baseball flick *Eight Men Out,* among others. As one might expect from his background, Amos has a creative bent, acting and singing in school musicals

and playing viola. (One day he may be a famous Amos.) When I
called his father about coaching, I told him Kipp was on the team,
with several other "wacky Nyackers" sure to join us after the
draft. Dan seemed amenable. He'd talk to Amos, and get back to
me. Later, I learned that he called Richards to check it out.
Richards told him: "Do it. We'll have fun." Dan then talked to
Amos, who said, sure, he'd love to play.

The core of an entertaining team was now in place, and I knew
we'd have a fine year—if I didn't screw up the draft which, of
course, was all too possible.

4

The computer revolution had finally come to Nyack/Valley Cottage Little League. For the first time, the league provided a roster of players eligible for the draft along with addresses and phone numbers. Yet the list alarmed me, for I realized I was unfamiliar with most of the players and only had my tryout notes to go on. And many of these kids hadn't even tried out. Former big league skipper Birdie Tebbetts once revealed a trade secret. "If you want to be a good manager," he explained, "get good ballplayers." I'd flown blind in the draft the previous year and vowed never to repeat that mistake.

The draft list was evenly divided between players from last year's minors and younger kids hoping to ascend from the International League, nearly all of them strangers to me. To rate them I'd have to draw on my professional skills—as a compulsive researcher. Mainly I wanted to know what kind of kids they were and what their parents were like, for I hoped to recruit enthusiastic role players as well as all-stars. It would be easy to contact the kids' parents, even if they were not exactly objective observers.

So I started calling. I have to admit to a bit of sexism here: If a kid answered the phone, I'd ask to speak to his father. If the father answered, I'd assume he was the baseball facilitator in the family. On the other hand, if a woman answered, I'd ask who handled Little League in the household. A surprising number of women

39

said they did. And some of the men admitted, a bit sheepishly, "Oh, I'm not involved with that, my wife is the one who does it." Most of these fathers were from Nyack, of course.

Introducing myself as a manager, I'd try to extract basic information, such as what positions their son played, without asking for any analysis. After winning their confidence, I'd ask, "Did he have fun last year?" This conveyed something positive about me—I cared about the kids having fun—while attempting to learn something about their family values. "Oh, he had a ball, even though he hardly played all year," one mother said. On the other hand, a father replied, "It's about fun? He hit great and his team won, isn't that what counts?"

Only after all that would I gently inquire: "Well, how did he play overall?" A few of the fathers—but none of the mothers—responded with brutal honesty, confessing, "He was just okay," or "He's really not much of an athlete—but that Chesterman kid, you ought to get him, he's good!" When your own father steers a coach to another prospect it's time to find a new sport, or another dad. A few of the mothers—but none of the fathers—cast such a rosy glow on Junior's achievements it was almost meaningless. "Oh, he pitched super and never made out," one woman revealed, "and he brought Powerade for everyone." (Sorry, Mom, we have an exclusive contract with Gatorade.)

A few parents admitted their kids had a bad year, but blamed it all on the manager. It was interesting to hear the parents vent, as if they'd been waiting for months to unload on someone about their son's cruel, disorganized coach who never let him play any position but right field. Others dumped more profound problems on me. One kid, I learned, was a foster child who'd recently been returned to his natural father. The foster mother was almost in tears, predicting that the father wouldn't bother to keep the kid in baseball. She asked me to phone the dad and, if it was true, to call back and tell her. And what would she do with this information? Go to child services? This was a little scarier than judging whether a kid knew how to bunt.

Many parents couldn't remember much, weren't even sure which league the kid had played in. Some of them had probably used Little League as nothing more than a baby-sitting service. All I got out of them was "He had a good year," which might mean nothing more than "He didn't get hurt," or "We didn't have to bring his coach up on charges."

Of course, my own prejudice came to the fore as well. I found myself calling mainly parents from Nyack. Part of it was simply that their kids would be easier to round up for practice, but there was an undeniable, unfair, cultural bias, as well. After all, when we left Manhattan in 1989, we could have moved anywhere in Rockland County, but chose Nyack. So we must be "Nyack types"—whatever that is.

Now don't get me wrong. I have nothing against Valley Cottage. It fits George Will's description of a "good community to grow up in": where Little Leaguers are allowed to play long after the local radio station has signed off for the night. Indeed, I know plenty of fine parents, coaches, and kids from Valley Cottage, but most Nyackers reflect a less, shall we say, *intense* view of sports.

In many ways the two communities could hardly be more different. These are not value judgments, just the way things are, and the way people in each place apparently like it. Nyack is denim shirt, Valley Cottage white collar. Nyack is thirty percent black, Valley Cottage three percent black. Nyack is bursting with liberal Democrats, while Valley Cottage leans to the right. Nyack has a tiny storefront video store, Valley Cottage has Blockbuster. One has Thai, Japanese, and Mexican restaurants, the other has Ed's Chowder House.

Certainly, there's plenty of overlap. Most of the kids mix in the schools without stress. But if you want a house with a big back-yard, away from Nyack's parking problems and weekend tourists, then Valley Cottage is the place for you. One Valley Cottage man-ager told me, with a grin, "We know what Karen Finley does with chocolate and we want to stay as far away from that as possi-ble." (In performance Finley sometimes spreads chocolate over her naked body.) Asked to describe the difference between the adjoining towns, he called his community "mainstream middle class" while Nyack is "artsy-fartsy."

Nyack, indeed, has long been an artsy enclave. Edward Hopper painted many local scenes (his boyhood home now serves as an art gallery on North Broadway). Carson McCullers moved here in 1944 at the age of twenty-seven and later proclaimed, "I love Nyack more than anything else in the world." At her home she entertained Arthur Miller and Marilyn Monroe, Gore Vidal and Truman Capote, and died in Nyack Hospital after a series of strokes in 1967. Helen Hayes and writer Charles MacArthur called their twenty-two-room Victorian overlooking the river Pretty Penny (because that's what they paid for it). One day they took F. Scott Fitzgerald up the Hudson by boat to have a look at Sing Sing prison.

The town's most famous eccentric was Dr. Pierre Bernard, the man who brought yoga to America. He founded the first yoga school in Manhattan, but preferred Nyack, organizing in the 1920s a kind of ashram centered around several dozen buildings, tennis courts, gardens, orchards—and an elephant house—on the hills overlooking the river (about a half-mile from where I now live). Thousands came from around the world to study Eastern thought and practice new breathing exercises. Locals called him "Oom the Omnipotent."

Nyack still appeals to slightly bohemian urban-dwellers with young children looking for a home with a (small) backyard out of the city, but not in a cookie-cutter suburb. When friends in New York City say to them, skeptically, "You're moving to *Rockland County?*" they tend to correct them—"No, we'll be living in *Nyack.*"

Soon after the Tappan Zee Bridge opened in the mid-1950s, as a lifeline to Westchester and New York City, the county's population doubled. Farms disappeared, and Nyack lost much of its business to the new strip malls out on Route 59. Shuttered storefronts pockmarked Nyack's once-vibrant Main Street. It even experienced a race riot in 1967. But after decades of decline, Nyack revived as an antiques and arts center in the 1970s, and housing prices soared a decade later (unfortunately, about the time we moved here).

In the late 1980s, celebrities discovered Nyack, and there were sightings of Madonna, Uma Thurman, and Geraldo Rivera looking at properties. Helen Hayes passed away, and Madonna's *A League of Their Own* pal Rosie O'Donnell bought her place. Rosie made Nyack a household name for about a week, via her talk show, when she repeatedly poked fun at the new Palisades Center that opened just west of here. She hinted darkly that the humongous mall was plunging into the old waste pit it rests on. She called it the Incredible Sinking Mall—but clearly, funky Nyack's fortunes are rising.

After taking a welcome break for a Bob Dylan/Van Morrison concert—the "Leave It to Geezers" show, as I called it—in New York, I continued my telephone polling for the draft. As I talked to parents, I kept hearing about a Nyack kid named Mark Downey. Several parents recommended him as a player, and his father seemed eager to help out at practices. Mark was an ace soccer player, but his dad promised there'd be no conflicts with baseball practices or games in the spring.

Then there was Stephen Albert, a nine-year-old who had played on our winning Rookies team in '96, a little lefty with a huge glove that seemed to have glue in it. He's nuts about baseball, a real Norman Rockwell throwback, but he was coming off a nearly wasted year in the International League. He didn't like the coach, and Stephen "needs a certain comfort level to play well," according to his mother, Donna. At least the manager let Steve pitch, and he did pretty well. It was that pitching experience, however slight, that caught my ear in talking to Donna. She even said the magic word, "strikes"—he could really throw them. You can never have too many pitchers, especially lefty relievers with swell parents. So maybe I'd take Little Stevie Wonder with my final pick.

My favorite dark horse prospect, however, was a kid named Gerard, who had recently moved to Nyack from California. His father, after getting custody of Gerard in a divorce case, resettled in Nyack to be closer to the magazine biz in Manhattan. He was a well-known photographer—fashion, travel, rock stars, the works. His new wife was French, also something of a novelty in our Little League. He said Gerard had played Little League out in San Diego, and was a tough out and fine fielder. For some reason I believed him. I wanted to believe him. Out in California the kids can play ball year-round so the quality of play is generally better. Gerard might be the real ringer in the draft, and no other manager was nuts enough to call so many parents, so no one else would know about him.

All the while, I was ranking kids on the word processor and moving them up and down on the draft list as I received more information. No, I did not "have a life," or rather, this was it. The alternative was to return to work—writing a book about capital punishment. Still, the draft was no picnic. It taxed my brain, and I had to ponder difficult issues. If I took too many pitchers, for example, it might be hard to justify pitching my son. Yet I needed at least two good hurlers so I wouldn't put *too much* pressure on Andy. Also, I hoped to draft a couple of Andy's friends, and one or two kids with appealing mothers for my wife. In other words, I wanted something for everyone in the family to keep them happy.

With most of the top players already off the board (because their fathers were coaching), the list of compelling first-rounders seemed thin. The kid who topped my list was another sleeper. A husky kid named Matt Scimeca had showed up at the tryout with a broken foot—from playing tag in the school yard—and had limped through a poor performance. He also wore glasses. Fair or not, he didn't look like much of a player. But his old manager, Mike Witte, told me he had a strong arm, and besides, he was a very "sweet" kid with a nice mother. I called his mom right away, to check on his foot. Vicky Scimeca said he was fine, adding that he'd attended the official Little League camp in Bristol, Connecticut, last summer and came home with great pitching mechanics.

This was almost too good to be true. Vicky mentioned that he was about to leave on a ski trip. Losing my mind completely, I asked her to call me if he came back with any new injury! I didn't want damaged goods. Fortunately, she laughed—a good sign, parentwise.

One player I'd really hoped to grab for our new team was our old catcher, Enrique Pabon. I loved just saying his name . . . En-REE-kay Pa-BONE . . . it was so musical. Latino catchers were thriving in the big leagues, from Sandy Alomar to Pudge Rodriguez. Enrique didn't have quite that potential, but he had the grit, the style, and he certainly looked the part: short legs, compact body, stoic but with some flair—take a picture of him and put it in a youth baseball guide under "catcher."

For many of us, the lingering image of a catcher is Pete Rose bar-

45

reling over Ray Fosse at the plate in the 1970 All-Star game, knocking him unconscious. Why do you think they call catcher's gear "the tools of ignorance"?

Now, it's true that Enrique had trouble throwing out runners, but unlike many young backstops he could catch a pitch that didn't bounce, and he "stoppeth one in three" that did. *Enrique Pabon won't you please come home?* Still, there was no guarantee that I'd get to pick him before someone else did.

It was draft eve. I drew up a final ranking, then changed it five minutes later, and fifteen minutes after that. Then I held a mock draft, guessing how it might go, but I had no idea where I'd be picking in each round. Needing additional useless information, I made a couple of late calls, then asked Mike Witte if I could stop by his place and swipe his notes from the tryouts.

His son Drew had made majors so Mike wasn't coaching minors this year, meaning he no longer had anything to hide. I hustled over to his place, about five minutes away in Nyack. Mike, an artist who has done illustrations for *The Atlantic, The New Yorker,* and other publications, lives in an old house so lovely it's sometimes rented for commercial photo shoots. When I got there, Mike was just finishing a magazine spread with a dozen sketches of celebrities. I was feeling like a caricature myself—of an obsessed baseball manager.

Mike's a real veteran of the Little League wars, and I often call him for advice. He has the relaxed manner of a professor but starts chattering when the subject turns to baseball. Growing up outside St. Louis as a Cardinals fan in the days of Stan Musial, Mike was only an average player and drifted from baseball until, as he says, he was "blessed with three sons." That means he coached nearly continuously for fifteen years. His oldest son, Griff, switched to tennis after Little League. "He'd had it with me teaching mechanics," Mike laughs, knowingly. But another son, Spencer, now stars on the Nyack High baseball team.

To help Spence impress college coaches, Mike took him to the aptly named Baseball Factory in Pennsylvania, where they put kids through drills, tape the results, and write evaluations. Mike knows Spence is up against daunting odds in pursuing a pro career. Only about one in a thousand high school stars even gets drafted by a pro team.

Mike believes that by learning the proper mechanics many average Little League players can surpass the naturals. He once showed me a shelf filled with video tapes on hitting, featuring Griffey and Gwynn and all the greats. "They always say Hank Aaron had 'quick wrists,' but they forget to say it wasn't just natural, it was something he did mechanically," he explains. Mike has made homemade tapes of sluggers' swings, and claims he's discovered secrets they try to keep to themselves, but when he tries to explain one of them to me, a Mark McGwire trick—"showing the knob of the bat" to the first baseman, or something like that—he loses me after about twenty seconds.

Mechanics give Mike something to focus on, besides winning, and he admits he needs that. (Talking to him I always think of the old rock group, Mike and the Mechanics.) During his early Little League years, in fact, he had some "bad moments," he admits, but he's calmed down a lot; as he observes, "I've had three chances to get it right, unlike most fathers." As much as winning, Mike takes satisfaction in seeing a kid blossom before his eyes. "One of my players in the minors, not much of an athlete, he hit a home run at the end of the year," Mike boasts, "but then missed third base! But I'm sure it's still a meaningful moment in his life, and that's what's important."

He agrees our league is low-key compared to some, but he says he's seen some "ugly" things over the years. One manager allegedly hired goons to settle a dispute with a player's father.

Another manager choked a parent after a game. In recent years, "there's often an undercurrent of hostility around the field, the threat of violence always there," Mike complains. Last year two managers who had been battling for years had a dispute over a makeup game, and one of them suggested they settle it in the parking lot. (It was starting to sound like the World Wrestling Federation—except not fake.) Another manager, in the midst of a tantrum, kicked a batting helmet that struck one of his star players, causing the kid's mother to briefly consider a lawsuit. Some managers "want to win the championship for themselves, with their kid as surrogate, and will do virtually anything," Mike observes. "I did a few questionable things, long ago, so I understand it well."

Going over Mike's notes on the tryout I was pleased to learn that they largely confirmed my rankings. From Mike I got a last-minute recommendation, a kid named Julian Del Campo, who played on his team the previous year. "I'm shocked he didn't make the majors," he offered, warning that Julian was thinking of sitting out the year rather than play another season in minors.

Finally draft day dawned. No word from Matt Scimeca's mom, so presumably he'd survived his ski trip intact. I phoned her anyway. Yes, he was fine. I also called the Del Campos, and they affirmed that Julian would not play minors while waiting to get called up to the majors. So scratch that idea. I went down to the computer and scrambled the rankings yet again. Then I printed out the list, shoved it in a folder with some of my notes, grabbed a yellow pad, and staggered out to the car, in a pouring rain.

My stomach churned as I drove eight miles to the volunteer ambulance station north of Valley Cottage that would serve as draft headquarters. Arriving ten minutes early, I drove past the site to an empty parking lot, turned on the overhead light and looked at my list a final time. After all that market research and rumination, I still had no idea who I'd take in the first round if Matt Scimeca was gone. One option was a tall kid from Valley Cottage who could really motor. Apparently he'd had a lot of practice— running from the cops. He also had a bully for a father. This put my values and priorities right on the line: How badly did I want to win? Not *that* badly.

Back at the ambulance station I found most of the other managers ready to start. Some had brought a coach to consult with, while I was riding solo. Eddie Badger had also come alone but appeared in no mood for male bonding. He seemed jittery, and asserted a bit too self-consciously that he didn't know any of the players and was simply going to guess. When I joked to the crowd, "Do we have to pick our own sons?" he bristled, as if this was directed at him and his kid. Clearly Eddie was feeling defensive already, and we hadn't even selected teams yet.

Steve Wanamaker, the minors' director, called the meeting to order. He's a big guy, who comes from a long line of local Wanamakers, and played football for Penn State under Joe Paterno and even made it to the Sugar Bowl. One of his sons is a high school star, the other the best pitcher in Little League majors. Wanamaker passed out a list of those eligible for the draft. Julian Del Campo was still on the sheet. I considered letting someone waste a high pick on him, but I finally announced that if selected he likely would not serve. Steve then assigned each of us a team name. I was delighted to get the Athletics—as a fan of the Bay Area, but mainly because I loved the green and gold caps.

Finally, Steve went over the list of coaches so we could cross their sons off the draft list. My jaw dropped when he revealed that Eddie Badger had grabbed Rocco's dad and the father of another stellar player. Rocco would likely be the best player in the league, and the other boy, Matt Reingold, wouldn't be far behind. That gave Eddie (who'd only been *playing* dumb) easily the best team on paper, so far. Fast Eddie—the name fit.

Then the key moment arrived: the picking of a draft order, literally out of a hat, or in this case, cap. When I unfolded the paper and read aloud, "Number two," I tried to disguise a sigh of relief. Matt Scimeca ought to be there that early! To even things out, however, each round reverses; so the team that picks near the top in the first round picks near the end in the second. So my first pick had better be good.

And thus we began. The fellow at my right, Dennis O'Neill, a congenial magazine publisher, consulted with his coach a bit too long. I could almost hear him whispering to his aide, "Scimeca . . . what do you know about . . . his broken foot?" He then picked another kid, a good little player, but thank God! Pausing to contain my excitement, I intoned, "Matt Scimeca."

No one said anything in response, indeed, no one said much of anything throughout the draft, no comments like, "Are you joking?" or "Nice pick—I hear he just got busted for assaulting his gym coach." No one wanted to tip off disappointment or risk offending anyone.

Badger had the next pick, and selected a kid who had some talent but was known for never swinging the bat—I mean, never. The next few picks went as expected, and now Eddie stepped to the plate again. "I'll take Del Campo," he announced, smirking. Everyone else hooted. "Mitchell's probably trying to pull a fast one," Eddie muttered, Nixon-like, looking directly at me. (In fact, I'd just written a book about Nixon and now realized that experience might come in handy this season.) Apparently he thought I was plotting to scare everyone off and grab Del Campo myself.

"Eddie, if you want to waste your second pick on him, go

right ahead," I said. "I'm relieved because that means I can now take Ian Rocker." He was a Nyack kid who'd skipped the tryout but came recommended by Mike Witte. The next round I grabbed Mark Downey, then crossed my fingers hoping that my sleeper, Gerard, and my catcher, Enrique, would go unclaimed. And so it came to pass, and I was able to take them with my next two picks.

As a bonus, I reeled in four more Nyack kids, including Andy's friend, Jeremy Safran. Then I selected John Marley, a smallish kid with great Nyack parents. At that, Dennis O'Neill exclaimed, "Darn, I wanted to pick him. Funny kid." He'd coached him last year, but I resisted blurting out, "Okay, you can have him." (Though I wondered, what does he mean by "funny"?) Finally, with my last pick, I grabbed Stevie Albert, and now I had my little lefty closer, the next John Franco.

At this, the draft ended and Wanamaker announced we could make trades if we wanted. But everyone was in a hurry to get home and notify his new players—one of the real pleasures, especially when you knew the parents, or the kid doubted he'd get picked at all. As we gathered up our yellow pads, Wanamaker told Eddie Badger he could pick another player for his team, the Tigers, if Del Campo didn't work out. Eddie exclaimed, "I bet I get him to play," then pointed at me and said, "This guy is sneaky."

What a way to end a good day. "What are you talking about?" I asked. "I spelled out the whole Del Campo story. I could have kept it a secret." But Fast Eddie would have none of it. "Okay," he replied, "I'll trade him to you—how about for Scimeca?" I had to laugh, but Eddie wasn't joking.

Driving home in the rain I still felt high, jangled, pleased with myself, overall. My scouting via Ma Bell had paid off, but something nagged at me. Maybe it was Eddie Badger's behavior, or his roster. He had a solid base with the two coaches' kids—and what if Del Campo decided to play after all? Even so, I figured my nucleus, with Amos and Kipp, was pretty strong, too, and Andy (and his mom) now had buddies on the team, so . . . bring it on! Opening day was less than two months away.

5

The day after the draft I called parents to inform them they were stuck with me as manager, and authority figure, for their kid over the next four months. Several didn't know me from Adam. Others said, "Aren't you that [crazy] guy who called twice last week?" I told them that virtually everyone on the team was from Nyack so we'd probably be a little flaky, but car pooling might be easy.

Fortunately, no one called to find out if I'd picked their kid in the draft. Nothing's more heartbreaking than telling a mom or dad that their precious angel got passed over by all the "judges." One year, the morning after the draft, a father called me from a portable phone with a poor connection. He was out on the balcony of a distant hotel and I could hear a rumbling not far away. He explained that a trolley was passing by.

"Oh, where are you, San Francisco?" I wondered.

"No, Bulgaria," he replied. Well, I guess the call was worth it, since he learned that, indeed, I'd selected his kid.

This year, when I talked to John Marley's mother, Betsy, she offered to be team parent, a thankless task that means helping the manager make phone calls, schedule team photos, and provide "volunteers" for concession stand duty. "Boy, the season is starting early," she declared.

"How's that?" I wondered. "I don't have a schedule yet."

"No, I meant, I saw a team practicing at Upper Nyack field this morning."

"You're joking," I replied. The temperature hadn't gone above 40 all day, with occasional snow flurries, which shouldn't have been surprising, since it was February 15. "Who was it?"

"No idea, but they looked too small for majors," she said. Could have been anyone, I figured, and quickly forgot about it.

When I called the Alberts to let them know their son had made the team, they were grateful, though Little Stevie grilled me about the level of play in the minors. Would he be able to handle fast pitching? I had no idea, but told him he surely could—an example of what Vonnegut calls the sweet lies that set us free.

Even if he didn't hit a lick, Steve would be an asset. He's my kind of player. With our Rookies team, at the age of seven, he was one of the few players who didn't constantly fidget on the bench, climb the fence, or squirt Gatorade at teammates. (One of the kids, a history buff, actually mapped out Civil War battles in the dirt.) Steve studied the game. One time he stood in the batter's box staring so intently at the pitcher he didn't hear us yelling instructions. Bob Giacobbe finally had to walk out, grab his batting helmet, and turn Steve's head in our direction to break his concentration.

His parents, Jon and Donna, suspected Stephen was a bit unusual when he started reading *Sports Illustrated* at the age of two in the baby stroller. People would stop and stare. At the age of three he demanded that his parents recite the backs of baseball cards, including the player's stats, as bedtime stories. His first words may have been, "Turn it to Sports Channel." He constantly asked his father to go out and throw the ball around, which Jon was happy to do. Jon's one of those rare Nyackers who actually grew up here—down the street from where I now live—and played Little League in town, with his father as coach.

The Alberts have a photo of Stephen at the age of four, wearing a Mets shirt, showing off his pitching form, his leg up and arm back—his mechanics already better than some Little League pitchers I've seen. He wore a glove his father had used in Nyack Little League. Jon's first mitt, in turn, was passed along by *his* dad. This baseball tradition was possible only because each of these Alberts is left-handed.

When Steve was assigned to our Rookies team, I had no idea who he was. One of his teammates was Robby Keiser, who lives across the street from him. When I'd told Robby's mother, Arlene, that Stephen was on our team, she exclaimed happily, "Oh, we have the Homeless Boy!" I didn't know what to make of that and, frankly, was afraid to ask. Then, over the next few weeks, a couple of other parents from that neighborhood said the same thing. Apparently Steve was locally famous—but for what? Abandoned by his parents at age five? Raised by stray cats and dogs in the field at the end of his street?

I finally asked Arlene about it, and she said, "Oh, everyone calls him the Homeless Boy because he's always outside on the sidewalk or in the street, no matter the weather or time of year, playing some kind of sport by himself." She'd first heard the expression at a party in Valley Cottage. A woman she didn't know said, "You live near the corner of Midland and Castle Heights? You must know the Homeless Boy." Steve would wear a Jets helmet and throw passes to himself, or swing a golf club, or act out Olympic events, or toss a ball up and hit it, always announcing a play-by-play in the wind. "*. . . Stephen comes to the plate, and there it goes, a game-winning grand slam home run into the upper deck, ROOOOARRRRR. . . .*"

People took note because it's so unusual for kids to do that these days. Usually they're inside zapping the TV or pushing Nintendo buttons. Neighbors, driving up the hill approaching Steve's house, would make friendly wagers, not on whether he'd be outside playing (a safe bet) but which sport it would be. In other words, he was a throwback—to me. That was *me* as a child. There were just more kids like me back then. And unlike me, Steve had another option—*he* could play catch with his father.

> *Baseball is continuous, like nothing else among American*
> *things, an endless game of repeated summers, joining the long*
> *generations of all the fathers and all the sons.*
> —Donald Hall, "Fathers Playing
> Catch with Sons"

My father played catch with me exactly once. It might have been 1960, I was about twelve years old, and we were up at our cottage on a small lake two hours from Niagara Falls. It was an overcast day, and maybe he didn't feel like hauling out the fishing tackle (fearing it would rain) or felt guilty, for once, about making me dig out the dirt basement. In any case, he suddenly appeared in the yard with the extra baseball mitt stuck awkwardly on his left hand. I got out my Eddie Yost glove and we tossed a ball around for a while.

Then it was over. Perhaps the phone rang or my mother called or he heard the fish jumping as the sky cleared. Afterward I sensed that this was a seismic event, and when I put away the glove and picked up the shovel I did it cheerfully, for a change.

Of course, it never happened again, although opportunities—hundreds of them—continued to present themselves. We went to the cottage every weekend during the spring and autumn, and for the entire summer, and I was usually outside throwing a rubber ball against the side of the house, *thud*, or tossing a Wiffle ball in the air and clubbing it with a plastic bat, *ping*. What was Dad thinking as he tinkered inside, outside, or under the house and heard those sounds? True, he was older than most kids' fathers, but he was lean, able-bodied (for an accountant), and not afraid of physical exertion when it came to digging out the cellar or walking up and down the hill to go fishing.

We never talked about why my father, who had few other major faults, played catch with me only that one time. This would long remain a mystery. But then, in my family, we did not discuss a lot of things. I don't recall ever complaining about it to my mother, who at least watched the World Series every year (to root against the Yankees), something my father never did. Perhaps I sensed it was a lost cause, knowing that my baseball career had already ended before it began.

For the die was cast years before, when we bought the cottage. I was an extraordinary sandlot player in Niagara Falls. It was a good time to grow up there, during boom times, the population swelling to more than 100,000. The local chemical industry percolated and tourists kept arriving in waves. Later this would all change as cheap air travel carried honeymooners to more exotic destinations and, thanks to criminal disposal practices, the city became best known as the home of Love Canal, a chemical graveyard.

Niagara Falls has a colorful history, of course, with daredevils crossing the gorge on high wires or conquering the cataracts in a barrel. It even contributed to baseball lore on July 2, 1903, when Big Ed Delehanty, a future Hall of Famer, a .346 lifetime hitter, plunged into the Niagara River in a drunken stupor and drowned at the age of thirty-five.

Since then, few players have emerged from Niagara Falls. One was Benny Bengough, catcher for the legendary 1927 Yankees. When I was growing up our claim to fame was Sal Maglie, "the Barber," closing out his storied career with the Dodgers and Yankees after an earlier stint with the Giants. The only big league player from my generation to come out of Niagara Falls was Rick Manning, who played center field for the Indians for several years—so I guess the odds of me making it were always slim.

Growing up in a neighborhood with 3.2 children per household, there were always a half-dozen kids to play ball with. We toiled in backyards, churchyards, schoolyards, junkyards. I'm not sure that I ever touched a softball or hardball. We used rubber balls, tennis balls, and rolled-up socks covered in electrical tape— "black sox," as we called them. Then some genius invented the Wiffle ball, and we used that.

Baseball was not something I did "after school." School was a way to kill time before playing baseball. Of course, I had Little League aspirations, which were soon dashed. With the purchase of our cabin, way out in the sticks, I'd be away from home when it mattered most, that is, spring and summer. (Why couldn't the general manager of my childhood have worked out a trade to another family? I wouldn't have minded being placed on waivers, or even getting my unconditional release.) I continued my practice routine up at the cottage—including playing catch with Susan, my obedient little sister, and my older brother, Brian—but now I had the tragic sense that it would not lead to Cooperstown, or even Cleveland.

For Little League was out. George Will, who calls himself "a born right fielder"—even beyond the political sense—once observed that a reason for baseball's appeal is that "we are all failed players." That is not precisely true in my case since I never really had a chance to fail. By the time I was old enough to stay home in Niagara Falls by myself on weekends, I was too far behind my peers to even contemplate trying out for an American Legion team or high school squad. Much later I'd play in Central Park softball leagues, occasionally with or against celebrities. That wasn't bad, but it wasn't hardball.

. . .

During high school I played for my church softball team—my closest walk with God—but during college my baseball enthusiasm waned. Partly it was the period, the late 1960s, and all the musical and political tumult that I embraced. In my circle, and many others, baseball was not "cool" anymore. Who could imagine Bob Dylan at a *ballgame?* (Little did we know he would one day write a song about Catfish Hunter.) Baseball was in decline across the country, as older stars, including my own Willie Mays, began to fade, and football fit the violent temper of the times much better.

When I moved to New York City in 1970, I thought that the baseball fanatic in me might re-emerge, with close proximity (at long last) to big league ballparks. But my colleagues at an "alternative" magazine with the whimsical name *Zygote* were thoroughly anti-sports. Then one day, the editor of the magazine, Peter Knobler, who had grown up in Manhattan, let slip that he was, of all things, a diehard Willie Mays fan. Finally I'd found someone else who agreed with Tallulah Bankhead—there were only two "authentic" geniuses, Willie Shakespeare and Willie Mays (and we weren't so sure about the Bard).

Peter and I bonded that day and have remained friends since. (He has gone on to write books with Kareem Abdul-Jabbar, James Carville and Mary Matalin, and Daniel Petrocelli, among others.) Like me, Peter had played a lot of ball growing up, often on asphalt, but missed out on Little League and rarely had a catch with *his* dad, a busy businessman. After suppressing our love for baseball in the counter-culture sixties, we were now free in the "Me" decade to indulge it.

While enjoying baseball as a belated Yankees/Mets fan, I still wasn't playing much ball, didn't even own a glove. Still, Peter and I had a tradition of meeting somewhere in Greenwich Village, where we lived and worked, on the first warm day of spring to hit and catch a few balls (barehanded). One year, on the morning after, a picture of Peter appeared in the New York *Daily News*, walking up Sixth Avenue with a bat over his shoulder, and the caption, "With warm weather a boy's fancy turns to baseball." Still a boy at twenty-seven! That's why we love baseball. But that's about as far as our ballplaying went. We didn't hang out at blue-collar taverns, so we didn't know anything about bar leagues.

Then it happened. It was early spring with an unseasonably warm weekend on tap. On Friday one of us said something like, "Gosh, we really ought to get out there and play a little ball tomorrow." We worked in the same office, editing *Crawdaddy* (the pioneering rock 'n' roll magazine), and obviously we were still kids at heart. We decided to invite a few friends to meet us the following morning at a small park off Hudson Street a couple of blocks from my apartment in the West Village.

Then reality set in: We didn't own any gloves, balls, or bases. When Peter got home he found a black wooden bat he had saved from a frat house fire in college. That was it. So we went out and bought new Wilson gloves and a couple of softballs. Now we were ready for re-opening day.

The next morning we arrived at the field, a few other guys showed up and we split into teams. As co-organizer I got to pick my position and chose my old church league spot at third base, with Peter at shortstop. (We would remain what Peter called "the solid left side of the infield" for years.) It was amazing to *play* ball after only watching and listening to games for so long. When anyone hit a shot over the left field fence onto Morton Street—where John Belushi lived—we'd call it "going uptown," toward the Empire State Building.

Now we were hooked and started playing, informally, every weekend. Since Peter and I were single at the time, we invited young women to join us, even though it sort of shattered the boyhood nostalgia aspect. Often we had to battle other, mean-looking, teams for the rights to the field, usually settling it by challenging them to a game. This being Greenwich Village there was often a bizarre edge to it. One time a squad of big, tough, gay guys, some wearing chains, literally wanted to fight us for the field. They were a bar team—perhaps the notorious Anvil Bar. Fortunately, the team manager, a profane guy in a clerical collar, showed up to restore order. We called him the Hoodlum Priest, and he could deal a pretty mean curve. They really "threw some leather" at us, but we beat them, and everyone went away smiling.

After that, we heard about a Central Park softball league that seemed only mildly competitive, so we paid our fee and joined. There were no uniforms, just T-shirts. We did pretty well that first year, finishing second, as I recall. Mitch Glazer, who went on to become a Hollywood screenwriter and marry actress Kelly Lynch, played a little outfield for us. So did Timothy White, now the editor of *Billboard*. Another teammate was the sports editor of the Communist newspaper the *Daily World*. Naturally, we called this fellow "Red."

> *He could throw that speedball by you*
> *Make you feel like a fool, boy*
> —Bruce Springsteen, "Glory Days"

Probably the highlight of our team's history came in 1976 when we journeyed to the swamps of Jersey to take on Bruce Springsteen and the E Street Band in a doubleheader. Bruce and I went way back—well, four years, at that point.

One of my few claims to fame was (with Peter) "discovering" Bruce, at least in the journalistic sense. We were the only writers to fall for an outrageous publicity stunt staged by Bruce's manager Mike Appel, before his first record came out. Mike had scheduled Bruce's first New York area gig since signing with Columbia Records at a big hall upstate—Sing Sing prison. We were suckers for anyone called a "new Dylan," and had never set foot in the pen, so we showed up. Lucky for us, no other writers did.

"Blinded by the Light" didn't go down too well in the Sing Sing concert hall (the prison chapel), so Brucie, dressed in a gray hooded sweatshirt, let the band riff endlessly on "Them Changes." In the middle of another R & B number, a muscular black con in the back suddenly leaped to his feet, ran down the aisle, and jumped onstage. I was about to see the Future of Rock 'n' Roll . . . knifed in the back! Instead, the con whipped a tiny alto sax out of his shirt and started wailing, giving Clarence Clemons a run for his money. The crowd exploded, and this was one audience you didn't want to get overexcited. Still, Brucie couldn't resist a risky little joke before playing his final number.

"When the assembly's over," he announced from the stage, grinning, "you can all go home!"

The cons might not have thought much of the white boy from Asbury Park, but we went back and wrote the first article ever about him, and we put his name on our cover even though no one had heard of him. Then we kept writing about him, helping keep his career afloat until his big breakthrough three years later with *Born to Run*.

Early on, when I visited Bruce at an upstairs apartment in Jersey he shared with a girlfriend, he took me outside on the street for a catch. It was only a rubber ball, but, hey, the kid could throw and go get 'em. Turns out, Brucie was something of a baseball fan— not in the sense of following the pennant races or knowing what year Joe DiMaggio hit in fifty-six straight games, but in a pure love for the game that he had played with great desperate joy as a kid. "Wait till I get you guys on the field," he'd tell us.

One evening we ran into him at a press party and told him we had an extra ticket for the annual Yanks–Mets "Mayor's Trophy Game" that night, and did he want to go? "Sure!" he boomed, and off we went, sitting behind the screen in back of home plate at Shea and having the time of our lives. By then, Bruce was battered by rock 'n' roll life—the darkness on the edge of town—but he was still a kid at heart when it came to baseball, with that innocent enthusiasm and high-pitched laugh he still displays onstage. He rooted for the Yanks, his team growing up in Jersey. "Would listen to Yankee games all the time on the radio," he said, "when I wasn't listenin' to Dylan or the Beatles."

He told us about his days in Freehold Little League, from 1959 to 1961, recalling specifically that his team was the Indians, and his manager a fellow named Fred Rowe. By the early 1960s Bruce had discovered Elvis, but at the time felt he had a better shot at making the American League than *American Bandstand*. Characteristically, in describing all of this, he was quite modest, not claiming too much for himself ("average player, man, but I had my moments"). He recalled daydreaming one time in the outfield and letting a ball fly over his head. Another time, he said, guys arrived at his house to pick him up for a ballgame, but he'd passed out on his bed after staying up all night playing guitar. Baseball's loss would be rock 'n' roll's gain.

That night at Shea he suggested we haul the *Crawdaddy* team to Jersey to take on his collection of backstreet Jersey "hitters." It finally came to pass on a golden autumn day in 1976. The E Streeters, who had invested hundreds of dollars in fancy gloves and pro bats, occasionally played radio stations and record company teams, and after one grueling contest, Bruce had uttered the immortal line, "The Thrill of Victory, the Agony of My Feet." He was now a big star, having appeared on the cover of *Time* and *Newsweek*, and we wouldn't see much more of him socially after this. But at least we had the satisfaction of sweeping the twin bill that day.

Bruce, as it turned out, played second base. This was surprising, since that's not the glamour position on the ball field—and
since he was "the Boss" he could play anywhere. One expected to
find him at shortstop or center field or pitcher, but apparently he
knew his limitations (good range, shaky glove) and really
wanted to win. He might have been born to run, but not make the
backhand stab in the hole at short.

Perhaps to distract us, Brucie started telling Polish and Italian
jokes every inning but always failed to finish them. His sidekick, Miami Steve Van Zandt (the future Soprano), kept things
loose. He heckled our hurler, who lobbed the ball to the plate in
a high arc, ordering him to "Pitch like a *man* . . . man." Between
games, Steve changed from a double-knit Yankees uniform into
his trademark Hawaiian shirt and Panama hat, and took a drink
out to center field with him. When a ball came his way, he took
one for the team—dropping the drink to dive for a liner (he
dropped that, too). Bruce, meanwhile, made good contact at bat
but grew frustrated as we pulled off several sterling defensive
plays against him.

The last time I saw Springsteen, a couple years back, he told me
he was playing a lot of ball with his son, Evan, who was then
about eight. Bruce thought he might coach the following year in
Little League, I presume in New Jersey, where he now lives most
of the year. Apparently his kid has a pretty good arm, though he
probably can't throw that speedball by anyone just yet. Father
and son are now so into it, Bruce once canceled a band rehearsal
so he could stay home and watch the Little League World Series
with Evan.

Not long after that he took his son to a game at Yankee Stadium,
causing quite a stir when he visited the home team clubhouse.
Bernie Williams, a noted guitarist in his own right, asked for an
autograph, and Bruce wrote, "To Bernie, if you ever get tired of

baseball . . ." Apparently Bruce didn't ask for Bernie's autograph, which I guess reflects the relative standing of baseball stars and rock stars these days.

Finally, Bruce pointed to long-retired Reggie Jackson across the room, and told his son that at one time he was "the greatest home run hitter in baseball."

"Really," his son asked, looking at the chunky, balding former athlete dressed in street clothes. "*Him?*"

The year after we played Brucie's band our team went into a funk—and not the musical genre, either. Then I left *Crawdaddy* and went solo, freelancing as both writer and ballplayer. For several years I played in a publishing league in Central Park, and fulfilled a lifetime dream of playing shortstop. I recall a game against *Sports Illustrated* when I leaped to catch a line drive, and later raced in back of third to catch a high pop near the line—the greatest inning of my life (but *SI* still did not put me on the cover).

Sometimes we battled teams with minor or major celebrities. Jodie Foster played against us when she worked at *Esquire;* she was quite friendly and a swell little hitter. Not long after she jumped into the Washington tidal basin with Congressman Wilbur Mills, Fanne Foxe pitched against us for *Screw* magazine. Naturally, we joked about sending her "to the showers." A memorable moment came in a game against *Gallery,* another skin mag, with porn queen Marilyn Chambers hurling. Marilyn, the former Ivory Snow girl, was still young and fresh-faced, dressed in short-shorts, with blond hair spilling out underneath her cap, and it was rather hard to concentrate on her pitches, but I did smack an easy serve into center for a single. I never reached home that game, so I was able to tell incredulous friends that I had gotten to first base with Marilyn Chambers but did not score.

Peter, meanwhile, had joined a more serious team, from the famed rock 'n' roll radio station WNEW-FM. They wore full uniforms, including *stirrups*. I tried out and made the team, but was relegated to the bench, on merit. Years of playing loosey-goosey had sapped my skills, and now I couldn't do much right (except pull hotheaded Peter out of fights).

My only "human highlight" play came when we faced a team whose star player was loud, rotund rock singer Meat Loaf, then in his prime. His teammates called him "Mr. Loaf," honoring *The New York Times'* stodgy name for him. Meat pitched and was quite good at it, but he was murder on infield pop-ups. Imagine hitting the ball high up over the mound and then hearing that bat-out-of-hell voice screaming, "I GOTTTTTTT ITTTT!"

One inning when I was playing short-center, Meat hit a clean single up the middle. Now, Meat did not . . . loaf . . . but let's say he was not exactly fleet afoot. For once, I fielded the ball cleanly and, noticing that this Meat was not traveling well, I fired to first, and he was . . . meat.

You can imagine what happened next. "AWWWW . . . *YOU'RE CRAZY UMPPPPP!!!* . . . NOOOOOOOOOOO!"

My baseball career almost had to go downhill from there, so following that season, I quit as a player, for good, hanging up my cleats at the still-tender age of thirty-nine. Ted Williams hit .388 when he was thirty-nine, but by now it was apparent that I would never be another Teddy Ballgame. The following year, however, Andy was born, so my baseball mitt wouldn't remain retired for long.

With the Little League draft over, I left for a whirlwind West Coast author's tour for my Nixon book with a satisfied mind, and returned ready for spring. Nixon's problem, by the way, was that he was an old *football* player, and never played baseball.

At a meeting for coaches and parents, I felt for the first time like an insider, a Little League V.I.P., as I'd worked my way up to one of the top twelve managing slots. Couldn't help it, I felt proud to walk up and collect my team folder, and green and gold A's uniforms, from our tireless league president Brian Thomas. Parents are always invited to these sessions to raise complaints or propose changes, but turnout is always poor. Of the more than four hundred families with kids in Little League, no more than one in eight ever attend, and the league has trouble getting people to run for the board.

Various reasons for this are offered. Today's parents are busy, especially on school nights, but many leagues seem to inspire more adult interest (often too much of it). Some, therefore, blame the alleged anti-jock culture of Nyack. Or you can look at the turnout in a positive light: It suggests parents believe that league officials and coaches are doing a good job and deserve little heat. The league has a good safety record, it appears to handle its nearly $200,000 annual budget responsibly, and few managers or coaches have been accused of physically harming kids, even if they may sock *each other* from time to time. When parents complain that the same core group dominates league affairs year after year, board members argue that few others are willing to put in the time.

At the close of the meeting, coaches huddled with their league directors for some final advice. A couple of guys complained to Steve Wanamaker that one of the managers had already held a full practice—the day after the draft, on a wintry morning. That had to be the Sunday morning practice John Marley's mother had told me about, and the manager must have been Eddie Badger, since he was the only one absent from tonight's meeting. "That just sets the wrong tone for the year, it's way too early. I'll have to talk to Badger about it," Wanamaker said. So Fast Eddie was already making waves.

"And guess what?" Tommy Gannon, one of the other managers, said. "Julian Del Campo showed up at Badger's practice." Eddie had gambled on Del Campo—and heckled me—and won? I knew I hadn't tried to mislead anyone, but now it might look like I did, and Badger would have the last laugh.

6

Spring beckoned, not necessarily a good thing for a free-lancer with too much flex time on his hands. I wasn't ready to practice yet, but I decided to have a team meeting so we could move decisively when warm weather descended. Besides, I was curious about our little Athletics community, so I reserved a room at Andy's school and brought along potato chips, cookies, soda, and spring water. Nearly the entire team, with parents in tow, came, so perhaps they were just as curious about me.

"Hello, Athletics," I said to break the ice, "or Athletics supporters, as the case may be."

Steve Albert, our youngest player at nine, was smaller than I remembered; so was John Marley, one year older. A couple others were stockier than I recalled from the tryouts. I was happy to meet my ringer from California, Gerard, a graceful, handsome kid with dark hair and delicate features. Matt Scimeca, my number one pick, looked like a star bowler—which, in fact, he was. But I knew he loved baseball enough to attend summer camps, and he'd tried out for majors in October on a broken foot. That showed me something. When I met Matt, I realized he'd played a key role in one of our two measly wins last year. He'd struck out on a 3–2 pitch with the bases loaded to end the contest. The pitcher: Andy Mitchell. Now they were teammates.

The meeting, from my perspective, went very well. I emphasized safety issues, claiming that no one on my teams had ever gotten seriously hurt, except one kid who fell out of a tree; this was sure to please the parents (I was already sucking up to them). As vaguely as possible, I promised that everyone would have "a shot" at playing every position and not get stuck on the bench most of the year. I insisted that we "just want to have fun," which should have set off alarms since this is what all coaches say and fun appears to be the last thing on their minds once the season begins. Of course, I was an exception (I told myself). But I knew that if we wanted to enjoy ourselves *thoroughly,* we'd have to steal a victory now and then. My goal was to win about half our games, play better as the season wore on, and go deep into the playoffs.

I also revealed that I planned to publish a weekly A's newsletter from my home. It's not an original idea, but I'd never heard of anyone in our league attempting it. (How many former magazine editors had ever managed a team?) Hell, I had the time, I had the computer program, why not bang out a couple pages a week to promote communication? Kids were sure to love the notion of a newsletter, even if they never read it.

As luck had it, the first 70-degree day of the late winter was forecast for the following day, so I announced that I planned to take Andy down to Memorial Park after school and if anyone else wanted to show up we could throw the ball around. In other words, I wanted to practice without anyone accusing me of holding a practice. As the meeting broke up, with good feelings all around, Gerard's father, the photographer, came up to me and brought me down to earth with the always-dreaded phrase: "My son is thinking of not playing."

"Yikes, why's that?"

"He's started taking aikido and he's so into it he doesn't think he'll have time for baseball." Rallying, I suggested Gerard show up for our unpractice the next day, figuring that surely he'd catch baseball fever again.

• • •

Fortunately, the forecasters had it right, and as Andy and I drove down to Memorial the next afternoon the river was ablaze with light. To my surprise, eight kids were out on the field already, five from our team, including Gerard. My first thought was: Nice turnout but I hope you loosened up your arms first.

John Marley had just arrived. He's about half Andy's size, but he's a floppy-haired, sturdy little fellow—a real Scots-man—and he cracked me up when I asked him to stretch before throwing. He went through an elaborate routine, pumping his arms as if asked to "make a muscle," but rapid-fire—like he was on speed—with his hands waving above his shoulders. Where had he learned that? From Hans and Franz, those goofy weightlifters on *Saturday Night Live*? At least his elbows got warmed up.

After that, I organized a pickup game, promising to do all the pitching myself. "You're stuck with me on the mound," I told them. "No one in the bullpen. I trained for this my entire child-hood, I just got to Little League forty years late."

John Marley, who probably didn't have the faintest idea what I was babbling about, had a question.

"Why do they call it a *bullpen*?" he wanted to know.

Naturally, I had no idea. "Because the relief pitchers . . . like to shoot the bull out there," I replied with a straight face.

"Shoot the bull?" Andy pondered. "And then . . . poor bull . . . where do they dispose of the body?"

I was getting into the spirit of it. "In the *locker* room, of course," I explained, as the two imps ran onto the field.

It was still the first week of March, and most of the kids didn't look so hot, at bat or with the glove. Playing first base, Andy fanned on a couple of throws, but Gerard was a revelation, hitting the ball hard and playing a very mobile shortstop. He could be the best player on the team, if not in the entire league. Best of all, it looked like he was having a ball out there, and when I drove him home afterward, I said, "So, you're going to play baseball, huh?" He nodded happily. I started making plans to shift my son from short to third to make room for Gerard.

A few days later, when I called Gerard's dad to tell him about our first "real" practice coming up that weekend, he announced, "I don't think Gerard will make it. He's going to quit the team."

"He had a great time the other day," I argued. "He can do aikido *and* baseball. You don't even use the same muscle groups. He can practice aikido between pitches at shortstop. These games can get awfully slow." I was making this up, but I was in a panic. "He doesn't have to attend any practices. Promise!" So much for equal treatment of all players. "Just show up in April."

"It's not that," he said. "He's upset he's not in the majors, he's too good for the minors, maybe." This was true, of course, but playing in the majors was not possible right now.

"Look," I replied, trying to sound calm. "The level of play is pretty good, and he'll start all the time, probably at shortstop, and he'll get a lot of hits, and be one of the stars of the league . . . and might yet get called up to the majors."

"I'm sure that's true," he said, "but I think Gerard just wants to concentrate on aikido for now. . . ." I wasn't ready to give up that easily, so I told him I'd wait for days—weeks!—to replace Gerard, to give him plenty of time to change his mind.

Well, at least I wasn't alone, facing a roster move. Julian Del Campo had been summoned to the majors at last. Now Eddie Badger, who'd wasted his second pick in the draft (as I'd warned), would have to find someone to fill his spot.

Over a couple of evenings, I visited the kids' homes, distributing our team uniforms. The gray pants often don't fit, and the shirts are nothing special, but the hats were an embarrassment: puffed up with foam rubber, with "Nyack/Valley Cottage Little League" on the front instead of even a team initial. Only the color of the hats, which vaguely matched your uniform, distinguished each team.

One day, at a local mall, I saw a really nice gold and green replica A's cap on sale for $7. If the store could sell it for that, they must get it for less, and so I visited my favorite outlet in Nanuet, a hole-in-the-wall baseball shop run by an old bird named Marty who used to sell stuff to New York ballplayers, such as Willie Mays and Monte Irvin, down on 125th Street in Manhattan in the 1950s. Marty manages to cram hundreds of discount gloves, bats, and jerseys into two small rooms, along with some memorabilia, but my favorite item is a machine (patent pending) that can pound a deep pocket into a stiff new baseball mitt. It's basically a metal ball on a bar that punches the glove over and over with a deafening growl, so you want to pick out your merchandise, plunk down your money, and flee Marty's in a hurry—if you can get him to cut short that Roy Campanella anecdote (but do you really want to?).

". . . and as I was telling Campy—we always called him Campy—"

Anyway, Marty the Maven looked at a catalog and said those neat A's caps would only cost me five bucks a pop. I figured this was a smart investment: Look sharp, play sharp. If I passed the caps out at the first practice it might bring us together as a team right away. And, who knows, maybe it would make the kids appreciate me (I was sucking up to *them*, too). Sixty-five dollars seemed like a small price to pay for all that.

With rain predicted for our first practice (of course), I rented gym space at our local "sports center" in Valley Cottage. It's a modest place, located in a long, low, brick building off Route 303, the hamlet's main drag, and includes half a dozen batting cages and two half-courts for basketball and kids' parties. Actually, I didn't mind the drizzle. It was sure to be a cool, raw day anyway, and now I could get the pre-season off to a good start in a warm, controlled setting without worrying about the kids' fingers turning numb.

To help plan an indoor practice, I consulted a couple of coaches' manuals, and surfed the Internet, where I discovered the Dickie Thon Literary Review, a web page devoted to Wedo Martini (who pitched three games for the Philadelphia A's in 1935), and an area devoted to Life Expectancy Among Nineteenth Century Players. Another site carries a long list of parodies of *Casey at the Bat*, including Ray Bradbury's *Ahab at the Helm*, and the Grantland Rice classic, *Mudville's Fate* ("Alas! The town's deserted now, and only rank weeds grow").

On the practical side, major league stars, such as Roger Clemens, provide mini-tutorials, and pro hitting and pitching coaches offer to turn your kid into a future star—if you'll just send along a few hundred bucks for a newsletter and nine how-to videos. But you don't have to be a pro to dispense advice. It seems like every manager only marginally more experienced than me has his own web site. "Hi, my name is Kyle, and I've coached Little League with my brother Hector in Upper Badhop, Missouri, for four years, and I'd like to share a few insights with you. . . ."

Some of the sites, such as Web Ball, are quite elaborate, with detailed diagrams of drills and message boards where you can post questions for the "experts." Many of the queries are quite good, even touching. One manager wrote that he had a nine-year-old on his team with fingers on one hand and stubs on the other. Should he teach him to bat "two-handed" or let him use one arm to swing the bat? The on-line coach replied that one-handed was best, citing the example of one-armed outfielder

Pete Gray, who played seventy-seven games for the St. Louis Browns in 1945.

But other questions are downright scary. One father wanted to know why, after he'd spent $5,000 on private batting lessons, his son (age ten) still couldn't hit the ball over the fence—on a consistent basis. The nerve of the kid! But thanks, pal, you just saved me five grand.

Having scanned most of the coaching sites, let me assure you: There is *no* final word on whether a pitcher should "push off the rubber" or a batter "release his top hand." Still, it makes for rewarding reading, as you realize that either no one, or everyone, knows what they're talking about (even me). I also enjoy the debates over which $220 bat to buy for your kid. Hardly anyone suggests this is an obscene price to pay for a baseball bat.

Fathers who survived Little League are also eager to advise you via the Internet. Even kids have their own sites and disburse batting tips. Some of them list their yearly Little League stats going back to T-ball. One kid claimed he'd hit .800 for three years straight. I almost e-mailed him to find out if he felt like relocating to Nyack and taking Gerard's place on our team.

One bit of useful advice I gleaned from the Net: Always carry a clipboard. It marks you as the manager, not just another coach or parent, and shows that you're well organized and know what you're doing, even if you don't. So I bought a new clipboard—green, team colors—and typed out a practice plan to clip on it, with notations such as:

12:40: Instruction on throwing
12:45: Throwing easy, then harder
12:50: Throwing from knee and sitting position

Fortunately, we only had ninety minutes, or I might have had them throwing backward between their legs.

. . .

Andy and I arrived for the first practice in high spirits. To com-
memorate the occasion, I decided to buy the team a new bat. The
sports center displayed many of the high-end models. Some of
these aluminum alloy bats are filled with pressurized gas (just
like the typical Little League manager) and "piezoelectric
dampers" to curb vibrations. These weapons can speed the ball
back at the pitcher before he has a chance to react. Due to a frightening rise in injuries to hurlers, the NCAA now restricts their
use in college games, and some teams are even returning to
wooden bats.

Bat manufacturers naturally oppose a return to wood. (There
aren't many ways to fancy up a wood bat and boost its price past
$40.) They claim they only want to make it easier for kids to hit.
"If you make hitting harder than it already is," a spokesman for
Louisville Slugger said, "kids will turn to soccer." Hey, they're
already turning to soccer. Maybe if they'd ban metal bats, and let
Little Leaguers wrap their hands around a nice stick of ash, kids
will do less kicking and more swinging.

Thumbing my nose at the new technology, I purchased a modest $45 green Mizuno model, and Andy cheerfully laid it out on
the basketball court with our other bats, bases, and batting tees,
and waited for his teammates to arrive. And waited. Fewer than
half showed up at the starting time, and they continued to straggle
in for another fifteen minutes. "Hey, guys, the meter is running
and it's my dime!" I felt like shouting. Instead, I remained Mr.
Congeniality, even as my carefully plotted schedule went right out
the window.

A birthday party raged on the adjoining court, with screaming
seven-year-olds playing volleyball. How do you offer "instruction
on throwing" over that din? Okay, guys, just hit a Wiffle ball off
the tee for a while. Except few of them could do it. They kept
smashing the plastic tube below the ball, sending it flying. When

the coaches got tired of reassembling the damn thing, we moved on to something else.

Following on-line coaching hints, I tried to make the practice fun, with a relay race and a brief intrasquad game, but the highlight of the day came in handing out the A's caps. As I'd hoped, the kids were thrilled, and they did look sharp and now seemed like a real team, even if they couldn't smack a plastic ball off a tee.

Finally following my advice, Andy and his friends had dropped We Don't Suck as the name of their rock band. It was sure to provoke heckling, so they replaced it with We Five, which was not likely to inspire a response any stronger than "huh?" If they'd known that a folk-rock group by that name briefly rose to fame in the much-despised 1960s with the hit "You Were on My Mind" they surely would have rejected it. We Five was okay for a week, but then one of the band members dropped out. This drove them into a tizzy over a new name; why We Four wasn't as good as We Five no one could explain.

It was an odd little group anyway. For starters, no one wanted to sing, even when they got sick of playing instrumentals. They had a terrific violin player, but he played keyboards in the band (and they already had an excellent keyboard player). My son was clearly the best guitarist, but he often handed over solos to his good friend, Casey, who was the best drummer—but did not drum with the band. That was Quentin's job. Practices therefore were always held in Quentin's basement. At that age you go where the drum set leads you.

Andy sometimes has trouble asserting himself, though never with a ball in his hand on the mound. Sometimes it's just a matter of being a nice kid. After all, he has already appeared in *The New York Times* in an article headlined: "Savings From Allowance Helps Boy, 9, To Aid Needy." It explained how this kid from Nyack, on visits to Manhattan, hated to see people "living inside boxes," so he'd asked his mother to send the newspaper's Neediest Cases fund $20 from his savings. I was proud of him, despite feeling jealous; he'd made the *Times* at a far younger age than I did.

But other times with Andy it's just low confidence. Sometimes, when he chooses MTV over batting practice, he seems lazy, but perhaps he's just afraid of going out there and hitting poorly—even if it doesn't bother *me*. If he emerges today and smashes line drives all over the yard, he'll volunteer to try again tomorrow; but if he has a tough day, he'll resist for a month. As I've pointed out to him, this may be human nature, and certainly his nature, but it's also self-defeating, for if he's doing badly at something he needs more, not less, practice.

It's not just baseball; he acts the same way with some of his schoolwork. Like most kids, he's anxious for positive results, *now*. This puts parents in a tough spot. We don't want to make our children practice more, or hire homework tutors, especially when the kids protest. It can lead to bad feelings—and little improvement. But if you do make that extra push it may produce a "breakthrough" for the kid; success, in turn, breeds enthusiasm *and* enjoyment. Yet how likely does such a positive result appear, in advance? It's far easier to write off your kid as just an "average player" or "average student" who "does not apply himself."

Andy wants to be a better ballplayer, even sometimes asserts that he (still) wants to grow up to be a big leaguer, but that desire does not burn bright and I will stoke it only so much. Which is okay, believe me . . . so long as he continues to give baseball a fair shot—for as long as *he* chooses to play it.

Honestly, I'd be just as happy if he became another Eric Clapton. Okay, maybe that's setting too high a standard, so let's say . . . Neil Young. Andy practices regularly on his Les Paul guitar and appears committed to it, but here, as with baseball, I'm worried he won't keep at it or try to be the best-he-can-be. It's easier to simply listen to music (or "watch" it on TV) than play it.

With that in mind I found myself intervening in the weekly band rehearsals, hanging around the periphery (like girls will do, eventually), while suggesting changes in the instrumental lineup and the repertoire. "Look," I advised, "I know you like Third Eye Blind, but their songs are too hard for you to play right now, you ought to start, like everyone else does, with 'Louie Louie' or 'Wild Thing' or even 'Sunshine of Your Love.'"

"Oh, that's sixties stuff, probably *Bob Dylan,* forget it," the band's spokesman replied, then played a harsh E minor chord on guitar, giving me additional feedback, as it were. The spokesman, of course, was my son. Andy thinks Bob Dylan is old and over the hill. That's to be expected. The problem is: He thinks *Jakob* Dylan is old and over the hill.

Anyway, I retreated from his band after a while, dropping off Andy and his equipment at Quentin's and picking him up later. In other words, I was his roadie. I'd ask how things went, and he'd always say "fine," but far as I could tell, they were foundering without a couple of fun, easy songs to play from beginning to end. Yet I was learning to just let it go and allow Andy to make his own mistakes (if that's what they were) and proceed at his own pace. I promised myself to do that with baseball, too. And who knows, maybe he'll end up as one of those major leaguer pitchers, like Jack McDowell and Scott Radinsky, who get most of their "playing time" with a rock band.

It was a rough time to be a schoolkid in America even if your father wasn't screaming at you about homework. There was the lewd spectacle of the ongoing Lewinsky scandal and the shattering of dignity surrounding the American presidency. Now, a couple of kids in Jonesboro, Arkansas, had shot up their school and killed four of their classmates and a teacher. Andy seemed a bit shaken, since Nyack schools have their share of discipline problems—and modest security—in the lower grades. Our middle school has survived several bomb scares recently.

At this moment, playing baseball with friends in the sunshine might be a useful antidote, or at least a distraction (I told myself). The weather was still too raw for a full outdoor practice, but I wanted to get a look at my pitching staff, so on a Saturday morning I invited a few kids to meet me at Memorial.

A chill wind blew off the river, but a bright sun eased the ordeal. The field was mushy from the snow, but the clay mound was still packed solid from the previous year. Who knew what might be buried under that clay? Memorial Park is old Native American land. Well into the twentieth century, visitors to the park were still finding broken clam and oyster shells in the dirt, suggesting that the Indians fished from the river and ate on this shore.

No one knows how Nyack got its name, but clearly, it's Indian in origin. The Nyack tribe helped sell Long Island to the white man—near Coney Island—in the 1600s, and some historians assume members of the tribe moved thirty miles up the Hudson and lent their name to this area near the river. One problem with that theory: Indians were already here, using it as a fishing camp and trading post. Rugged cliffs known as the Palisades line the river on the west bank all the way up from New York, and Nyack is one of the few spots with flat land right along the water. This ends abruptly at the natural northern border, a spectacular six-hundred-foot sheer cliff known as Hook Mountain (visible from right field at Memorial Park).

Henry Hudson anchored his *Half Moon* off here in 1609 (looking for his passage to China) and went ashore, later extolling in his diary the "beautiful" land, "pleasant with grass and flowers and goodly trees . . ." Right now, the flowers he found so pleasant were only a promise, the trees bare, the pale green grass matted grimly to the earth, but the sound of hardballs popping into leather—like Marty the Maven's pocket-pounding machine, minus the growl—sure sounded like spring to me. No birds could sing so sweet.

One potential pitcher who showed up that morning at Memorial was Mark Downey. This was our first meeting, since he'd missed the team meeting and indoor practice. From his soccer connection I'd expected a more brawny kid, but instead found a pale, slender blond. Little Stevie Albert arrived, as did Matt Scimeca, and Andy, of course. Andy had done well at that winter pitching clinic—the one that nearly sparked a divorce—and I'd picked up a few tips, too, as the only father who bothered to stick around and take notes. Let's face it, I wanted Andy to have the chance to pitch that I missed way back when. Pitching was my passion. There's something so artful, yet so primitive, about it. Bart Giamatti, the former Yale president, reduced pitching to its essence: "A man on a hill prepares to throw a rock at a man slightly below him, who holds a club."

After they warmed up a bit, I asked each of my junior cavemen to throw a few pitches to me. What suspense—I'd know a lot more about our season in the next few minutes. I figured Andy for one of our pitchers, but we desperately needed more help. Mark Downey looked promising, but like most young lefties threw the ball everywhere but over the plate. Steve, another lefty, actually threw the ball straight but was so small his throws didn't quite reach me. (He could have used a cutoff man.) Andy looked pretty good, and then handed the ball to Matt. Imagine my relief—no, joy—when Matt went into a full windup, showing strong mechanics, and not only fired a strike, but a fast one, which broke to the low outside corner! And it was only March.

"Whoa!" I said. "What was *that?* You throwing a curve or something?"

"Just natural movement," he replied, then threw another. He got a little erratic after that but looked like a sure starter for us, maybe one of the best in the league. How did he improve so much since last year? Just from that Little League summer camp? (Where could I sign Andy up for next year?)

But I was still riding a roller coaster. For every positive sign there was always at least one negative. I'd had big hopes for a big kid named Joe Reynolds. He was young but strong, I'd heard he could really punish the ball, and might pitch as well. Occasionally, I'd noticed, he lacked focus, but his mother, Gerry, had him in the Big Brother program and this seemed to help. Now Gerry, a single mom, called with some bad news. Big Joe had fractured his right wrist—his throwing arm, naturally—in gym class at school. Doing a cartwheel, as instructed. What was this football lineman doing with his hands on a mat and his feet in the air? A wrist was bound to collapse, and apparently it did. I swear, more Little Leaguers get hurt in gym class than on any ball field.

The doctor said Joe would be out for at least four weeks, meaning he'd miss the entire pre-season but might return for our first game. So now we were missing Joe, with Gerard still in limbo. Suddenly winning even half our games looked like a pipe dream.

7

Finally, on a chilly but bright sunny day in early April, we had our first full outdoor practice up at a middle school field. Some of the kids were Athletic in name only, but most of them played okay. Ian rocked a couple of long shots, Jeremy made a nice stop at second, and, best of all, Andy conducted himself rather humbly, only occasionally acting like the coach's son.

Gerard was a no-show. We might have seen the last of him, and our pennant hopes, but I loved watching John Marley flap around out there. He was only in third grade, so his concentration was not quite equal to his enthusiasm. He had all sorts of engaging tics and quirks and funny mannerisms, such as windmilling the bat over his head three or four times as he stood in the batter's box. You had to smile when you looked at John or tried to field one of his many, many questions. The classic *Why do they call it a foul pole when it's actually fair?* is far too pedestrian for him. He came up with mindbenders such as, "Why do they call a strike-out a *K*?"

"Well, John, I guess because there's a K in *strike*."

"So why don't they call it a *T* or an *R*?"

"John, go to left field."

Now I knew why his old manager Dennis O'Neill wanted to draft him—and why he called him "funny."

In any case, it appeared John could hit and, rare for this age, got a good jump on line drives in the outfield. He made a circus catch—actually the ball was hit right to him but he turned it into a spectacular play with a dive and somersault, and then he made a muscle. (Better to make one than pull one.) I started thinking of him as Little John—not for his size but because he reminded me of Robin Hood's brave, sturdy sidekick.

The truth was, I missed the golden age of the baseball nickname. Today it's just Derek This and Pedro That. Nicknames these days only get about as wild as "Chipper." Oh, for the days of Foghorn Myatt, Boob McNair, Fats Fothergill, Battleship Gremminger, Phenomenal Smith, and Moe "The Rabbi of Swat" Solomon. But we were off to a good start with the A's, reversing this trend. We had the Kippster, and Matt the Bat, and Little Stevie Wonder, though I hadn't thought of a nickname yet for my own son. He was the proverbial "player to be named later."

This was just as well. The novelist Robert Coover once suggested that you had to be careful in passing out baseball nicknames, as they carried hidden emotional weight—and there was enough pressure on my son already.

Dan Wolff, our batting coach, made some adjustments after noticing that several kids (including Andy) were not "lining up their knuckles" as they gripped the bat. Still, one of our players, Jesse Moskowitz, didn't come close to hitting the ball and kept asking how many more minutes until the practice ended. Clearly he didn't want to be there. It might even have been torture; apparently his parents had urged him to give baseball one last try. It was a shame it wasn't working out, because he was such a smart, quirky kid. "Jesse," I said to him at one point, "that's fascinating what you're telling me about Beowulf, but would you mind picking up that ball you've just stopped and throwing it to first base?"

Mike Reilly looked pretty good at bat. Playing first base he blocked a bad hop with his nose, and went down. Fortunately, we had an ice bag and got it on his nose in a hurry, but it still swelled a bit. So much for my spotless safety record.

John Marley, the Question Man, comes from a real baseball home, which is music to the ears of any coach. There are only two kinds of baseball parents: those who'd do almost anything to get their kid to practices and games, and those who whine about it and secretly wish their child would join the Chess Club. John's bedroom walls are plastered with Yankee posters—but he didn't put them there. The biggest baseball fans in the Marley household are his teenage sisters, Claire and Julianne, who are rabid Yankee fans, and John simply inherited their room. When the Yankees are playing, the TV *and* radio are always on around the Marley house, providing ambient noise, and the girls often stay up late, even on school nights, listening to a West Coast game in bed. That sounds like me as a kid, and I'd wondered if anyone still did that, let alone teenage girls.

As a tyke John played a lot of ball out in the street. His mother, Betsy Hastedt, used to pitch to him out there, and he became a pretty good hitter, she says, because there was no backstop and he had to chase any pitch he missed. John got an identity in the neighborhood as a good little hitter—"which makes it easier for *any* boy to grow up," as his lanky father, Jim (who played Little League back in Queens) explains. But it wasn't until he saw the movie *Angels in the Outfield* that John became obsessed with baseball.

Then he started watching games on TV, or perhaps more accurately, memorizing them. John is one of those kids with a highly selective photographic memory. Not for schoolwork. Not for remembering to bring a water bottle to practice. But baseball scores, play-by-play, and statistics—forget it! Or rather, he doesn't forget it. If his father misses part of a Yankees game on the radio, no problem, John is sure to update him in almost pitch-by-pitch detail. Ask John what happened the last time the Mets played the Cards, and he won't simply answer, "They swept," but instead report, "10–4, 9–6, 8–7 in ten innings."

John has a lot on his mind, so he often daydreams in the field. He imagines he's in a big league game and gets in trouble when fantasy overtakes reality. In his very first T-ball game he snapped to attention when a grounder bounced his way in left field. He trapped it and fired it to third base, just like Barry Bonds, which might have been the right play—if the third sacker had been at the bag instead of picking dandelions near the mound.

Little John loves the rituals of baseball as much as the game itself. This was evident when Dennis O'Neill asked him one day if he wanted to catch. Before Dennis knew it, John had all the equipment on, some of it backward. John trooped out to the mound and, Mike Piazza style, rested the mask on his hip while he draped one arm around the pitcher's waist and gave him a pep talk. ("Who is this guy?" the pitcher must have asked himself.) The only thing missing was tobacco juice shooting out between his teeth. Then John went back behind the plate and started flashing signs.

The team had no signs. That was immaterial.

The day after practice I got a phone call I'd secretly expected: It was Jesse's mother announcing that he'd quit the team. The parents had made some kind of deal with him—he'd get some reward if he gave baseball one more shot, but clearly it wasn't worth the effort. Nothing I could have done about it. Thanks for trying, Coach. This was, no doubt, a plus for the team—not an admirable thought, but an undeniable one. Yet it meant I'd have to call up from a lower league not one but two new players (if Gerard quit), and I hadn't been able to identify even one player passed over in the draft that I craved.

My first desperate thought was: Can I convince Robby Keiser and his parents to get off the dime? I couldn't seem to get any of the

Keisers to commit to Little League for another year, but now I had to try again.

Robby had average range in the field, but had come on strong at the end of the previous year as a hitter, earning from my wife the nickname "RBI Keiser." He'd grown a couple of inches since then, and was now wearing glasses, which could only help his hitting. He also had a maturity that might help in clutch situations, plus it would be nice to add a couple more great parents to our mix. But when I informed the Keisers they had a second chance to sign on, they were still divided. Robby already faced a busy spring with music, golf, school, and so forth.

So I had to go to my Hail Mary strategy: Examine the list of players already passed over once this year.

Unfortunately, that list wasn't very promising. It was the inevitable collection of nine- and ten-year-olds knee high to a grasshopper. Perhaps we ought to follow the example of the Little League team in Live Oaks, Florida, back in 1991. When the Kansas City Royals released Bo Jackson, the Little Leaguers claimed him off waivers for the standard $1 fee. (Bo didn't report.) Maybe we could sign free agent Michael Jordan.

Returning to my notes from the tryout and conversations with parents, the only name that jumped out at me was Thaddeus Bell—not a very jocky name, but I'd been told he had an older brother who was a star in the majors, so the bloodlines were good. Richards knew his parents, Duncan and Sally, and said they were low-key Nyackers. When I talked to Duncan to arrange a special tryout, he said his son was fairly small, but had improved a lot in the past year and was lightning fast. He added that his nickname was "Taddy." Now, Taddy Bell—that sounded like a ballplayer!

Still, I called all of the managers in the lower-level International League seeking another recommendation. Fat chance! No one wanted to lose his best player. Without fail the managers told me that Johnny was too young, too small, or his parents wouldn't want him to get called up. However, they freely recommended star players on *other teams*. But when I talked to the skippers of those teams, they'd scoff ("He's not that good, hell, he can't hit a knuckle-curve to save his life") . Taddy Bell's manager questioned whether *he* belonged in a higher league. Given the logic of all this, that probably meant that he *did*.

When I met Taddy at his tryout he seemed pretty damn small but looked like an athlete and had an engaging manner. When he chased after the grounders that went through his legs he was a blur, like a bug skimming across the grass without ever touching ground. (We'd have to call him "Cool Taddy" Bell.) At the plate he made good contact. Well, he was an appealing character, blond-haired and charismatic.

His father, I later learned, was judging me as well. He worried that Tad, though he'd improved, was not qualified for the minors. Duncan invents robots, at the nearby Lederle Laboratory, that can study twenty thousand compounds at a time. Ironically, he believes that in baseball the most important thing is that kids not be the "tools" of their manager.

It was looking like Taddy Bell, by acclamation.

When Andy and I made our way to Williamsport, birthplace of Little League, it was just another fun road trip for him, four hours by car from Nyack, but a kind of return to my roots for me. It even looks a lot like Lock Haven, my mother's hometown just to the west, and has a similar rugged, riverside setting, shadowed by mountains. It's nothing like that other baseball mecca, pastoral Cooperstown. Baseball hardly dominates Williamsport. You can walk for blocks and see no evidence of Little League or indeed baseball itself. It's hard to find a vintage baseball card for sale, probably a good thing, given my experience in Cooperstown.

The field where they first played Little League is still there, marked by a statue of Carl Stotz, but it's on the edge of town. We discovered the organization's headquarters and museum across the broad Susquehanna on a forty-two-acre tract with Lamade Stadium (and a few other ballfields) down the hill out back. The Little League museum, which cost over $2 million to build and opened in 1982, occupies a red-brick, colonial-type structure, its collection scattered over two floors. It's a pleasant place, surprisingly substantial, but easy to breeze through in an hour or two.

Andy liked it a lot, not feeling intimidated as he did at Cooperstown. This museum does not throw thousands of names and statistics at you, so Andy didn't feel stupid about not knowing who Tris Speaker was or how many no-hitters Sandy Koufax hurled. The dusty old baseball equipment only went back half a century, not to the nineteenth century. He knew most of the players who donated old Little League gear, like Mike Schmidt, though he drew a blank on Kent Tekulve. Andy got a kick out of a photo showing American and Japanese teams facing each other before the start of a World Series final—the Americans erect in their warm-up jackets, the Japanese kids in robes, bowing.

My favorite moment came in the museum's Hall of Excellence, honoring a wild mix of people who have helped further youth baseball: from former Little Leaguers like Nolan Ryan to baseball enthusiasts George Will, Tom Selleck, Dave Barry, and Dan Quayle. (Quick, Dan, how do you spell *rhubarb?*) It's quite a select group, less than two dozen in number, and I laughed heartily when I saw mounted on the wall a picture of Bruce Springsteen. The tribute to Bruce reported that he played Little League in Freehold and often recalls this experience in his onstage raps.

Andy, who knows the Boss mainly from movie soundtrack ballads, barely nodded. It was like Springsteen's son trying to figure out why Reggie Jackson mattered so much.

After the requisite visit to the gift shop, we wandered outside and down the hill that overlooks Lamade Stadium. It's a perfect little ballpark with glistening grass, a roof covering the grandstand in back of home and 10,000 seats, making it larger than some minor league stadiums. I wondered if anyone plays there except at the World Series in August; perhaps it's kept in pristine shape mainly for another purpose—to admire from afar. Andy couldn't get over how much it looked like a big league park but still had Little League dimensions. The outfield fence was the same distance from home as it is at Liberty Field in Valley Cottage (two hundred feet). A home run at Liberty would fly out of this stadium, too.

"Let's bring Mom here, tomorrow," Andy said. For a fleeting moment, I believe, he felt a part of something larger, an entire nation, even world, of juvenile ballplayers, playing on nearly identical fields—Little Big League.

When I called Duncan Bell to tell him Taddy was now an Athletic, he seemed genuinely pleased, which made me pleased. The next day, however, the other shoe dropped: Gerard's father reported that he had positively decided not to play. "I think he's making a mistake," he explained, "but I can't get him to change his mind. He's just into this aikido thing."

And so, on the eve of the roster deadline, away from home on a brief business trip, I tried the Keisers again—from an airport in Cleveland or Pittsburgh (who can tell the difference?) connecting back to Newark. The Keisers were away from home, too, in Atlanta. That was how desperate I was. Arlene said they'd talk to Robby about it, and this time she said, "Maybe." Now I had a slight smile on my face at the Cleveland (Pittsburgh?) airport waiting for that US Airways flight.

When I got home I called the Keisers at their hotel about ten P.M. "Nah, I don't think Robby can do it, his plate is full," Arlene said. Dejectedly, I started shuffling through my files again—or could I play the season one body short? Twenty minutes later, the phone rang; it was the Keisers, saying they had talked it over with Robby again and apparently he'd said, "Why not?" He had friends on the team and he liked to play baseball, even if he wasn't an armchair fan. Whatever.

Now things were looking up again. Robby could hit and had experience. Taddy could run and was sure to be fun. Maybe we could win a few games after all.

With our first game only a couple of weeks off, I drove out to Modell's on Route 59 and picked out a new jockstrap for Andy. He already had two others, which he may or may not have out-grown. There was no way to tell, since he'd never worn them. He probably wouldn't wear this one either, but at least it was new and he might like the bright yellow packaging.

I was the same way growing up. Since I never played Little League, this was a non–issue until seventh grade, when our gym teacher suggested that boys start wearing jocks to protect "the family jewels." I never did. I couldn't. I'd take my chances with the family jewels, which weren't much to speak of then. Maybe it was the way the gym teacher loved to say the word *rup-ture*. He made it sound dirty. Not many of the other kids wore a jock either, but the ones who did always seemed to be "hoods." This only reinforced the sexual connotation, since it was widely assumed these guys were already "getting some."

This wasn't exactly logical. About the only thing jockstraps have to do with sex is that they embrace the male sex organ; an accident of anatomy. Quite possibly I confused them with condoms. I also doubted I could ask my mother to buy me one—simply out of the question! It would have been like asking her to buy me a rubber. So I never wore a jock all through high school, but was never seriously injured (maybe because I did not play on any school teams).

The real danger arose playing intramural football in college, and still, I would not buy a jockstrap. I wouldn't even know what size to order—and what would the size refer to anyway? I knew the difference between a jock and a condom by then, but it made no difference. I lacked what Dizzy Dean, that master of the malaprop, once called "testicle fortitude." So what I did was stuff a pair of socks down there before trotting out on the football field. It gave me a nice manly bulge, too.

Little League rules require that every kid wear a jock, and catchers must wear cups. It's pretty hard to enforce, short of doing a kick-test. Many of the kids don't wear the equipment, but will lie to your face claiming that they do. I don't take it as seriously as I should, partly because of my own experience, and because I've yet to see a Little League kid get nailed down there and badly hurt. For the sake of future generations I do carry a couple of extra cups in the equipment bag for my catchers, as they really are in harm's way.

In buying Andy yet another jock I felt I was making a good faith effort to be a responsible coach and parent. When I gave it to him I asked him to try it on, with the warning that "this year you have to wear one." I knew I wouldn't press the point, at least until opening day. Maybe he'd figure out the sock trick himself.

"You know, he's just a guy you want to *beat*," one of my fellow managers said, referring to Eddie Badger, when we ran into each other one evening at the local Grand Union. I said we hadn't crossed paths since the draft, so we hadn't yet crossed swords. "We were in the middle of practice last week," he explained, "and he shows up with his team and says, 'You have to get off the field, we have a two-hour practice scheduled and we *have* to get started.' Of course, no one can reserve the field, but just because he has something planned, our little team should just get out of the way. He's too intense for me, and the season hasn't even started."

Our next outdoor workout in early April proved uneventful.

With no practice whatsoever, RBI Keiser hit a bunch of line drives and fielded well. He could bat cleanup for me every game if I wanted, and I probably would.

Little Stevie fielded smoothly at second base, with just one problem—whoever heard of a left-handed second sacker? Forget the struggles they have with scissors and can openers: It's baseball that's most cruel to lefties. Because of one little rule—you have to run counterclockwise around the bases—they are essentially prohibited from playing four key positions: catcher, second, short, and third. It's just too hard for them to turn their bodies and throw to first base from those spots. As someone once observed, the national pastime basically says to lefties: "Go home, kid, get an outfielder's glove and maybe we can talk."

Or in Steve's case, his father's old first baseman's mitt. Steve could also pitch, of course, and I'd made a significant change in his pitching motion, meaning he could now reach the plate—most of the time. He had better control than our other two starters, Matt and Andy, though they threw harder. Still, I fretted because I knew I'd need at least four pitchers, and no one else showed much in that department.

At the practice the Kippster made a couple of nice grabs in center field. Like his friends Robby and Amos, Kipp is not a huge baseball fan, he just likes to play. From his first game as an eight-year-old, when he actually caught a pop fly, it was apparent that Kipp was that rare kid more adept in the outfield than the infield. John Marley may be the Question Man, but Kipp is the Philosopher. He likes center field because there's less tension out there, it's quiet, and he can hear himself think. "It's a nice way to spend a warm spring evening," he'll say, "standin' in the outfield, lookin' in at everything goin' on." Move over, Walt Whitman!

Andy, as usual, hit erratically at our practice. During the past three years he'd tried roughly twenty-three different stances, and none had panned out in the long run. Hands high, hands low; elbow up or elbow down; the Orlando Cepeda closed stance or the Andres Galarraga open stance—nothing seemed to work. How many times, out front in Mudville, had I said to Andy, "We're finally over the hump," after he'd slashed a dozen line drives? Now we went back to a golden oldie, Batting Potion #9—simply "See the ball, hit the ball."

Also, since we'd started concentrating on pitching last year, Andy's range at shortstop had shrunk. He was getting gangly and losing the ability to scoot after balls. And he was still having trouble drifting back on pop-ups over his head, preferring to backpedal—the old Statue of Liberty play—which can end in embarrassment with a little dunker falling just out of reach, untouched, behind him. This could have been fixed with practice, which we hadn't done.

Maybe what all this meant was—I was a mediocre coach. And a coach's son with serious flaws in his game makes some parents wonder why the league lets you manage in the first place. Bertrand Russell once observed that the "fundamental defect of fathers is that they want their children to be a credit to them." That's bad enough, but the parents of players on your team also want your kid to be a credit to you—and they get nervous if they think he isn't. You're with your son all the time, and if you can't get *him* to master certain basics, why should you be put in charge of *their* kid?

With Andy's hitting and fielding still uneven, we were betting that his baseball future was on the mound. But could either of us stand the pressure?

The A's were looking pretty good in practice, but as former Yankees general manager Gabe Paul once put it, "The great thing about baseball is that there is a crisis every day." While calling to give me a date for our season opener, Steve

Wanamaker reminded me that minors' games would be played according to majors' rules, as detailed in the official Little League manual.

"Except for the limit on steals, right?" I interjected.

"No, we got rid of that restriction, remember?" Somehow I'd missed the announcement. The previous year in the minors your team could only steal three bases per inning, to prevent managers from running you to death—winning that way without developing other skills. Now they'd lifted that limit, having found that the league needed to develop young catchers. That meant I'd have to spend much of our final practice on base stealing, when we still had so much else to cover. And I'd have to find an alternative in case Enrique couldn't throw anyone out.

Catching's a tough position, even in Little League. Home plate collisions are rare—in fact, discouraged—but the catchers take a pounding every inning from balls in the dirt banging off their legs and arms. (Is this where the expression "catching hell" comes from?) They also must scramble back to the screen to retrieve wild pitches, and then fling the ball toward second base in a vain attempt to nab a base runner. Some go an entire season without throwing anyone out, and it's often not their fault.

Still, as Casey Stengel once pointed out, "you gotta have a catcher, or you'll have a lot of passed balls."

At an earlier practice I'd asked if anyone, besides Enrique, would like to catch. No one bit at first. Matt smiled playfully, as he often did, and reminded me that he'd caught a little last year, but I didn't want to get him hurt or too worn out to pitch. Same for Andy, in spades. We didn't have anyone else with experience—or anyone who could reach second base regularly with an accurate peg, hardly Enrique's strong point, either.

Developing catchers is one of the toughest things for any Little League coach to do. In lower leagues a lot of kids will try it. Like

John Marley, they'll put on the equipment, at least for a few minutes, but as the kids advance, the pitches get faster and more lethal and the gear gets uncomfortable after an inning or two, especially in June. So, to get kids to catch, you must appeal to their desire to be at the center of action. Still, few want to do it. Those fastballs and foul balls can be felt right through the padding. (Not that I'd know. You'd never catch *me* catching.)

Now, Enrique could take a licking and keep on ticking, and he was a delight to have on the team. Born in the Bronx, he moved to Nyack when he was about three. His father, Big Enrique, grew up fairly close to Yankee Stadium and played stickball in the streets with his Puerto Rican friends and his two older brothers. They also played softball, but the only field nearby was a bank parking lot, and it was there Big Enrique dove for a ball and broke a finger, which remains twisted today.

When his wife gave birth to Little Enrique, sports were not much on their minds. They lived in apartments, first in the Bronx and then in Nyack, so for many years the only throwing the kid did was indoors with something soft; perhaps this explains his lack of a "gun" for an arm. As he started up the ladder in Little League, Enrique realized he was not an exceptional hitter or fielder and so he followed the age-old advice: If you really want to play, volunteer to catch. He did—and he did.

I'd drafted him blind the previous year, thanks to his musical name and the vague sense that Latins have a special flair for baseball. Alas, when we first encountered Enrique on the ballfield, we noticed that he had one of the worst uppercuts we'd ever seen. But he soon won us over with his heart and his smile—displaying Trix-colored braces on his teeth—even if he never quite curbed that uppercut. What he could do, we found out, was catch and, even more unusual, he was eager to take charge, and take his lumps, back there. In truth, he was a magnet for foul tips. Still, he'd hang in there, and in our final playoff game that year—

played at noon in 95-degree sun—he refused to come out until the last inning, drenched in sweat.

Best of all, in my mind, Andy enjoyed throwing to him, because he set a good target and pumped up his pitchers between batters. But what if other teams ran wild and bunted well? Could Enrique, or anyone else on our team, stop them?

8

Our final practice started low and ended high. Once again, we met at the middle school's upper field, which I figured would be free. It's usually free because it's a lousy baseball field, used mainly for lacrosse and soccer. At first I couldn't identify any positive omens. Big Joe Reynolds still hadn't been cleared to play, Mark Downey again did not show, and I had to open the practice admitting I'd screwed up, overlooking the new base-stealing rules. So we started off with Enrique and a few others pegging throws to second base—inevitably on a bounce (or two).

Okay, time out. Let's go over the signs, or rather, sign. For now the only sign I'd flash from the third base coaching box: pointing to my throat, ordering the batter not to swing at the next pitch. (T for take, get it?) I was afraid to have a bunt signal. Then I might use it, and it didn't look like anyone could bunt.

Naturally, John Marley piped up with a question. "Why do they call them 'signs'?" Little John wondered. "A sign is a board or metal thing and everyone can read it. It's not a coach pointing to something like it's a big *secret*."

He had me there. I had to think fast.

"John, coaches used to take *actual signs* out there, but then, you know, the other teams started to . . . steal their signs."

He looked like he only half believed me. He had that look down pat. The look said, *Are you kidding . . . or what?*

98

But there was a deeper problem. "What do you mean by 'take the next pitch'?" Little John asked. "You don't mean *on purpose?*" Funny kid. It was going to be an interesting season.

Once again, I asked if anyone wanted to try catching, sugar-coating it by promising they'd get to play more often (hell, I'd throw in a free dinner at Pizza Hut and the keys to the car, too). Amos made my day by saying he'd give it a try. He certainly had the build for it—a perfect Carlton Fisk to Enrique's Thurman Munson. I got him in the gear, always half the battle, and then asked him to peg a few to second. Amos revealed a reasonably strong arm, plus his size might intimidate base runners.

"Nice idea, Amos catching," Richards observed, dryly. "You know what that gives us when your son pitches?"

"What does it give us?"

"A battery of Amos 'n' Andy."

I noticed, however, that Amos was not flipping off his mask, the way catchers do when they make throws to second or try to locate foul pops.

"Oh, I did that the first throw," he explained.

"And what happened?"

"My glasses flew off with the mask." I hadn't thought of that. Must be the reason there have been so few bespectacled catchers in baseball history—Carl Sawatski, Clint Courtney, Darrell Porter, and now, Amos Wolff.

"Okay, just leave the mask on for now," I answered, grateful for anything.

Being big for his age, which was eleven, wasn't easy for Amos. Many of his friends in sixth grade were already in the majors and Amos was bigger than most of them. Now he'd be playing in a lower league with mainly younger kids, some of them two-thirds his size. Still, he seemed to have a good attitude about it. Amos was the strong, sensitive type—strapping but with soft features, very smart, and creative (with mother a dancer and father a writer). Among other categories, we led the league in most players wearing glasses (three).

Since T-ball, Amos's father has usually been one of his coaches. One day I asked Amos if (like Andy) he sometimes got sick of having his father always around the ball field.

"No," he answered quickly, "he's a great assistant coach but I might not want him as manager."

"Why's that?"

"You know him, he'd probably play every kid the same number of innings and at every position so we wouldn't win many games."

"Don't worry," I assured him, "I'm not *that* idealistic."

As our final practice continued I realized we hadn't done much sliding all spring. Of course, there was no infield dirt to slide on. We had to do something, so I ordered a few kids in long pants to try sliding on the grass. The first kid tore up his pants, and we noticed there were pebbles and little bits of glass in the grass.

So much for that. I was out of ideas. Even with unlimited Internet access I didn't know a lot of baseball drills, and what I knew I often botched. Marty Schupak, the most successful manager in our league in recent years, feels that, with proper planning, no practice needs to be longer than about an hour. He's even produced an excellent video, *The 59 Minute Baseball Practice,* to prove it. I was already an hour into today's practice and felt I'd hardly accomplished a thing.

Clearly, we'd have to rely on team spirit, not technique, this year. "The heck with this, let's just have fun," I said, and ordered an intrasquad game—kids versus parents. I'd even let the A's pitch to the old folks. Matt's father had trouble hitting his boy, and Jon Albert struggled against Steve, but at least he had an excuse—

lefty vs. lefty. I decided to catch for both sides so I wouldn't have
to face my son (manager's prerogative).

The other parents had a grand time in the field. Sally Bell
played short and laughed when two balls in a row rolled between
her legs. Her hotshot son Nathan played center field, giving the
youngsters something to aspire to. Pete Rocker hit a hard shot—off
his son's leg at first. Tall, white-haired, and long-legged, Jim
Marley looked like he could still go nine innings, running grace-
fully for fly balls. "Show time," he called it. But poor Richards
dove for a ball in the outfield and came up hurting—having
landed on the keys in his pocket.

He was more concerned about something else. "I'm *so* out of
shape," he moaned.

When Little John blooped a single to right, he "styled" his jog
to first and barely beat the throw from the outfield. "Way to go,
John," I shouted to him, "you've got your home run trot down,
now all you have to do is hit one over the fence!"

"I do?" he replied.

When five o'clock, the scheduled end of practice, arrived, no
one wanted to quit, so we played another twenty minutes. It was
a sunny day, 60 degrees in mid-April, and it felt like the best day
of our (adult) lives. We were having fun with our kids, not
"practicing," and no one could take it away from us. The entire
Nyack High football team could have appeared for a spring practice and threatened us with bodily harm and we wouldn't have
surrendered the field. Smells like team spirit! Now we were *really*
ready for opening day.

A parade through downtown Nyack (all eight blocks of it) tradi-
tionally kicks off the Little League season. In some towns it's a big
deal, but here it's little more than a few hundred players and
coaches marching a mile behind a fire truck. They've even abol-
ished the practice of putting last year's champs on the engine—for

insurance reasons. As expected, about half our team turned out. I
had to admit, we *looked* the best out there, in our green and gold
A's caps, while the other teams wore their bland Little League
hats, identical except for color. I feared that other managers might
feel I was upstaging them, but only Dennis O'Neill commented,
ambiguously, "I hope you play as good as you look."

Baseball in Nyack goes back well over a century. Nyack
Library has a photo of the town's "professional team" from 1886.
Growing up in the 1930s and 1940s, pre-Little League, Nyack kids
played pickup games on the local sandlots and scheduled (via telephone) "away" games with other fanatics down the river in
Piermont or over in Tappan. Then they'd pack their gloves and
lunch, and catch a train (for a nickel) to their destination—like
the Yankees riding the rails to Boston.

Professional ball came back to Nyack after World War II, a franchise in the Class D North Atlantic League. These were the original "Rockies" (short for "Rocklands"), and they lasted three
seasons. One of their players, Fred Hahn, went on to pitch—two
innings—for the St. Louis Cardinals. As far as we know, he is the
only native Nyacker to reach the majors. And who is the most
famous ballplayer to emerge from Rockland County? One candidate would be: John Henry Peterman, yes, J. Peterman of mail-
order catalog and *Seinfeld* fame. He starred in high school a few
miles from Nyack, got drafted by the pros, and advanced through
the minors before his promising career was cut short by injuries.
Those who played against him still speak with awe of "Johnny"
Peterman.

It fell to Nyack, along with Haverstraw up north, to form the first
Little Leagues in Rockland, in 1952. A group of businessmen and
local boosters did the deed. Valley Cottage, just emerging as a siz-
able community, sent few if any kids to what was then known
simply as Nyack Little League.

Civic clubs helped fund the first teams and bought their uniforms. The league adapted the softball field at Memorial Park for Little League, planting home plate near the Hudson and erecting an outfield fence. Batters hit toward town. One drawback to this arrangement: Errant throws and foul balls could roll into the river. Then, as now, there were no lights for night play. Players passed through the crowd with coffee cans collecting donations to buy balls and new equipment, and parents (who didn't have to pay sign-up fees then) willingly tossed in a few coins.

Little League caught on quickly in the village. Officials moved home plate at Memorial to another corner of the park so the batters now hit toward the Hudson. One who claims he "went river" a couple of times is Dave Siegriest, now head coach of the Nyack High team (and once Andy's gym coach). He hit so many home runs, parents would take out dollar bills when he came to bat and wave them in the air, and if he banged one out, they'd pass the bills over to him. Dave claims he made enough money this way to buy a new bicycle.

Then, as now, there were disputes within the Little League board, and one longtime president was deposed in a palace coup. In the late 1960s, the league treasurer absconded with the funds (about $2,500), and fled the county, forcing the league to scramble for money door-to-door. The quality of play in the league was only fair (judging by its showing in county tournaments), at least partly because the quality of coaching declined in the 1970s. In many other leagues, a manager might spend ten to twenty years in the dugout, but in our area that was very rare. And some of the best athletes here showed less interest in baseball. Blacks had always favored football in Nyack, and by the 1980s, basketball became the rage. Everyone wanted to be like Mike (Jordan). Few wanted to be like Junior (Griffey).

In recent years, our league has bounced back and now competes for top honors in the county. Some claim that improved coaching—the league now sponsors clinics for managers—has something to do with that. I had a feeling I'd put that theory to the test very soon.

Only two matters remained to be settled before our opener: the identity of our starting pitcher—and our team mascot.

I don't know where I got the idea we needed a mascot. I've never seen a Little League team with one. Perhaps, as with our caps and weekly newsletter, I just wanted us to be different—and a little goofy, to emphasize the element of fun (while we seriously tried to win). Let's face it, I wasn't that smart a "baseball man," but I was good at atmospherics. Andy nominated our hamster, Stuart, for mascot but I didn't think a live animal could survive several weeks around a dozen pre-pubescent boys—or even one week. I was thinking of getting a huge Nixon mask, but that seemed like too much of an inside joke. When I couldn't think of anything else, I shelved the plan.

Now I looked around the house again for inspiration. Then I spotted, in Andy's room, sitting on a shelf, his leftover Halloween costume, a human-sized, rubber Alien head. You know the look: fat forehead, narrow chin, enormous insect eyes. . . . I'd always visualized our players rubbing *some* object for good luck before batting (or to jump-start a rally), so from the beginning I probably had in mind something bald, like a Don Zimmer or Billy Corgan head. The Alien seemed perfect— it had a lot of head to rub, and almost every kid thinks aliens are cool.

But would Andy go for it? When he came home from school, I announced, "Meet the Mascot" and produced the Alien head. Andy laughed, then said, "Great, and it's an *A* like the A's— we could call ourselves the A-liens." Perfect! I was so proud I gave him a hug, just as if he'd hit a grand slam, for he had.

What about our opening day starter? It looked like Matt, Steve, and Andy would form our rotation—a collection of *ifs*. Stevie was probably throwing better than anyone, but he was so small I was afraid he'd get hammered. Andy was the "coach's son," and so everyone expected he'd start the opener, and nearly every game afterward. A father and son named Mike and Luke Ryan once wrote a book revealing how a youth league manager decides who plays where. According to the Ryans, the skipper consults his coaches and then "does what everybody on the team knew he would do from the get-go": He sends one of his best players out to shortstop, another to first, fills in the rest, "and then, without bias or favoritism, he selects his son as the pitcher. Nothing could be fairer. The team's destiny now rides on the arm of his heir and namesake."

Well, I planned to break the mold, knowing that starting my heir/namesake, Andy, right away would be bad politics, and perhaps not even the wise choice in baseball terms. That left Matt, who had continued to show good stuff—but stuff that often drifted off the plate. An umpire who was a stickler on the strike zone might call every close pitch a ball. Any one of our pitchers was a risk, but it was easy to settle on Matt. Nervous already about the first game, I'd find it unbearable worrying about Andy on the mound (and parents gossiping about nepotism). So, go get 'em, Matt!

Because of a late Easter, Little League opening day would not arrive until April 20, and by now the big league season was already well under way. As Will Rogers once observed at the start of another baseball season, "The country is all right now. We get real news every morning from now on." And that meant quite a change in my life. As if managing a local team, and practicing out in Mudville, wasn't enough, I'd also have to find time, and lots of it, to follow the Yankees and Mets—and baseball in general, since pundits were predicting a run on Babe Ruth's single-season home run record.

If George Orwell could admit to a long, hopeless love affair with cricket, I suppose I can make a fetish of baseball. The difference, of course, is that he broke *his* habit when he was sixteen.

During the spring I can't devote all of my free time to Little League because I have to watch the Yanks or Mets on television, scan the box scores in the *Times* and the scuttlebutt in *Baseball Weekly*, surf the Net to see how the other games are going, or make plans to attend a contest at Shea or the Stadium (or at the minor league park in Fishkill). Did I mention the dozens of other baseball sites on the Net that I sometimes visit, with baseball news and views, tips on Little League coaching, baseball card chat, and links to other baseball sites? Or the phone calls from my friend John Demeter to gas about the Yanks, or from my collaborator Robert Jay Lifton (who grew up in Brooklyn) to deconstruct his Dodgers? On top of all that, what about the cumulative hours spent simply thinking about baseball in any of its forms?

Now, that *is* too much baseball, but it's not as much as it may appear. Nearly everything (including practicing with Andy in the front yard) is done in snatches nowadays, five minutes here, fifteen minutes there, reflecting the short attention span and electronic wizardry of our time. Until a few years ago, for example, you'd have to spin the radio dial to find an announcer reciting out-of-town scores if you wanted to stay on top of a pennant race. Now, you can get all the action on-line, for every game, literally pitch by pitch, updated every few seconds.

Still, if you add it all up, it amounts to an absurd amount of time, at least some of which could be better spent making money, making dinner, or making love. As Don DeLillo put it, "The game doesn't change the way you sleep or wash your face or chew your food. It changes nothing but your life." Need I add that baseball even gets in the way of *writing* about baseball? But so it goes, the diamond enclosing what I am.

Squandering half of my free time to baseball was nothing new for me. I had more than forty years of experience to draw on. In this case, as in so many others, the child was father to the man—or is it "fan"?

When I was eight, I received as a present my first adult book. (I was in second grade but reading at the big league level.) It was Willie Mays's autobiography, *Born to Play Ball,* and I was reasonably certain the title also referred to me. It was no small thing that the "Say Hey Kid" became my first black hero. There were few blacks on TV and in the movies and I sure wasn't ready for Little Richard. Willie was, in a sense, my Martin Luther King. Naturally, I became a Giants fan, although I remained loyal to the Red Sox in the American League.

Why was I a Red Sox fan? No one else in town dared make that claim. Niagara Falls was about halfway between New York and Cleveland; one of the local radio stations carried the Yankee games and the other the Indians. You could walk down a street and follow both teams' games from radios blaring through open windows: "Here's the pitch to Berra . . . and Colavito swings and misses!"

Most of my friends liked the Yankees. It's funny how kids at that age can be chauvinistic about their home state, and we were "New Yorkers." We also rooted, ineffectually, for Miss New York to win Miss America and Nelson Rockefeller to become President. We were proud when our obscure local congressman was named Barry Goldwater's running mate in 1964. (Here's the answer to that trivia question: William Miller.)

The likely explanation for my Red Sox affliction is a simple one: Ted Williams was the best hitter around, and since the Bosox were in the American League they could, theoretically, beat out the Yankees for the pennant, which would have delighted my mother. Like my dad, my mom didn't care much about baseball, except for the All-Star game (when she could root against individual Yankees) and the World Series (when she could rail against the entire Yankee team). Why was she so rabidly anti-Yank? Perhaps because she lived in Brooklyn as a young woman, working there as a nurse in the 1930s. Or maybe she just liked rooting for the underdog. She did it on Academy Awards night, too, but drew the line on election night (unless the underdog was a Republican).

Except for hating the Yankees she pretty much kept her feelings inside, leading to an ulcer, a weight problem—she had too little of it—and a cigarette habit that would kill her by and by.

Many men of my age have fond memories of their mothers ironing, back in the 1950s, before permanent-press. I recall running home from school to catch the last couple innings of the World Series—remember day games?—and finding my mother, iron in one hand, cigarette in the other, standing in front of the TV in the living room ready to fill me in on "the situation." We always pulled for the same team—whoever was facing the Yankees. We generally rooted in vain, an experience that no doubt forged a bond more common between sons and *fathers*.

Distressingly, the Red Sox never did overtake the Yanks, and when Ted Williams quit, I abandoned the Bosox, and just followed Willie Mays and his Giants. Admittedly, this was difficult, since they'd fled New York for San Francisco. But after college I moved to New York City, the Giants traded Willie to the Mets, and life suddenly became a whole lot simpler, and sweeter.

After settling on a starting pitcher, there was nothing left to do before opening day but fiddle with lineups. It reminded me of fantasy leagues, which I'd been involved with off and on for years, going back to getting my first baseball board game, known simply as APBA, for my eleventh birthday.

I'd discovered APBA through full-page ads in the back of *Sport* magazine. The ads always said, YOU BE THE MAN-AGER, which was (and apparently still is) pretty hard for me to resist, accompanied by a picture of a famous player's card filled with tiny numbers, next to a couple of dice. When I started devoting most of my waking hours to playing the game, my grades plummeted. My parents never gave me grief about that because at least I wasn't watching television all the time or running around outside with my friends throwing eggs at passing cars; and rolling dice kept my hands busy (one form of playing with myself they endorsed).

Long before "Rotisserie" leagues, my friends and I drafted APBA teams. Many years later, I'd manage a team in an APBA computer league. Coaching a team in Little League was a far cry from fantasy baseball, however. These were actual, not virtual, players and they'd one day appear on a real ball field, not merely on a tabletop or computer screen, and play real opponents. Here I did not have the option of quitting, demanding a new team, or switching to another league—and trading was prohibited. And these players had parents I'd have to deal with, too.

Our starting lineup wasn't that hard to figure. Matt would pitch and Enrique would catch. Robby and Steve would form the right side of the infield and Amos would play the hot corner. I had qualms about Andy starting at shortstop, but I had graver doubts about others. And what about the Aliens in the outfield? Kipp gave us a solid center fielder, and it didn't much matter who played left and right because with a "power pitcher" like Matt or Andy hurling, hardly anything would fly out there, so I went with the better hitters, Ian and Mark Downey (if he showed up). That left five on the bench—assuming Big Joe's wrist had healed.

Manipulating the bench would be a real challenge. I'd heard about the genius moves you could make, but had never attempted one. The previous year our team was so weak it didn't matter who played where or when or for how long, so we just winged it. But now every move could spell victory or defeat.

I'd watched big league ball for decades, and I knew all about "double switches" and other arcane strategies, but in Little League it's an entirely different game (beyond the fact the games last only six innings). You *have* to use your bench—everyone must bat at least once and play at least two innings in the field. The really cutthroat managers try to figure out a way to fulfill the minimum requirement for their bench players, making sure they don't play a single out beyond two innings and for God's sake don't bat more than once.

Some managers believe in front-loading—start some of the weaker players, then get them out of there so they can finish the game with their best lineup. Others space out their moves so that several reserves are never on the field at the same time. So there's an art to this, apparently, but I barely even understood the rules, let alone how to exploit them.

Nevertheless, I spent an hour that afternoon devising lineups and planning how to move players around in the field and at bat, inning-by-inning. I hated to relegate anyone to the bench, but like most managers I told myself that everyone would get a chance to start "once we get a win under our belt." After that one win, managers sometimes amend that to "a few wins" or "once we're in first place." We lie to ourselves, but we're not good liars, so we feel guilty about it. Once you're in first place do you really want to wreck it by putting your best players on the bench half the time? That wouldn't be fair to the team as a whole (we tell ourselves); competing for a title supposedly pleases everyone, except maybe those not playing much.

My goal, then, was to rely on the more experienced players at first but work overtime with the others so that eventually they would challenge for starting roles and become interchangeable with the regulars. That would be fun for the players—and the manager. But for now the opening bench would be: Taddy, Jeremy, Mike Reilly, Little John, Big Joe. Not an easy out among them.

9

It already looked like our lucky year. Rain clouds broke during the night and opening day, April 21, dawned sunny and warm. I hadn't slept much, and was up to see the sunrise. As the day wore on, I could not concentrate on writing for more than ten minutes at a spell, so I took my nervous energy down to Memorial to inspect the field.

Two other teams had played the night before in a light drizzle and, as I expected, the infield was a mess. There's little or no maintenance at the Nyack field between games, since the village prohibits Little League from keeping a shed there with rakes, shovels, and other landscaping utensils. The infield already had more pockmarks than Beavis (or is it Butt-head?). I can live with that, but since my son is a pitcher I get obsessive about the mound. At most youth league fields the area around the rubber is a disaster area. The kids love to kick at the dirt in front of the rubber, invariably causing a hole—no, a small crater—by the second inning. This helps them get leverage but it can cause other problems, from losing balance to twisting ankles.

So I try to stop by the field on game day and fill in the hole left over from the previous night, scooping dirt from a nearby clay pile and packing it solidly, like concrete. If the opposing hurler wants to blast it out he'll have to use his spikes like a jackhammer, taking out his aggression on the mound instead of one of my batters.

That task completed, I went home and fretted some more. Then I finished my list of twenty-nine things to go over with the kids in the sixty seconds we'd have together on the bench before the game. *Have fun, relax. . . . Pee between innings, not during. . . . Chatter in infield?* And so forth. One thing I wouldn't have to worry about was "keeping the book," as it's called. That was Richards's thing, so all I had to do was write the starting lineup in the scorebook and he'd take it from there.

Richards had lived up to his billing. He attended every practice, loved to joke about our ups and downs on the phone, and was a steady presence around the kids—and around me, when I got (overly) worried. But if he knew a lot about baseball he was keeping it pretty close to his sweater-vest.

Growing up in the Philadelphia suburb of Berwyn, Richards never made Little League majors, but kept on playing (setting a happy example for his son today). He watched ball games on TV only when a pennant or World Series was at stake. After college, he went to India, lived in Halifax, got married, had a daughter, divorced, moved to New York, built lofts, met his wife, Pat, an editor and writer. About the closest he got to baseball was attending the victory parade after the Mets won the Series in '86 (funny, I don't remember seeing him there). Then the Jardens decided to move out of Manhattan and drew a circle on a map twenty-five miles around to see what fell within it. Their choice came down to Red Bank, New Jersey, or Nyack, and they chose Nyack.

Okay. The pre-game routine. Kid comes home from school, no time to mellow out, has to rush to get homework done before leaving. Not a bad thing, keeps him from sitting around worrying about game. Doesn't seem to be worrying anyway, leaving it to father. Father wishes he had homework so he could forget about game.

Then everyone has to get dressed. Son has all the luck. He gets to wear uniform—green A's shirt, gray pants, cleats—so no choices to make (except he chooses not to wear jockstrap, I'm sure). But father/coach has to decide on a "look"—athletic apparel, yuppie casual, or normal schlubby everyday attire? Aim for something slightly conceptual: plain T-shirt, jeans, denim jacket (Springsteen-on-the-ball-field). Check equipment bag, make sure have scorebook, game balls, two gloves, five bats, bottle of Gatorade for Andy (which he never remembers), and water bottle for the manager.

As we gathered up our stuff, the phone rang. It could only be bad news. It was the mother of the mercurial Mark Downey, with a request. She and her husband both had to work late; could I take him home after the game? No problem, I told her, knowing they live only a mile or so from the field. It was a promise I'd soon regret.

I'd told the kids to get to the field by 5:30 for the 6:00 start, but Andy and I left a little early at 5:15, wife to follow. In our Honda on the way, Andy seemed calm, humming a new Wallflowers tune (speaking of fathers and sons) while I chattered, reminding him to crouch at the plate, pause in his pitching delivery, and so on. "Yeah, yeah," he responded. "What kind of Gatorade did you get?"

It was a lovely night, warm for mid-April, the lowering sun dancing on the river as a few sailboats piloted by commuters just off the train headed out for an hour of blowing off New York City soot. We parked in the lot between the outfield and the river and lugged equipment to our bench, including the Alien head, which I'd bundled in a bag for secrecy. A couple of Pirates were already out on the field throwing the ball around. Andy unpacked the bats and helmets and lined them up next to the fence. There was no dugout, of course, just a wooden bench behind a chain link fence, with another fence behind that to keep the parents out of our hair

(or what was left of it). Since there are no bleachers at Memorial, some of the fathers use the fence to lean on the entire game, as they direct encouragement or abuse at their little slugger.

It felt good to be out there. Other players arrived, and we did look good in our A's caps. Dan Wolff threw batting practice, while I concentrated on our hurlers. If pitching is, according to cliché, 80 percent of big league baseball, then it must be twice that in Little League (as Yogi Berra might put it), so I warmed up Andy, Matt, and Steve for about five minutes each. Then I made out the lineup. I decided to bat Andy sixth—pretty far down for a coach's son, but not so low as to embarrass him (parents I can tune out, but this guy I have to live with).

And now we were ready to go, at last, six months after the try-outs last October.

As the players grabbed some pine, I went over my laundry list of enigmatic instructions, including "Be aggressive at the plate but take a walk" and "Just throw strikes but don't let them hit it." I sounded like Casey Stengel—when his mind started to go. After a minute or two of this foolishness the kids started pounding their gloves and poking each other in the ribs and I realized they just wanted to play ball—come wild swing or wild pitch—so I canned the rest of the lecture. I was afraid that if I said anything about on-deck batters, Little John would ask why it's called on *deck* when you're standing on *flat dirt*.

"Look, you guys, don't be afraid to make a mistake out there," I advised. "You know Bill Bradley, the basketball star and U.S. Senator? His Little League team made it to the regionals in Iowa and he cost them the game when he got tagged out at first on the old 'hidden ball' trick. And look what happened to *him* after-ward."

"They wouldn't let him play baseball anymore so he had to play basketball?" Kipp cracked.

"Who's Bill Bradley?" three other kids asked at once.

Good example, coach.

I didn't tell them that Bradley once said that a reason he wanted to run for President was to go back and win the Iowa caucus to avenge the hidden ball play.

Then I pulled out the mascot, to squeals of delight, and Andy announced that the A's were now the Aliens. Then I told them to "just have fun"—a coach's way of saying, "You'll have fun, if we win"—and after making them rub the mascot's bald ugly head, sent the Aliens out to the field.

Robby headed for first while Stephen took second, which must have surprised a few onlookers—whoever heard of a lefty second sacker? Steve had a good laugh about it, yelling over to me, "What's wrong with this picture?" But I reasoned that he provided an awfully short target for throws to first, and had better range than Robby at second, so why not defy convention?

"Play ball!" the umpire bellowed (as he knew he should, and laughed at himself). All of the umps in our league are volunteers, from the ranks of coaches, so he was just another unpaid amateur, probably a Little League dad.

Matt struck out the leadoff hitter, a good sign. Then he labored to find the plate, walking the next three batters, with a run scoring on a passed ball. The season was only five minutes old and we were already down a run. Matt's moving fastball made him hard to hit—but the ball inevitably broke outside to right-handed hitters. And it was hard for the catcher to catch.

Then we caught a break. Matt threw a pitch so wild it sailed over Enrique's head and struck the screen behind him on a fly. The runner on third naturally thought he could score, but the ball caromed back to Enrique, who tossed it underhand to Matt covering home, and he tagged the runner easily for the second out. Then he fanned the next batter to get out of the inning. Okay, I figured, we can live with that—one run shouldn't mean much at this stage of the season.

Kipp was the senior player on the team, but admitted to feeling nervous at the start of a game, and he struck out swinging at a bad pitch. Amos followed with a single, Robby walked, Ian reached on an error, and Stevie stroked a single. Andy interrupted the onslaught with a strike out, flailing at an awful pitch (would this be a repeat of last season?), but two more walks and wild pitches gave us a total of four runs. The knot began to loosen in my stomach.

We put the game away in the next frame, scoring seven runs on a bunch of walks and singles, including a hard shot to right by Andy. Our batters were already in "scoring position" when they stepped to the plate. Leading 11–2, I made mass substitutions, in light of what is known as the "ten-run rule"—a game must end after four or five innings if one team trails by ten or more runs. When I told John Marley I was sending him up to bat for Mark Downey, he naturally took advantage of the opportunity to ask me a question.

"Why do they call it *pinch-hitting?*" he wondered. Sportswriters talk about "wheels spinning" in the minds of managers, plotting strategy, but the only time it happened to me was when I confronted one of John's queries.

"Umm . . . back in the old days . . . managers didn't want the other team to know they were about to send up a substitute, so instead of pointing at the player they'd walk past and *pinch* him. So they became known as pinch-hitters." Seemed as good an explanation as any.

"Pinch them on the butt, or what?" Andy asked. Kids can't resist saying "butt" at least four times per game.

"If that works for you."

When Matt walked another batter in the Pirates' third, I summoned Andy to the mound, anxious to get a look at him in action and knowing he had a huge cushion to work with. He promptly struck out the next two hitters. Then we went out and got four more runs, and I was thrilled to see the little guys, Taddy and John, get on base, knowing how happy it made them and their folks. Then Andy struck out the side, and it was all over.

What a night. All of our kids had played well, we notched that first win, and Andy had performed above expectations. "I'm relieved," he said when we embraced briefly at the bench, "after last year." Parents walked past beaming. Like the players, they too need that first win under their belt, "to relax," as Jim Marley put it.

It was still pleasantly warm as Richards helped me pack up the equipment. Then the night came crashing down. I heard a shy woman's voice behind me say, "Is Mark here?" I turned around and a young black woman smiled at me. "I'm supposed to take him home," I said, "his mother called."

She looked perplexed. "She called *me* a couple of hours ago and told *me* to pick him up," she replied. "I'm the baby-sitter." Well, this was surprising, but swell—she'd save me a trip and I could stand around and gas with Richards a little longer. The problem was, the boy in question was nowhere to be seen. Apparently he'd split—or been abducted—as soon as the game ended without telling anyone, and the sitter looking the other way.

"Oh shit," I said to Richards. My afterglow was gone as I scanned the hillside (where drug sellers are known to gather during and after games) and parking lot. No luck. It didn't seem likely he'd simply decided to walk home, as it was now getting dark. Richards retrieved the cell phone from his car to call Mark's parents, the police, or both, but discovered his battery dead.

"I'll drive around and look for him," Richards improvised. "Me too," said the baby-sitter. By this time a sheriff's car had appeared in the parking lot—perhaps looking for child molesters or kidnappers—so I ran out there to report Mark missing and provided a description. The cop sped off, leaving me alone in the park—me and the potheads and our equipment bag. (If anyone hassled me I'd don the Alien mask and scare them out of their wits.)

I thought I'd better stick around in case Mark climbed out of the river after going for a twilight swim, but after ten minutes that got old, so I set off for his home myself. When I got there I noticed a car in the driveway and a light on. I knocked on the door and Mark's dad appeared, and I was relieved to see his son still in his uniform back toward the kitchen.

"Hi, wow, he made it home, good," I said.

"Just got here, and the police just left," his father answered, looking grim and unhappy. I thought he might apologize or at least explain the mixup, or thank me for sending out a search party, but instead he said, "Mark tells me he only played two innings and only got up twice."

My jaw almost dropped to my chest.

"First," I said, evenly, "we only played four innings, hardly anyone got up more than twice. Second, what happened after the game, he had three people in a panic?"

"Oh, my wife got home in time and decided to pick him up."

"After telling the baby-sitter and me to look after him, she shows up and doesn't tell anyone?"

Finally, he looked a bit abashed. "Just an oversight, sorry," he said, but he didn't look sorry, and still didn't thank me for mobilizing the troops to look for his son.

"Christ," was all I could say. "Next game is Thursday. Good night."

The postgame frenzy had taken the edge off our victory, but when I finally got home we still tried to make the most of it. And I was happy to learn that B.B. had enjoyed watching the "paint

dry" with her friends in the peanut gallery. The Aliens had
landed!

The Pirates did not appear to have much of a team, but something
significant set them apart. They were the only team in the league
with two black players. In fact, they were just about the only team
in the league with *any* black players.

In four years of Little League, Andy rarely had a black teammate. I'd always assumed the demographics would change as he
advanced, but that had not occurred. Why was the local Little
League so white when there were so many African-Americans and
Haitian-Americans living in our baseball community—or at least
the Nyack half of it? There are, to be sure, money issues (signing
up for Little League costs well over $100 a year) and transporta-
tion problems (many parents here do not own cars, or work odd
hours). With few black kids in Little League, there's no peer pressure to play baseball—perhaps it's even seen as *uncool*. The white
sport. It certainly is white—locally.

And increasingly, nationally. Baseball once was a showcase for
black athletes, in the wake of Jackie Robinson. Just a generation or
so ago most of the best players in baseball were African-American:
Willie Mays, Henry Aaron, Frank Robinson, Ernie Banks, Bob
Gibson, Willie McCovey, Joe Morgan, Lou Brock, Willie Stargell.
Then young black superstars emerged, including Dave Winfield,
Eddie Murray, Tony Gwynn, Barry Bonds, Ken Griffey Jr., Frank
Thomas, Barry Larkin, and Albert Belle. But this steady flow of tal-
ent has slowed to a trickle.

Nearly all of the star rookies who've come along in recent years
are white or Latin. In fact, it's becoming hard to name a black
superstar under the age of thirty. This is partly cultural—nothing
hip-hop has ever attached itself to baseball, except maybe for
Yankees' caps worn backward in music videos. But it's also partly
practical, as black kids and parents have explained to me. It's a

heck of a lot easier to find a friend for some one-on-one hoops than try to organize a pickup baseball game with ten other kids, especially since even white kids don't hang out at the sandlots anymore. And you can even play basketball by yourself.

Of course, I played *baseball* by myself for hours—days—at a time, but that was then, and that was me. According to a recent survey, twelve million kids now play organized basketball, seven million soccer, and five million baseball.

Many of the African-American kids have stars in their eyes, having witnessed young men seemingly just like them vault out of college—even high school—directly into the NBA, with multi-million-dollar contracts. They overlook the fact that they will not likely grow to be 6'4" or taller and thus have almost no chance to follow in those giant footsteps. Diehard baseball coaches plead with them to give Little League a shot, pointing out that they have a much better chance for a professional career in baseball where size doesn't matter (as much).

Finally, one must admit that many kids today, of all races, tend to see baseball as, well . . . a little . . . dull, in an age of joystick action and instant gratification. There's not much running in baseball, it's mostly finesse, meaning natural athletes don't often get to strut their stuff, and in fact, they can remain very weak players if they never learn to hit—witness Michael Jordan. One of Andy's Haitian classmates once said to me, "Baseball's too hard, it's easier shooting a basket." The following year, he belatedly played Little League and, after a while, hit the ball pretty well. He didn't own a glove, however, so I let him borrow one of my extras all season.

Marty Schupak, the respected local manager, recalls a similar situation a few years back. A kid new to baseball came to practice one day without his glove. "Make sure you have it for the next game," Marty told him.

"It's in the trunk of my uncle's car," the kid said, smiling.

"Good, then it's no problem."

"My uncle's car is in Georgia."

Dave Siegriest, the Nyack High baseball coach, says the best black athletes tell him that baseball is simply "boring."

One of the most prominent black Little League families around here are the Baltimores. Bryan Baltimore and younger brother Terry became all-stars, and their affable dad, Stu, an insurance agent, has always coached and presently serves on the league's board. Stu himself was a Little League and high school star across the river in Dobbs Ferry. His father might have been good enough to play pro if there had been no color line, and one of his wife's cousins made it to Triple A with the Astros a few years ago.

When I talked to Stu once about the "race issue," he said even in his own household baseball may not be number one. "My kids don't watch baseball," he says, "which is how I learned the game when I was growing up. Instead they'll play a video game—even a baseball video game." Terry frankly favors football and basketball because there's "more action" and "less pressure on one player," his father explains.

Low minority enrollment has come back to haunt the league in other ways. Nyack officials often use it as a reason (or excuse) for not providing more funds for the league or for improving facilities at Memorial Park. For years the league took the approach "We can't make anyone play who doesn't want to," but recently began a recruitment drive, signing up black kids at football games and offering to reduce fees if necessary. Minority enrollment is up only slightly.

And nationally, the racial divide in baseball continues to widen. Not a single black kid made the latest USA Today high school All-American team. Will baseball keep getting whiter and basketball blacker? With what consequences for kids—and racial harmony as a whole?

• • •

The Aliens, who had just rocketed into space, now appeared ready to crash. Three of our best hitters would miss all or part of the next game against the Yankees, who had also won their first game. Mark Downey, of course, had a soccer conflict, Stephen was out of town, and Arlene Keiser told me Robby could not miss his piano lesson because of an upcoming recital (but he'd try to make it to the field later).

I was also nervous because Andy would start on the mound. Coming on in relief, your team may already be way ahead or far behind, but if you pitch poorly as a starter it's hard to miss, and you might take your team out of the game right away. Also, the opposing team puts its best hitters up first, so your starter always faces a challenging first inning. Later in the game, as a reliever, you're bound to face a few weak reserves.

Our players drifted down to Memorial uncomfortably close to game time, but I'd never stressed pre-game warm-ups. I knew kids had homework and music practice, and in some families both parents work full-time. In the old Donna Reed days, Mom would always be around to drop Junior off at a game, but now Donna might be on the 5:12 out of Grand Central. In fact, in Nyack, it was often the freelance father who was around the house most of the day and performed the schlepping duties.

I enjoyed the ritualized arrival of the players. Here they'd come, across the outfield, with their bat bag or cleats slung over their shoulders, a bottle of water or Gatorade in one hand, glove in the other, happy and alone for the moment, but soon part of a noisy ensemble. It was easy to say a few words of greeting to each, ask how they were feeling, and compliment them on something they'd done the previous game. Then they'd joke with their teammates, slap on batting gloves and other unnecessary accessories, and run onto the field to take a few swings or stretch those arms! To warm up the pitchers, I'd try to find a grassy spot behind the screen that parents hadn't already colonized with lawn chairs and blankets.

Last game, three of our kids had missed my "take" sign. Maybe Little John was right: I ought to take a poster out there with "Take the next pitch" written on it in big letters. Instead, I told them to forget the signs for now—but "always take on 3 and o."

"Unless the 3 and o pitch is good," Taddy said confidently.

"You still have to take it. Because you might walk on the next pitch."

"Why would anyone want to do *that?*" Little John wondered. He found the notion of not hacking at any pitch near the strike zone unthinkable. I could erect a billboard in back of second base with TAKE THE DAMN PITCH emblazoned on it and he'd still act like a tiny Travis Bickle, you know—*You talking to ME?*

Facing the Yanks, we scored a run in the first and then Andy took the mound. A walk and infield single left runners on first and third with two outs and Andy faced his first personal crisis of the season. The batter was a cocky classmate who has always given Andy grief over the years, for no apparent reason. Now he was up at bat. The count went 3–2 and then he swung and missed and Andy bounded off the mound. I felt so good for him I could have kissed him ("but it would have been wrong").

We scored three more in the second, with the Kippster delivering his second hit of the game, and it looked like we might breeze after all. Making the Alien our mascot was already paying dividends. A lot of kids stroked his bald noggin before going up to hit. Some did it because they hadn't gotten untracked at the plate and wanted a lit-tle edge. Others had been hitting well, having rubbed the head since the first game, and didn't want to break the spell. And I'd thought only adults were childish enough to be superstitious.

The Yanks scored two runs, but we matched that in the third, with Big Joe, one of our mighty subs, blasting a double in the gap (apparently his wrist felt fine), and we were up again 6–2. Andy started losing it the next inning, but kept the Yanks off the board with the most spectacular play of the season so far—at shortstop, even though he was still pitching. A kid named Conor stroked a double to left center. Amos, playing short, went out for the relay, and Joe's throw sailed over his head. But Andy was backing up and the ball landed on the fly in his glove right at the shortstop position. Conor, seeing the relay sail over the cutoff man, had rounded second and headed for third—but the ball and his rump met as Andy applied the tag. It was a big league play.

I got Andy out of there on that high note, and Matt came in to pitch a perfect fourth. But in the fifth it all came apart for the Aliens, with walks, errors, and hits leading to five runs. Unnerved, Matt muttered to himself on the mound, "Get it together," but the more he tried to calm himself the more uptight he got, and now we trailed 7–6.

Andy led off for us in the fifth, and no doubt, last inning. It's often said, "There's no clock in baseball," but whoever coined that phrase never watched a game at Memorial Park. Because the village won't put in lights, umps call many games because of darkness after just four or five innings. Baseball at Memorial confirms another adage, Yogi Berra's "It gets late early out there." This keeps managers on their toes, knowing you may have to engineer a rally sooner rather than later. Sometimes the falling darkness assures a comeback, as fielders lose balls in the dusk.

"Get on base—or we'll kill you," Robby Keiser said in encouragement, and Andy shook with laughter. (Rob had made it to the game after all.) Hey, we were loose! Andy gritted his teeth and worked out a walk—and then came around to score the tying run on steals and wild pitches. With the moon rising over the Hudson they called the game, and we escaped with a 7–7 tie.

Shaking hands with Yanks' skipper Glenn Meyerson, I said, "Great outcome because no one deserved to lose," but I was a little down afterward. As George Brett once said, a tie is like kissing a girl—your sister.

. . .

When I got home, I remained melancholy, which was strange, from a personal standpoint, in that Andy had again pitched well, made a spectacular tag play in the field, and scored the tying run. "Why the long face?" B.B. asked, as I sipped a beer, trying to relax. This cracked me up, as I recalled a stupid joke the late song-writer Townes Van Zandt once told: A horse goes into a bar and orders a drink, and the bartender asks him, "Why the long face?"

As I reflected, over my brew, I realized that I cared desperately about the Aliens as a team, and wanted them to get off to a strong start, gain confidence, and have fun. If I only cared about how Andy played, I'd be elated right now, but I was not. Strangely, recognizing this finally got me out of my funk. Maybe I'd make a good manager after all.

My wife admitted that, whatever my baseball excesses, I was probably right about Andy and pitching. It did seem to be his thing. The kind of focus he finds on the mound is rare for him. We don't see it that often, except sometimes when he's sketching, fin-ishing a Lego project, or playing guitar. Overhearing our conver-sation, Andy explained, "It's just you, the batter, and the catcher. And the ball. Sometimes I think of the catcher's glove as a magnet and forget about everything else. It's relaxing somehow."

"Tunnel vision," I observed.

"It may be calming for you, Andy," his mom advised, "but it's nerve-wracking for me!"

"Hey, Andy," I said, "maybe we ought to send *her* to pitching camp."

Still, I kept wondering: If we could only tie the Yanks, how could we possibly beat or even compete with Eddie Badger's Tigers? They'd devoured the Yanks 16–4, with a fourteen-run inning. And what if the other teams we hadn't faced were better than us, too? It wouldn't take long to start finding out, with the mighty Tigers up next.

10

When it started drizzling the morning of the Tigers game I rooted for a rainout. I had a bad feeling about today's contest. It would be our first game at the big ballpark in Valley Cottage, where few of our kids had played before, and our first day game. If we did play, the field would be wet, and it was horribly humid. Who said when it rains it pours? Never on a game day when you need it.

Arriving at Liberty a bit early, I found the Tigers already well into batting practice, and using a pitching machine. Had they been there since breakfast? None of our guys had arrived, so I had to stand in the outfield warming up my one player—Andy—while various Tigers hit or chased line drives in the gap. After most of our team showed up, I asked Eddie Badger if he was ready to relinquish the field, and he said, okay, then threw to three or four more batters.

Batting practice, of course, is nearly meaningless. Anyone can hit off a coach but it's a different story when they have to face a kid with a jerky motion and absolutely no idea where the ball might go next—toward the batter's skull, for example. But clearly, Badger was in battle mode. Few Tigers dare crack a smile until they left the field. They already had their game faces on (they had no choice).

I'd heard that the Tigers had narrowly avoided an upset in their recent game against the Pirates. With Danny Stroud pitching, the Pirates led 2–1 after four innings. Eddie then informed opposing manager John Miller that league rules dictated that no one could hurl more than four innings in a game. This was nonsense, of course. Pitchers are limited to six innings per week, but you can use all of them in one game if you wish. But Miller, new to the league, removed Stroud, and watched the Tigers get three in the fifth to win the game 4–2.

Still, I tried to be friendly, suspecting we were about to get squashed and wanting to communicate that we didn't take winning seriously. Exchanging lineups, Eddie couldn't resist needling me. "I hear Matt Scimeca is throwing a curve," he said. Everyone knows kids at this level shouldn't throw breaking balls, to protect their arms, but that doesn't stop most coaches from showing their pitchers how to do it. I considered confirming this, as it would make Tigers' batters, and their manager, uptight facing Matt, but I didn't want to get a reputation for trying to win at any cost. Also, I was determined not to let Eddie rattle me.

"No curve," I teased, "but he does throw a wicked knuckleball. And a spitball."

"Oh sure," Eddie replied. "You're kidding . . . right?"

But with Matt's collapse in the previous game still in mind, I decided to start Andy. The last thing I wanted was for Andy to get whacked by a tough team, shattering his confidence, but for once I threw caution to the wind. It appeared to pay off as Andy pitched a perfect opening frame, striking out Eddie's son to close it.

We had our first, but far from last, run-in with the Tigers in the bottom of the inning. Kipp led off with a walk. After two more walks he came home with a run on a passed ball. The pitcher took the throw at home as Kipp slid. Although the Kippster barely brushed him, he collapsed at the plate, grabbing his leg—surely more upset about giving up a run than suffering some mortal wound. Without any evidence, Eddie rushed toward me, accusing

Kipp of wearing metal spikes. I could only chortle in response. "Eddie, come off it, no one wears metal spikes in this league—they're rubber. You think Kipp's another Ty Cobb or something?"

"Well, let's check, let's check," he blustered.

Then Andy went out to face the Tigers with a one-run lead. He got two quick strikes on his former teammate Rocco, but then the Rock fouled off three tough pitches on the way to working a walk. Andy struck out the next two batters and seemed in command, but then, facing the bottom of the order, he walked two more, two runs scored on steals, and we were down 2–1. Okay. Not bad.

We failed to score in the third, putting the pressure squarely on Andy, and he walked two more batters—his mechanics looked way off—then gave up a ringing double to Rocco, and by the time the uprising was over we were down 5–1. This wasn't good enough for one of the Tigers' parents, however. I could hear him in the stands constantly criticizing his son—at bat, in the field, even in the dugout (and his boy was a good player). When the kid got hit by a pitch, a painful shot to the ankle, Dad just laughed and shouted out to his son, who had collapsed in the batter's box, "That will leave a nice mark! Get up!"

Perhaps feeling his oats, Eddie burst over to our dugout between innings, and started waving his finger in my face. "Your players are swearing in front of my team and it has to stop!" he complained between clenched teeth. His right index finger was about an inch from my nose.

"Eddie, first off, get your finger out of my face," I said, still managing a smile, "I don't know where it's been. And second, what are you talking about?"

"Your guys are out there saying curse words to my kids, and I don't allow that kind of language," he said. That was funny, I'd heard him drop a few *hells* and *damns* during the first few innings.

"I'll talk to them about it," I promised, and he finally retreated.

As the Aliens assembled on the bench, preparing to hit, I asked if anyone knew anything about this. I hate trash talk, and I didn't expect anyone to confess, but I was surprised by the unanimity of the response: Four of our guys said that the kid who started it was the Tigers' shortstop. With that, I hoped to watch us score ten quick runs, but this was no field of dreams today. The Tigers mauled Matt the Bat and pulled away for a 14–5 trouncing. About the only positive sign: I got Stephen on the mound in the final inning, a perfect spot for his pitching debut, with no pressure, and he struck out the side.

When I asked Matt after the game what went wrong, he said that he was throwing harder than ever but the pitches "weren't going as fast."

"Maybe that magnetic field between the mound and home is slowing them down," I said, deadpan.

"Has that always been here?"

The highlight of the game came near the end. We were hopelessly out of it as Cool Taddy Bell came to bat. He hadn't had a good cut for a while, using a bat that was much too long and heavy for him. So I'd brought along a smaller one Andy had used two years ago. Tad scorned it, as it was an old, gray antique; the new, high-speed models all have fancy colors or designs, but I ordered him to try it. Naturally, on the first pitch, he stroked a solid single to right field and then stood delightedly on first. I was as happy for him as I was for myself, as I'd just reaffirmed my (now shaky) coaching credentials.

After the game I told the kids to forget about the Tigers, it was just one game and we'd done our best. Andy hates it when I say that, after a losing game, or when he does not do well. His reasoning is impeccable when you think about it. "If you do your best and still fail," he'll say, "then how good can you be? If you did your *best*."

I found Vicky Scimeca fidgeting out in the parking lot.

"Don't let Matt get too down about this," I said.

"Oh, don't worry, when he gets home he always looks at the positive side."

"That's what I tell everyone to do."

"He carries it a bit far, though," she explained. "Like, we'll say, 'You struck out on a really bad pitch.' You know, he should learn from that. And he'll say, 'But no one was on base.'"

"So if he gives up a three-run homer, he'll say it could have been a grand slam?"

"Something like that."

"Looking on the sunny side—there are worse things. Take it from me."

Well, Matt *did* get a few guys out. But I was drained by the long game, bad pitching, wretched errors, and childish behavior by certain adults. And I realized that I'd forgotten to ask the kids to rub the Alien's head at the start of the game—no wonder we lost. Unforgivable.

Added to this, the multiple Badger incidents made me wonder if it was all worth it. Maybe you really had to practice three times a week and arrive an hour before the game if you wanted to succeed. Maybe it was even good for the kids to get pushed hard and often, so they could improve and play up to their abilities—even if this turned off some players and parents. Maybe to win you had to treat every game like Gettysburg.

And let me say this about Badger: The fact that he was a zealot on the ball field doesn't necessarily mean he's a bad human being.

Kipp probably had the proper perspective, advising me after the game to "forget Eddie, he's just like a little kid who can't stand losing so he tries tricks." Even so, I didn't look forward to facing his antics for the rest of the year. Ty Cobb once said, "The great American game should be an unrelenting war of nerves," but I don't think he was talking about games between pre-teens. I found myself wishing that Bob Giacobbe had stayed on to manage another year so I could just be a lowly coach, in the background. Andy would still get to play and I could concentrate on coaching him. Now I had to go to bed with the foibles of thirteen other kids, and myself, in my head. And we were only three games into the season. . . .

The next day, to get my mind off this and yet remain in what Donald Hall calls "the country of baseball," I surfed the Net searching for a few laughs. I'd gotten hooked earlier in the spring searching for coaching tips, and now I was a web-ball junkie. Many of the baseball sites, if you don't take them seriously, can be quite entertaining. There's a site, for example, that lists every baseball song ever recorded, with most of the funny titles relating to the men in blue, such as: "The Umpire Is a Most Unhappy Man," "Let's Get the Umpire's Goat," and "Don't Kill the Umpire Until the Last Man Is Out." There is no truth to the rumor that this last ditty is set on a Little League field.

Speaking of Little League, there's an authoritative web site devoted to heckling, with hundreds of free samples for anyone feeling a little low on creativity before a big game. And there are three separate sites devoted to baseball nicknames coined by ESPN broadcaster Chris Berman. Here you'll find odes to Von "Purple" Hayes, Rick "See Ya Later" Aguilera, Ron "Born in the U.S." Cey, Vida "Tangled Up In" Blue, and the immortal John "I Am Not A" Kruk. My favorite wacko site, however, is the Mendoza Line. It explores the history and folklore of what it calls "the most famous line since Mason/Dixon," named after the weak-hitting big league infielder Mario Mendoza. As true fans know, a player is said to fall below the Mendoza Line when his batting average sinks past .200. Inevitably, a rock group from Athens, Georgia, now uses the name The Mendoza Line.

Damn, I was about to suggest that name to Andy for *his* group.

My favorite site for a few laughs, however, is the eBay auction area. Baseball fans, of course, will buy anything. Perhaps you've heard of the Pennsylvania woman who recently paid $7,475 for Ty Cobb's dentures. Now this is the beautiful part: Her father was a dentist for fifty-three years. The evil Cobb is famous for filing his spikes before a game; perhaps now we will learn whether he filed his teeth as well. At eBay you can spend hours (and some do, e.g., my friend Peter) scanning the baseball memorabilia, paraphernalia, and marginalia for sale, from Musial-era mitts as low as $20 to seats from Ebbets Field as high as $2,000. I buy old baseball cards off eBay from time to time, but that's serious business as it involves actually spending money. Window shopping is much more fun.

On this Sunday afternoon, I really "scored" without spending a buck. There was, literally, an embarrassment of riches to peruse. Someone was selling a menu from Willie Mays's Grilled & Roasted Chicken restaurant (long deceased) in Menlo Park, New Jersey. It included a printed message from Willie himself: "Taste my chicken and you'll Say Hey." For a one-of-a-kind buy, however, you'd have to consider: a Christmas menu (unknown date) from a federal penitentiary in Texas autographed by several former Kansas City Royals doing time there for drugs: Willie Wilson, Vida Blue, Willie Aikens, Jerry Martin. Surprise your friends with that one! Bidding started at $75.

But if you really wanted to impress them: How about Babe Ruth's underwear? No, not shorts he'd worn himself—that would have been priceless, not a lousy $152 (which was what these were going for)—but rather a piece of vintage clothing with the Babe's facsimile signature in red on the label. "You probably won't ever get a chance at one of these again," the seller boasted, and for once eBay hyperbole rang true.

Yet you could purchase an even more intimate item of apparel if you chose. Take a look, there's even a color snapshot of it: a jockstrap worn, and signed, by Mark McGwire during his rookie season in 1987 with the Oakland A's. You had to wonder: How did the seller happen to get this piece? According to him, it came from the team trainer. The bigger question: Would anyone pay good money for such a . . . thing? When I checked, thirty-five people had already entered bids, and the price had cracked a thousand bucks, with two more days of auction left. "Just try getting Mark to sign one of these nowadays," the seller advised. "Good luck!" But if you bought it, what would you do with it? Wash and wear it? Mount it on the living room wall? Use it to carry groceries?

Fortunately, at least one eBay customer felt that this was going a bit far, and posted a parody item for sale starting at two bucks: *Rare Mark McGwire Chewed Gum!* On second thought: What if this wasn't a parody?

After taking a day to restore my sense of humor (and absurdity), I found I was still concerned about the behavior of certain baseball parents and coaches, so I decided to start investigating, for my own sake, what others think about the father/son dynamic in Little League. Over the next several weeks, I would consult books and magazines, and talk informally to other local coaches and parents, a current big leaguer, and one Hall of Famer.

Probably not a single Nyack dad will ever have the experience of watching his kid climb the mountain to the major leagues, but perhaps I could also learn something from those who have.

According to legend, Ted Williams carried his bat to class at high school in San Diego, his glove hooked to his belt. He received little encouragement from his father, who hardly noticed his son playing ball until he started reading stories in the newspaper about Ted's high school exploits. Later, Ted encouraged his own son's interest in baseball, but the boy, John Henry, never advanced far. Indeed few sons of ballplaying legends get anywhere near the majors. For every Moises Alou or Bret Boone there's a Dale Berra (who had a rocky major league career), a Pete Rose Jr. (who barely emerged from the minors), and a few thousand others who never even made it to college ball.

"Well, it's a hard act to follow," Ted once told writer Dick Wimmer, "and I think it's harder today for *any* kid to excel in sports as well as their fathers did. Because I don't think they have the time, they're lookin' at television, they're gonna have other interests, and all the major sports are involved now. But when I was a kid, it was baseball, baseball, baseball." Asked what he'd like *his* son to say about him, Ted uttered words that could spring from the lips of any Little League dad: "Well, I'd like my kid to say, 'Boy, my dad was a helluva guy and he loved me and he did everything he could for me and he gimme the right advice and he was an extra-special guy.'"

Perhaps the most famous ballplayer's son who didn't follow in his father's footsteps is country music superstar Tim McGraw, whose dad is former reliever Tug "Ya Gotta Believe" McGraw. According to press reports, Tim barely knew who his father was until he reached adulthood. Most sons of star players know all too well whose footsteps they're following.

Bosox immortal Carl Yastrzemski, who replaced Williams in left field when he came to the majors in 1960, had a pure baseball childhood. His father, who once had major league aspirations, farmed on Long Island from six to six every day, but set aside a couple of hours every night to practice with his boy—around home or with Dad's semipro team. At the end of his career Yaz suggested that baseball had *never* been fun, but "all hard work." He admitted that at first he merely wanted to live out his father's dream, but eventually, it became his dream, too.

Most star players do not complain that their fathers pushed them too hard, but rather that they disciplined them too much, back in Little League, because they were often the "coach's kid." One wonders if this rather benign view reflects reality or has been softened by years of success and riches. When first questioned about this, Mike Schmidt rhapsodized about the "loving, family-oriented environment" he came from. He said his dad encouraged him, bought him the best equipment, and helped run the leagues he played in. But on further probing he admitted that his father was critical of "everything I did. I was really never good enough for him. He was on me all the time." He could watch his son slug home runs and "not bat an eye," as Mike put it.

This emotional terrorism may have helped Schmidt become the player he was—just as it's driven many others to fail or quit base-ball entirely. Earl Weaver, the Orioles skipper, had it twice as hard as most. As a player he never made it to the majors, and his father rode him all the way. Then he became a manager and his dad acted as if "every damn move I made was wrong."

The late Cal Ripken Sr., was the only man in baseball history to manage two sons at the same time, but Jack Brett sent even more kids into pro ball. Everyone knows about George Brett, the Hall of Famer, and Ken Brett, a big league pitcher, but two other brothers made it to the minors. Yet the elder Brett became best known for never attending a single one of George's World Series or playoff games and generally refusing to talk about his boy. "You can't get too close to your sons," he once told reporters. "I think that with a friendly look, a little smile, and nodding your head, you can show your affection. If he hit four homers in a row, I would not say any-thing to him. . . . My attitude is, 'He had a great game, but he was lucky.'"

Keith Hernandez's father played a similar role. When the Mets were all the rage in New York in the latter half of the 1980s, Keith often talked about the postgame phone calls from his father, aimed at getting him out of a slump. "I've tried to pull away," Hernandez once said, "but he won't let me. I'd tell him, 'Dad, I'm a man. I don't want to be reliant on you for my career. Dad, I'm twenty-eight. . . . Dad, I'm thirty. . . ." His father, Keith said, wanted to take credit for his success, wanted everyone, particularly his son, to know he couldn't have made it without his dad pushing him. But this was more cliché than reality. Keith found it hard to believe that no great athlete *ever* made it without "a father that pushed and pushed and pushed."

After traveling the country talking to former players, Dick Wimmer decided that nearly all of them were "obsessive" about baseball, but got there from different angles. He calculated that roughly 40 percent had fathers who were distant, and another 40 percent had demanding fathers who were almost impossible to please. Few of these ballplayers ever seemed to rebel—"still striving to satisfy their real fathers or surrogate fathers in the form of managers or coaches. How many coaches, how many managers had they tried to please since they'd begun . . . and who'd told them what to do or *else?*"

Judging by what current big league players say, little has changed over the years. Many trace their success directly to their fathers, some of them admit their dads pushed a little too hard—the majority still rely on them for support or advice.

Many players cite the work habits of their fathers as inspiration for their dedication to the game. When Cal Ripken Jr. was a boy his father went out to do a little snowplowing on his tractor, and a crank flew off and struck him in the head, leaving a deep gash. Instead of heading to a hospital for treatment, he slapped a rag on the wound and resumed plowing. "When I get the feeling that things are a little low," Cal Jr. said years later, "that I need a little motivation, I visualize the tractor-crank story. That pushes me."

The Yankees' Andy Pettitte refers to his father as his pitching coach since the day he first picked up a baseball, but one year his dad worked the graveyard shift at a chemical plant instead of staying home and watching his son pitch in a playoff series against the Texas Rangers. He could no longer stand to hear announcers commenting that Andy had a "disappointing" season, despite winning sixteen games. "It's not fun listening to people beat up your kid," he explained (and we can all relate to that). But then he added, revealingly, "I've always been more critical of Andy than any New York fan or New York media, but he's my kid. I can do that. To hear other people ripping your kid hurts." Perhaps that paternal criticism explains why Andy is known for being too much of a perfectionist, often pitching "too fine" instead of letting his natural ability carry him.

His teammate, Derek Jeter, seems just the opposite, with preternatural ease and grace, always wearing a confident little half-grin. But he almost didn't get this far. His father, Charles Jeter, recalls a turning point one day in Little League back in Kalamazoo, Michigan, when his son refused to shake hands with the opposing team after a tough loss. Dad told Derek it might be "time to grab a tennis racket, since you obviously don't know how to play a team sport."

The rise of Mike Piazza to perennial All-Star status is one of the most amazing stories in sports. A mediocre youth player, he was drafted by the Dodgers in the final round purely as a favor to his father, a friend of Dodgers manager Tommy Lasorda. But he worked like a demon and eventually proved the doubters wrong. Apparently his work ethic was instilled by his father, Vince. Unlike most players today, Mike grew up in a cold, northern climate (Pennsylvania). To practice in the winter he'd hit balls into a mattress propped up against the basement wall. His father built a batting cage in the backyard and in winter Mike would shovel snow so he could keep hitting. Or his father would move furniture so Mike could hit Wiffle balls in the living room. "What I did with Mike then, if I did that now, they'd probably get me for child abuse," Vince Piazza once confessed, but unfortunately did not elaborate.

As I've mentioned, few major leaguers have come out of Rockland County. Perhaps it's too cold up here. Kids can only practice half the year, unlike their peers in the Sunbelt. Well, that probably doesn't matter—kids up here don't play all that much even during the six warm months.

Savvy shortstop Walt Weiss is perhaps the best-known player to emerge from Rockland, hailing from Suffern, at the other end of the county. C. J. Nitkowski, who also hails from Suffern, has pitched in the majors for quite a while with mixed success. Once a hot prospect as the Reds' number one draft pick out of college in '94, his career started slowly, even as he gained renown as the first baseball "web star." A few years ago, pitching for the Astros, he set up his own web site, and *USA Today* did a piece about this rookie hurler who came back to his hotel room after games and answered all his e-mail.

Always looking for expert pitching advice, I'd dropped him a line back then, via AOL, wondering what advice he'd pass along to my son. Perhaps worrying that I'd push Andy too hard, he told me not to let him lift weights or anything like that. "At nine, let him go, don't overdo it," he added. "I didn't know what mechanics were until I was sixteen."

This sounded like a levelheaded guy—for a left-hander—so I decided to send him another note, but this time my questions concerned not Andy's pitching but the father/son dynamic and some of the coaching shenanigans in Little League. How had things gone with Nitkowski and his dad?

C.J. e-mailed a reply promptly. He said he'd felt he was going to the big leagues "since the day I could talk," regardless of ups and downs. "I loved to play catch," he wrote. "My dad would throw me pop-ups, I could do that all day (and probably still could)." His father coached Little League, directing his son with a fairly light hand, and C.J. claimed he didn't take away a single negative thing from it. "The coaches I had were pretty laid-back," he revealed, "not like some of these lunatics you hear about today, screaming, yelling, complaining. I hate that, it's brutal. The game is for fun, let your kids enjoy it."

By the time he was a star at St. John's University, his dad focused not on the field but on his "career"—that is, when to sign a pro contract, and for how much. Somehow I doubt I'll ever be in that position, but I asked C.J. what advice he would offer to any Little League father? "Let your kids play the game," he wrote. "Little League memories last forever. Don't make them bad memories for your kids. Nobody wants to remember the horror of your dad yelling at you from the stands after you struck out."

Vowing to remain upbeat and laugh at controversy, I looked forward to our next game against the Rockies, who had gotten off to a rough start, including a 16–8 thrashing from the Tigers. It was a chilly, damp evening, but we were back in the friendly confines of Memorial Park. That scent of marijuana wafting down from the "upper deck" smelled like home cooking to us, but the boom boxes were starting to get to me.

Sometimes I'd ask a husky father to climb the hill and ask the revelers to turn it down, but never had the nerve to do it myself. A few years ago a manager had on his team a Nyack kid whose father had once been busted for dope. During a game at Memorial the music on the hill was blaring and, without thinking, the manager sent this fellow up there to ask for quiet. He didn't return for a while. "He probably went up there," the manager joked, "and said, 'Please turn down that stereo and, by the way, does anyone have some weed?'"

Most of our players arrived late—even by our standards—for pre-game warm-ups. Mike Reilly showed up balancing a slice of greasy pizza in his mitt (perhaps this was just his way of oiling his glove). When I complained to Stephen about his late arrival he said, "You know Mrs. Kennell and homework, and now I have to finish this Franklin D. Roosevelt report."

Don't let it be said that I ever let baseball stand between FDR and the next generation.

"We're worried about Stephen getting through the season," his mother told me. "Not because of baseball injuries but weariness from homework." For better or worse, this did not seem to be *my* son's problem.

Mark Downey again failed to show. He was more cipher than ballplayer. Always a soccer conflict. Wasn't that a fall sport? Hadn't his father sworn, up and down, there would be no conflicts? Richards had dubbed him "Mysterious Mark," and it looked likely to stick.

Learning my lesson from the last game, I made sure the team gathered around the Alien and rubbed his head for luck. We had our usual complement of fathers in our dugout, way over the league limit: me and the two official coaches (Richards and Dan), plus Bob Keiser and Jon Albert, who referred to himself as a "dugout groupie," and sometimes Jim Marley and Big Enrique. We could nearly field a second team—of fathers.

Most of them played a clearly defined role. Richards, of course, kept the book and announced who was up next. This is what you probably already suspect about Richards as a scorekeeper: He's never witnessed an error in Little League. Going by his book, none of our guys had booted a single ball all year. And those little grounders our players hit that scooted through one, sometimes two, pairs of legs? Now they all looked like line drives. (Apparently Richards's mission was to make sure all our players ended the season with a higher batting average than Tony

Gwynn.) The man simply never learned how to write the letter *E* back in grammar school.

Dan Wolff's job was to run the pre-game warm-ups, work with the hitters, and chat up the kids in the dugout, keeping them loose and at least vaguely aware of what was happening on the field. "What's the count?" he'd shout out to the gremlins on the bench. This was asking for trouble, unless you were willing to force them to pay attention, and he wasn't. Neither was I.

"Two and one," Taddy might say, just guessing.

"Three and two," Jeremy would correct him, also guessing.

"Why do they call it *the count?*" This was Guess Who.

Dan had egalitarian instincts and was quick to remind me to get the subs in the game. And when an umpire didn't show up, he was always the first parent off the bench to pinch-hit behind the plate, as he had a reputation for fairness. He even called his own son out on strikes one time. Still, I sensed he was enough of a jock himself to relish a hard-fought game. Although pushing fifty, he keeps in shape and still plays a lot of basketball and softball.

What Dan is best known for, around town, is not his Sam Cooke book, but his community activism. He's long been active with the local NAACP and on the board of Head Start. With his wife and others he helped start an ambitious group, Partners in Education, pushing for reforms in Nyack public schools. They believe in, among other things, making changes in teaching, tracking, and curriculum so that all kids, including blacks and the disadvantaged, get a chance to succeed and not be "profiled" as likely to fail. This rubs some white, middle-class parents the wrong way, as many of *their* kids are also struggling to keep up, or suffering because the school district spends relatively little on gifted programs. It's made Dan a lightning rod, the subject of Op-Ed columns and letters to the editor in the local paper, as defenders of the school system accuse him of political correctness, and worse.

Sometimes Dan coached first base for us, always a challenge. Typically, the coach down there would tell one of the Aliens to "steal on the next pitch." More often than not the kid would shake his head yes, then stay anchored to the bag.

"Why didn't you steal?"

"You really meant that?"

Often this would be repeated for two or three pitches. Maybe we should have tried Shakespeare with them. . . .

"When time is ripe, which will be suddenly, you will steal."

"My heels are your command—I run."

"Hence! Home, get you home!"

Big Bob Keiser was always welcome as a bouncer in our dugout whenever he could get away from work at IBM. He kept a semblance of order amid the chaos on the bench and made sure the on-deck batter wore a helmet and did not brain anyone with a bat (he called his job "crowd control"). Occasionally he'd comment wickedly about the overbearing behavior of opposing managers. He knew something about that, for he has the distinction of being the only parent in our league who once played for one of the legendary wildman coaches, Bobby Knight.

After completing Little League in a small town west of Ann Arbor, Michigan, Bob Keiser quit baseball, finding his 6'2" frame better suited to basketball and football ("I liked to hit people"). When he entered West Point he found himself playing freshman basketball at a time Bobby Knight coached the varsity. From time to time Knight "showed up to persecute the frosh," as Bob puts it. He recalls one Knight drill where he'd split the squad into two lines and then roll a ball between them. The two guys at the head of each line would dive for the ball, banging their bodies on the hardwood. The loser had to return to the head of his line; bruised and exhausted he had *no chance* against the next guy—and the guy after that.

Even more painful was a drill Knight ordered at the end of practice. Everyone had to shoot two free throws, and for each one you missed, your teammates had to run two windsprints. That meant "you'd get your ass kicked in the shower room" if you missed a lot. One day he watched Knight throw a chair into the trophy case in the gym. He had no idea why. Knight was "the devil incarnate," Bob thought. "He scared the shit out of me." Perhaps Bob was fortunate to get cut from the frosh team.

The Keisers moved to Nyack shortly after Robby was born in 1986. Bob, the old jock, is still more of a sports fan than his son. "I never pressured Rob on baseball," Bob once told me. "Maybe that's why he enjoys it when he does play."

As our game began, I looked forward to seeing how Amos fared catching. Enrique was doing fine, but he'd missed some pitches in the dirt the first few games, trotting back to the screen on a semi-regular basis. Too often the old Little League adage, "A walk means a run," had come true, though it was mainly our pitchers' fault. I'd wanted to try someone else back there to give us a part-time option, but felt nervous about insulting Enrique and his father. With Enrique scheduled to arrive late for this game, it gave me a perfect chance to try Amos, and he seemed enthusiastic about catching, which counts for a lot back there.

As it turned out, he did fairly well. He let a fair number of wild pitches elude him but he was quick to retrieve them, and tossed out two runners trying to steal home, pitcher covering—even though Amos never removed his mask because he was afraid his glasses would fly off. Andy pitched well, striking out seven in three innings, walking three, and giving up one dribbling hit. So maybe the Amos 'n' Andy show would be a long-running hit.

When Taddy went to the plate, I noticed that he'd switched back to his old bat after getting his first hit of the season in the previous game with the smaller stick I'd recommended. Now, using the heavier bat, he struck out.

As he passed me, running back to the bench (Tad never walks anywhere), I grabbed him and said, sweetly, "Why didn't you use that lucky bat from last game?"

"It was lucky once," he said, barely breaking stride. "But I think that bat . . . only has one hit in it."

"One hit in it?"

"And now it's used up."

I could barely keep a straight face long enough to summon Steve to the mound to close it out, and he did, as we held on for a 9–1 win.

11

We were back at Liberty for our first game of the season under the lights. No chance this game could be called because of darkness. A game at Liberty could go on forever—and many of them seemed to. It was a drizzly night. We were facing the Mets, who had gotten off to a surprisingly strong 4–1 start, but they were missing one of their best players, who had dislocated his shoulder—at a birthday party. This confirmed my belief that hardly anyone gets seriously hurt in Little League. It's always away from the game—doing cartwheels, falling out of trees or off porches, or tripping over Game Boys.

Once again, Mysterious Mark was nowhere to be seen. He was reminding me more and more of a character out of *Catch-22*. Was it Major Major whose existence was only a rumor?

"How'd you like catching last game?" I asked Amos.

"It was fun getting a lot of action," he answered, "but when a ball goes to the screen and a run scores and you're walking back to the plate, you feel kind of . . . naked."

"Even with all that equipment on?" But I knew what he meant. I felt that way whenever I had to go out and make a pitching change.

Dennis O'Neill managed the Mets, and I liked him a lot. He's an affable Valley Cottager, born in the Bronx, son of a New York City cop, and now publisher of the esteemed trade journal *Editor & Publisher*. His son Terence swings a good lefty stick. Like the rest of us, Dennis hoped to win his share of games, but he told me he also wanted to give kids a chance to play a wide variety of positions—almost daring the other team to hit the ball to them. We'd try to oblige.

Our schedule had us playing Dennis's team the following afternoon, too, kind of a night/day doubleheader, and I decided to hold Andy back for that game, hoping for better weather and a dryer ball. (And people wonder why fathers manage their sons' teams.) Problem was, we only had three pitchers, no one was likely to hurl a complete game at this juncture, and kids were forbidden by Williamsport to pitch on consecutive days. Simple math told me we'd need at least four pitchers this weekend, maybe more. I'd tried to develop more hurlers, with little success, and now I wondered why I hadn't made that more of a priority.

Fortunately we got off to a quick start with solid line drives by Steve, Andy, and the two third-graders, John and Taddy. Little John came back to the bench after his first hit of the season and shouted out to his parents, "I nailed it!" After three innings we were up 11–1, with Steve pitching well. With the game in hand, I let Kipp and Amos leave early to attend the middle school dance, joining Robby (who had passed up the game entirely). Kipp had turned into quite a break-dancer, I'd heard, just one more way to impress the girls. "No one would have missed him at the dance a few weeks ago," Richards told me, chuckling, "but now his absence would be *noted*—he has a *reputation.*"

With a big lead it was time to audition Ian on the mound, freeing Matt to relieve Andy the next day. At great risk I was rejecting one of Leo Durocher's commandments: *You don't save a pitcher for tomorrow. Tomorrow it may rain.* Ian gave up a hit, drilled a batter in the neck, yielded a single and double, and then, after retiring two batters, gave up another double and single. Now it was 11–6 with two runners on and half our team on a dance floor five miles south.

Even though it would leave me with no relief tomorrow, I had to bring on Matt to get out of it, and he did, retiring the one batter he faced on an easy grounder. Then we scored five ourselves, with Ian smashing his second hit, going ahead 16–6 and thus invoking the good old ten-run rule. So we'd survived our pitching shortage *and* the middle school dance.

Naturally, it rained the next day, and our game was postponed. I vowed I'd never ignore Durocher again.

Now we were only one game away from a rematch with the Tigers, and we'd be facing the Pirates, whom we'd demolished on opening day, on a warm sunny evening at Memorial Park. Gazing past the baseball diamond to the entire scene along the field, as I often did, I felt reassured that *everything was in its place.* I'd begun to see every game there as a theater piece with the main members of the cast—the kids and coaches—out front, and the supporting cast (parents), scenery, and props (water coolers, chairs, bicycles) in the background. The show could not go on unless everything was on its mark.

Most reliable of all were the mothers, arrayed in almost the exact configuration every game. B.B. referred to these maternal for-mations as "islands." Donna Albert supervised her youngest son in the playground in back of third base. Vicky Scimeca and her ex-husband, John, reclined on lounge chairs with a cooler (symboli-cally?) between them. Near her, Gerry Reynolds sat, but never for long, with Big Joe's little brother dashing about. Then the largest group, side-by-side on their lawn chairs just behind the backstop: my wife, Pat Jarden, and Arlene Keiser, and usually Sally Bell and Betsy Hastedt (John Marley's mom). Sometimes Marta Renzi, Amos's mother, joined them, but she tended to occupy a blanket.

It was a tableau of anticipation, chitchat, and dread.

"So what do you mothers talk about at the game?" I'd asked my wife a few days earlier. Every so often I try to find out what really goes on over there, beyond the shouts of encouragement based on a gradually increasing repertoire of baseball phrases: "Good eye!" "Good cut!" "Get the next one!" It's a question every Little League dad asks at one time or another; surely, none of us ever gets a satisfactory answer.

My wife greeted the latest query with a glint of amusement in her eyes. "What do we *talk* about?" she finally responded. "You mean, when we're not struggling with the concept of the Infield Fly Rule?"

"But seriously."

"You mean, after reciting the lengthy list of chores and home repairs that will never be completed in my lifetime because you are managing a Little League team?"

"That's just you. What about the others?"

"Hmmm . . . you mean you're really interested in the Alternatives to Pizza as a Major Food Group discussion?"

"There are no alternatives to pizza, or God would have invented them in the off season."

"By the way, *why* is 'a walk as good as a hit'? Isn't a hit a lot better, because—"

"Come ON. Just answer the question. You don't get to ask questions. Leave that to John Marley."

"I'm not going to tell you."

"You're not going to tell me?"

"Mitch, you manage your team, I'll keep my friends."

Nyack mothers and Valley Cottage mothers, on most teams, tend to stick with "their own," at least at the start of the season. A couple years back, one Nyack woman decided she'd try to get to know the mother of one of her son's teammates who hailed from Valley Cottage, kind of an anthropological project. She came to really like the Valley Cottage mother, who seemed "normal" compared to so many Nyackers who breathe the "rarefied air" of the arts or are too "touchy-feely" about education, as she put it. She enjoyed hearing the Valley Cottage perspective of Nyackers as freelance snobs who live "cushy" lives and whose kids are so sensitive they have trouble adapting to the rough and tumble social life of Nyack Middle School.

Wherever they hail from, moms heckle the umps and opposing players far less than their husbands do, which doesn't mean they don't. One of the funniest things I've heard, because it came from a woman and was meant tongue-in-cheek, occurred at a Little League all-star tournament a while back. In the bleachers, parents from our league huddled together waiting, and waiting, for our game to begin. The preceding contest dragged on, through extra innings, and it became clear that our game wouldn't even start until nine P.M. Finally, one team scored five runs in the top of the eleventh, and soon the other team was down to its last out. Then the pitcher threw a fastball that hit the batter in the leg, and he went down. Not a mortal blow, perhaps, but he stayed down for a while, further delaying the start of our game.

Suddenly this nice Valley Cottage mother next to me stood up and shouted toward the plate, "Oh, come on, get up!" She smiled, everyone laughed—because a *woman* had screamed it. A man couldn't have gotten away with it. Of course, a man probably would have meant it.

So far this year I hadn't heard about any major conflicts between parents, and no one seemed to hate me yet, either. Everyone seemed to like the A's newsletter, and in some households even the siblings of the players read it for laughs. Jim Marley felt it "codified" the team's existence, "like a bar team that posts its box score in the tavern." Parents appreciated the head's-up information and the kids loved the baseball jargon. And I got to write goofy headlines like Catch If Catch Can, Stat Thing You Do, CATCH PLENTY TOO, Spring Train Spotting, and Line Drive, He Said.

But now that we had a few games under our belts, certain patterns had emerged (some kids were playing less than others), so the natives were growing restless. Not everything was hunky-dory in A's land. One player's parents openly quarrelled on the sideline, with Dad getting on his son pretty hard and Mom assuring him that her boy "knows what he's doing" so "leave him alone." One father had already asked me when his son was going to start regularly. Another kid's folks rarely came to games, but there are worse things; someone else's mom and dad had just separated.

One mother complained to my wife, not about playing time, but the fact that her son's name didn't appear often enough in the newsletter. I counted the mentions (there were many) and asked my wife to pass the number along to her, and that was the last I heard of it. One father got ticked off when another dad volunteered to give his son a few tips on improving his foot speed, finding the offer "damn insulting." But maybe all the parents—not just me—were simply trying to be helpful, starting to feel they'd do *anything* to help this ragtag team win.

With all that support, we coasted that evening to another ten-run-rule shellacking of the Pirates, this time 13–2. Still, I was worried about our pitching. Matt the Bat had good stuff but walked six in two innings. Andy pitched an okay inning but seemed lost out there, experimenting with a different grip (across the seams) and holding his leg up higher. And Steve had staggered through his frame. With the Tigers next up I wondered if we could hold down the score. They were 5–0 and averaging fifteen runs a game. Rocco, I'd been told, was still batting a thousand and had reached base something like sixteen times in a row.

After this quick series of games, with a practice or two mixed in, I felt that Andy and I were starting to get burned out, playing ball. We needed a break, a respite from all that. A nice day away from home, out in the sun, far away from Little League. Where better to relax than at Shea Stadium? It was a vacation, all right, a busman's holiday for us both.

The Yanks were number one in New York and heading for perhaps a record season in the win column, but Andy and I prefer the Mets over Steinbrenner's invincibles. We like the drive to Shea better, and find the atmosphere in the park more wholesome, and certainly less noisy, than Yankee Stadium. Nothing makes me crazy like the pounding music and canned enthusiasm emanating from the Yankee Stadium scoreboard. Somehow I don't think Beethoven envisioned his Fifth Symphony as rally music in the South Bronx.

At Shea it's fun to find out which rock 'n' roll song the house deejay matches to each player as he comes to the plate or walks to the mound. John Franco, naturally, inspires "Johnny B. Goode." Al Leiter, a known Springsteen fanatic, always gets "Born to Run." This doesn't make much sense when he's *pitching*—better "You Can Look But You Better Not Touch." Leiter, a Jersey native, once met the Boss backstage after a local show, and invited him to a game at Shea. (Sorry Al, I got there first.)

Forget about playing shortstop for the Mets. Now my career goal is to spin the records . . . uh, CDs . . . at Shea.

Andy prefers attending games to watching them on the tube. His reasoning is perfectly logical: When you're in the crowd at a game you're free to "look at what you want to," while at home you're a prisoner of the camera. Problem is, a kid can sometimes see too much—his favorite player failing to run out a ground ball, for example, or a high-paid pitcher shouting back at the fans. Mitch Albom once wrote a parody, *Today's Casey Finds No Joy in Mudville,* which included the lines, "The fans began to boo and hiss—how long there must they linger?/Casey showed his deep concern by giving them the finger."

My son had attended his first big league game just the year before, at Shea, when he was nine. (I saw my first game at the same age, at Fenway, with Ted Williams in left field.) I would have taken him sooner, but he never insisted and I wanted the first experience to be memorable: a nice day, with great seats, and at least fifty bucks in my pocket. Who cares if it's a thrilling game at that age so long as the hot dogs are good?

At his first game, Andy got real spoiled real fast. One of my friends, John Doble, happens to know Dallas Green and his wife quite well. Wherever Dallas manages, John gets to sit in the manager's box seats almost anytime he wants, and bring a buddy. I saw quite a few Yanks and Mets games that way, before Dallas got axed by each team. The seats, inevitably, were in the first two rows behind the dugout.

Actually, Dallas and I go way back, too. I used to root for him when he pitched for the Buffalo Bisons on his way to the majors in the late 1950s. Now, here I was, nearly forty years later, sitting with his wife behind a major league dugout, my son by my side— the great "arc" of baseball described by Donald Hall nearly visible as a rainbow over Shea Stadium. Andy got to chat with the manager between innings, hear all sorts of inside gossip, and wheedle autographs from the players. Even more amazing: He came away with a foul ball.

Now, this is something of a sore point for me. Over the years, friends have asked me to stop complaining about the number of major league games I have attended—hundreds—without even *coming close* to getting a ball. In fact, any fan who really wants a chance at a ball should find out where I'm sitting and purchase a seat four or five sections away. And to think there's a kid in New York who's become famous for snagging over a thousand balls—an average of six per game. He's even written a how-to book about it.

At Andy's first big league game, the odds of getting a ball seemed reasonable, given our seat position, but I'd felt that way countless times before. Then it happened, as if by fate. Around the sixth inning, walking up the steps toward a restroom, we heard the crack of the bat. Glancing over my shoulder, I saw a foul ball heading our way. I didn't have a shot at catching it, but it happened to land in a row of unoccupied seats nearby. Forgetting Andy for the moment, I took a few steps, reached under a seat, and grasped it, and when I held the ball up, I got a nice hand from the crowd.

Grandstanding over, I turned and, in horror, saw that four kids, also going for the ball, had crushed Andy against a railing and he was grabbing his stomach in pain. Never having attended a game with a nine-year-old, and never before getting this close to a ball, it never occurred to me that he could get hurt in a stampede.

Fortunately, he recovered quickly, and took delight in getting the ball, especially since I insisted that *we* had retrieved it. It's magical to hold in your hand an inert sphere (Roger Angell calls it "a little lump of physics") that was just in the palm of a pitcher on the mound in a major league game. It's perfectly stitched and balanced, and surprisingly tan from the dirt rubbed into it by the umpires before the game. But what's astounding is how similar it is to a Little League ball—million-dollar professionals and fourth-grade amateurs play with pretty much the same equipment.

Of course, Andy could not appreciate the experience the way I did. The little rascal probably figured this is the way it always happens. You go to the game, sit behind the dugout with the manager's wife, and get a foul ball on the way to taking a leak. Talk about getting spoiled. His baseball fandom almost had to go downhill from there.

We still have that ball, signed with the date it was "caught" and encased in plastic, and we keep it right next to our "500 Home Run Club" ball signed by Ted Williams, Willie Mays, and Hank Aaron—and the game ball given to Andy in 1997 when he earned his first Little League victory.

It might be bland, even banal, but Shea is my favorite ball field in the big leagues. Going there with Andy unites my past, present, and future.

Although I consider myself a Yankee fan, and have witnessed some historic moments at the Stadium (going back to Chris Chambliss's pennant-winning homer in 1976), I can never quite shake the nagging sense that my mother would disapprove. But the Mets—she always liked the underdog. And my eternal devotion to the Mets was clinched in 1972 when they traded for Willie Mays.

How much did I love Willie? Among other things, he inspired my favorite passage in all of sports writing. When Willie caught the fly ball that ended the epic three-game playoff series with the Dodgers in 1962, he turned, laughed, and fired the ball into the stands. Murray Kempton observed, "It was his ball and he could do what he pleased with it. All of a sudden you remembered all of the promises the rich have made to the poor for the past thirteen years and the only one they kept was the promise about Willie Mays. They told us then that he would be the greatest baseball player we would ever see, and he was."

When Willie came home to New York in 1972 he naturally hit a home run in his first game at Shea. With my friend and fellow Willie freak, Peter Knobler, I attended as many Mets games as possible, even though it was sometimes painful to see our hero stumble around the bases or flail away at bat. If nothing else we enjoyed spotting his Cadillac in the parking lot with the "Say Hey" license plate.

In 1973, Willie made it official, this would be his last season—he was barely hitting his weight—and the Mets scheduled a farewell night for him near the end of the season, with the team, improbably, in a pennant race. Peter and I attended the wake, sadness so deep it made your chest ache. Willie got the usual car and other gifts from the team, and then stepped before a microphone. He never had a way with words, but he uttered a heartbreaking sentiment that night, now part of baseball lore. With tears streaming down his face, he admitted that it was finally time to "say good-bye to America." Peter and I could not stand up the rest of the night.

But it wasn't quite the end for Willie, or for our relationship with him. The Mets won their division with a record barely above .500, and faced the Big Red Machine in the playoffs. We got tickets for all the home games—this was actually possible then—and the first one featured the infamous Pete Rose–Buddy Harrelson brawl at second base. I confess I helped make history that afternoon. Late in the game the partisan crowd started screaming "Rose Eats Shit," so loudly it could be heard clearly by fans at home via television, the first time a profane ballpark chant ever carried across the country. It signaled a new era of uncouth behavior at ballparks, which I now lament.

The Mets-Reds series was tied at two games apiece going into the fifth and deciding game at Shea. Willie, aching all over—he'd banged up his shoulder playing *first base*—was relegated to pinch-hitting, replaced by the anonymous center field platoon of Dave Schneck and Don Hahn (or was it Dave Hahn and Don Schneck?).

What a day at Shea. Arriving at the ballpark I witnessed an incredible sight: Four young fans, balancing a fifteen-foot ladder, ran through the crowd outside the gates, propped the ladder against the side of Shea—and climbed up to a ramp and free admission to the sold-out contest! Who cares if they lost Dad's ladder in the process? Then, early in the game, the scoreboard flashed the news that Spiro Agnew, under threat of indictment, had resigned as vice president, and the always compassionate crowd chanted, "Spiro Sucks."

Finally a moment arrived that lingers today as my fondest ballpark memory. Midway in a tied game the Mets loaded the bases against Cincy ace Jack Billingham. Reds manager Sparky Anderson brought on hard-throwing young lefty Don Gullett to face lefty Ed Kranepool, so Mets skipper Yogi Berra (fearing it would get late early) made a switch, too. Out of the dugout, waving a bat, popped none other than the "Say Hey Kid." It was premature to go to the bench, but then look who was on the bench.

Peter and I went bonkers. "A bad sports novel couldn't get away with this scene!" he shouted in my ear. Pulp fiction, in fact, required that Willie hit one over the fence to win the pennant.

But at age forty-two, this was too much to ask, but Willie did what Willie could do. He fought off a tough pitch and, just making contact, chopped the ball in front of the plate, and somehow got his brittle legs churning toward first. The pitcher reached high for it but it stuck in his glove, and before he could shovel the ball home, Felix Millan slid in with the go-ahead run. It must have been the shortest single of Willie's career, but it counted. A ribby for Willie! Chants of "Willie! Willie" cascaded through the crowd. Spiro was out and Willie was on!

I think Willie came out of the game shortly after that—the Mets not trusting him to play much center field at this point—but we didn't care. In the ninth inning, with the Mets up by five runs and Tug "Tim's Dad" McGraw coming in to wrap it up, I got so carried away I leaned over the railing of the upper deck in right field and started chanting "Hondo! Hondo!" at mild-mannered Don Hahn, standing way down below. Hahn looked up and waved. Peter said something about Willie being the only person in whom he'd ever had complete faith his entire life—and now Willie had come through again—one last time.

Then we went downstairs, ran out on the field, and grabbed a few blades of grass from center field, Willie's turf, hallowed ground.

In years that followed, Peter and I attended dozens of other games at Shea, especially when the Mets soared in the mid-1980s. My teenage daughter, Jeni, from my first marriage, then living in Buffalo, had also become a rabid Mets fan (at my urging, of course). When Jeni was Andy's age, I'd dreamed she might play Little League in that early wave of female pioneers. A brilliant student, she didn't own a bat or glove, but she was a hell of a hitter with a sawed-off broomstick. I'd pitch crab apples that fell from a tree in her backyard and she'd smack the hell out of them. It was our equivalent of stickball. But Jeni, absorbed with schoolwork, piano, and other important things, never tried out.

Like me, she'd never know what kind of ballplayer she might have been. Unlike me, this did not bother her in the least.

Still, she embraced the goofy "Mookie-period" Mets, and we attended many games on her visits to New York. Superficial as it may seem, baseball was a godsend, helping draw together what divorce had driven apart. We both loved Lenny Dykstra, if in different ways. A few years later, she landed a summer job working for the Buffalo Bisons. Clearly, baseball was in her blood.

Recently, moonlighting as a waitress in Washington, D.C., where she has worked in various research positions, Jeni heard two patrons arguing and they called her over to settle the dispute. This happens quite often in Washington, but the question that needs to be resolved is normally, "Who takes over if the President and the Vice President are both impeached?" This time the question was far more weighty: Who played shortstop for the Mets in 1986? They knew it wasn't one of the Mets' high-priced all-stars but a rather obscure Latino named . . . they couldn't recall. But Jeni piped up immediately: "Rafael Santana." And then added, "But they called up Kevin Elster in September." That's my girl!

As the once-beaten Aliens prepared to meet the Tigers for a share of first place at Memorial Park, I found I wasn't as nervous about it as I'd feared. We'd won three in a row and were solidly ensconced in second place, which was about all I'd hoped for anyway, so we could afford a loss, though I hoped to avoid another thrashing. Andy could guarantee that if he pitched decently, but he was still fooling around with different windups and grips, as if he sensed he needed some kind of secret pitch versus the mighty

Tigers. Enrique was sick, giving me another chance to try out Amos at catcher.

Arriving at the field I found the Tigers at full throttle, banging the ball around the field like they'd been out there since school let out (yesterday). Eddie Badger was smashing wicked ground balls at his infielders, and his kids probably weren't wearing jocks, either. I'll say this for Eddie: He is even-tempered—he's uptight *all the time,* at least on a ball field. Once again, I practically had to threaten to call the cops to get him to give up the field and let us take a few swings.

"Eddie," I yelled out, "you said you'd give us the field ten minutes ago."

"I did not," he replied angrily.

Before I could answer, one of Badger's star players, over at first base, told him, "Yes you did!"

"Stay out of it," Eddie said, abashed. I could have kissed that kid.

In some ways, however, it was a typical Little League scene, despite Badger. Many of the players socialized before the game. Two of Andy's best friends, Owen and Ben, played for the Tigers and they never teased each other. And I always chatted a bit with John Bergin, Rocco's dad, a good guy, comparing notes on our kids; we congratulated each other for keeping them at a level where they might excel, and grow up a little, too.

The Tigers were not just beating their opponents, they were devouring them. I had to laugh, however, when I heard about their previous game at Memorial. Apparently an orchestra was rehearsing in front of the gazebo beyond center field, and Rocco hit a ball so hard it headed straight for the percussion section, as the usual cries of "heads up" died in the air. The ball missed the musicians but landed with a resounding CLANG against a cymbal, to cheers from players and fans. Hey, ump, what does the rule book say about that? Just a loud double?

Once again, I sent my son to the mound, which was easier on him than his mom. At the end of our bench, I had a bad angle on what was going on behind home plate, but that was just as well. According to B.B.'s friends, she had a hard time watching the field when Andy was pitching. She'd say, "I can't look," or "I need someone to hang on to," or most often, "What happened?" Or, superstitious, she'd ask a friend to hum the same tune she hummed the last time Andy got out of a jam. Or she'd just clasp the nearest pair of hands and hold on, for dear life.

One of the other mothers labeled her a "basket case," but that was probably an exaggeration. Still, when my wife got acutely nervous, Pat Jarden would say, "Come on, Barbara, *knock it off.*" (Easy for her to say, since her son never pitched.) Chastened, B.B. would lean forward, with fingers in front of her lips, breathing through them, slowly. If it was one of those long, walk-filled games, time passed so slowly it seemed to take shape and hang from the trees, she once told me, poetically.

Off to a quick start in tonight's game, we scored three in the first, with Matt the Bat living up to his nickname with a double. Then Andy went to the mound, yielding a run—but, sound the trumpets, he struck out Rocco, the first time the Rock had made out all year! In the second, however, Andy collapsed, walking two and giving up hits to their two weakest hitters, and all scored, and we were down 5–3. Between innings I asked him what he was doing differently and he admitted he had thrown nothing but across-the-seam fastballs.

"And you don't think you should maybe go back to the old fast-ball?" I asked, incredulous.

"Okay," he said meekly. He'd just learned what Crash Davis in *Bull Durham* called "lesson number one"—*Don't think, it can only hurt the ballclub.*

With that burst of assurance, I ordered everyone to rub the Alien's head and go out and score five runs, but they did me one better, tallying a half dozen, with Andy contributing a clutch hit-by-pitcher and Amos getting his second of three hits on the day. We were up 9–6—and the Tigers suddenly looked human. Eddie took out his frustration on his own team, not us, for a change, barking at them and waving his arms as they returned to the bench.

Throwing his old fastball, Andy yielded just one run in the third, but Rocco came on to pitch for them and he was blazing the ball past our hitters. I had to admit—he was not only a much better hitter than Andy, he also threw harder. Little John did reach Rocco for a line single to right, surprising everyone but himself, and he came back to the bench strutting, announcing, "I own him!" It was like, *Today I am a Man,* or some other primal ritual.

Andy had a decent fourth inning, yielding one run, and we were still up 9–7, but then the Tigers tied it, around Rocco's double, and when we failed to score in the top of the sixth it seemed inevitable that we'd lose. Even a rub of the Alien's head didn't guarantee anything. Steve came on to pitch, and looked tiny out there, but somehow struck out the first two Tigers. When the count went to three and two, the next batter hit a chop back to the mound, Stevie snared it and fired it recklessly to first even though he could have walked it over. I heard his father behind me mutter, "Oh no."

Fortunately, it was an accurate throw and Robby held on to it. Stevie jumped up and down as if we'd just won at Williamsport. I punched the twilight sky with my fist and bellowed "YEAH," and went out to pound on a few of our players as they left the field. Most of the Tigers' players wandered around in a daze, asking each other or their coaches, "Are we still undefeated?"

George Brett may be right, comparing a tie to kissing your sister— but in this case, your sister was Cindy Crawford.

The mother of one of the Tigers' players ventured over to our side of the field following the game. She knew some of our moms. "I wish my son was on *your* team," she told my wife. "You guys have more fun than we do." It was the finest compliment we'd received all year.

12

Who said baseball was like a day at the beach? Not in our case, as our next game was scheduled for the Saturday of Memorial Day weekend. Many kids today have trouble remembering which world war came first, one or two, but still, it's a major holiday. Luckily, all of our players but one (the Mysterious One) stuck around for the game, perhaps because we were suddenly in the thick of a pennant race.

It was a hot, humid day at Liberty and everyone felt a bit tense, even though we expected a fairly easy game, and always enjoyed playing on a "real" field. As usual, the Question Man helped break the tension, after I announced the starting lineup. "I was wondering," inquired Little John, "why do they call it a *shortstop*? He's just as close to second base as the second baseman. Why don't they call the second baseman the shortstop?"

"John, I have no idea. You've got me this time." At least no one asked me what I thought of the final *Seinfeld* episode. These kids seemed to be the only people in America, besides me, who had missed it.

I decided to give Little John a taste of his own medicine. "Hey, John," I asked, "why do people sing 'Take Me Out to the Ballgame' during the seventh inning stretch—when they're already *at* the ballgame?"

He gave me his best perplexed grin. I really had him.

"They sing it," he replied softly, "because maybe . . . they don't know the words to 'Y.M.C.A.'"

He was better at this than me.

We got three runs against the Rockies in the second inning, helped by Jeremy's double, and were coasting when Andy suddenly lost control, walking three straight to start the Rockies' next inning. It was clear he was getting "squeezed" by the umpire, one of the few semi-professionals in the league. This ump really looked the part, dressed in a starched blue shirt with the chest protector worn under his shirt (just like in the bigs). One wanted to be respectful, of course, but he seemed to be calling pitches down the middle *balls* and pitches that bounced in the dirt *strikes*. And Andy was not a low-ball pitcher.

Coaching at third base, Tommy Gannon, the Rockies' manager, couldn't believe the ump's calls either, even though most of them went in his favor. "He couldn't see the plate if his dinner was on it," Tommy observed.

Normally Andy is pretty impassive on the mound, but after the sixth blown call he looked at the ump and shook his head. Apparently the ump didn't like Andy's body language, and when his next pitch split the plate, he called that a ball, too. Okay, maybe in this Alice in Wonderland world a ball was a strike and a strike was a ball, but it seemed like he was simply teaching Andy a lesson about never showing up an ump. "I can't believe he did that," Big Enrique announced to the other fathers behind the fence. "It's just like in the big leagues when the umps retaliate, except here it's with ten-year-olds. It's so funny it's—scary." Then Andy walked two more and hit a batter and was lucky to get out of it with only three runs against him.

Next inning, after Andy popped out, he came back to the bench, ripped his helmet off, and threw it to the ground, where it bounced and hit another player on the leg—causing no damage, but now I had to discipline him, and so I ordered him to the bench.

Steve came on and quickly ran afoul of the phantom strike zone, walking four in a row. One of his teammates on the bench yelled, "Ring, ring. . . . Wake-up call, ump!" before I made him stop.

Noticing that the calls had almost reduced Stephen to tears, I came out to settle him down, but the next batter doubled, putting the Rockies ahead 6–5. That meant I had to bring on Matt the Bat, who was more emotional on the mound than anyone, but he struck out the next batter, and then got them out one-two-three in the fifth.

"It looks like Matt's developing a new pitch," Bob Keiser confided.

"Oh, really? What's that?"

"It's called a strike."

Top of the sixth, still down a run, I gathered the team around our totem, the Alien head, but the magic was gone. After Enrique led off with a walk, Taddy and Kipp fanned and we were down to our last out. Steve walked to move the tying run to second, and up stepped Robby. Soon he was down to his last strike.

But as the great Joaquin Andujar once put it, "There's only one word that describes baseball—*You never know.*" Robby lashed a single to right, and Enrique chugged around to tie the score, and the dugout went nuts. Then Matt the Bat singled in the go-ahead run, and soon we were up 9–6. But could Matt the Hurler hold them? Some of our fans rose to cheer him on, others remained seated, perhaps in prayer. (There are no atheists in the bleachers.)

"He might start walking guys," I warned Jon Albert.

"I don't think so," he replied, chuckling. "You know, when Matt throws pitches out of the strike zone, where do they go? They bounce in the dirt low and outside. That's the ump's strike zone today! So it's a piece of cake." Naturally, Matt went out and, for once, threw the ball consistently down the middle—walking three batters. But with the tying runs on base he retired the side for a stirring 9–7 win. Matt, you are my hero!

After the game, B.B. resurrected her old nickname for Robby from the previous year—"RBI Keiser." It had a nice ring to it, especially this day.

I could dish it out but could I take it? Everyone complains about the umpiring but no one does anything about it. Now I had my chance. It was time to do my duty (as defined by Nyack/VC Little League) and ump a game in the majors.

Spending three nights a week managing or practicing does not get you in enough marital hot water, and so all coaches are expected to ump four or five games a year as well. I'd already umped a game in a lower league, but that hardly counted. The most pressure I felt at that game came when Jonathan Demme complimented me for wearing a blue shirt—umpire's colors—and I didn't have a glib reply. (So much for my screen test.) Now it was time to slip on a mask and stand behind the plate in a game they played for keeps. Actually, I looked forward to it. I wanted to get a closer look at the trouble Andy would face next year in "the show."

Games in the majors are pretty intense. The kids are a little more athletic, the pitchers throw harder than in the minors—and the managers have had time to develop vendettas with rival skippers, or grow frustrated after failing to win titles in the past. (Many of the kids mimic them, or have ego problems of their own.) Some of the managerial feuds go way back, to when the coaches competed against each other in sports as kids. Few spectators know this. Most just think the two managers have simply lost their minds. "If you are already a fierce competitor in life," Vincent Fortanasce, a psychiatrist and legendary Little League manager, once observed, "Little League can bring you to the brink of insanity."

Everyone knows the classic Grantland Rice line: It's not whether you win or lose but how you play the game. Some Little League managers, however, seem closer in spirit to Gene Autry, when he owned the California Angels and said, referring to that famous quote, "Grantland Rice can go to hell, as far as I'm concerned."

Another spokesman for that point of view is former slugger-turned-Little-League-coach Jeff Burroughs. He complains about parents "who think winning is not important" or "even worse, that there is something inexcusable or psychologically wrong about teaching kids to win. Baloney!" Like others in this camp, Burroughs argues that winning "is what sports are all about" and, more than that, it's "what life is all about" in "the real world." In fact, Little League should "get kids ready for real life." He equates not caring about winning on the ball field to going to college and not caring what grades you get, or taking a job and not caring whether or not you advance.

Now, this approach has worked pretty well for Burroughs, personally. He's a former American League most valuable player, his son Sean is currently one of the top young prospects in all of baseball, and he twice coached a team to the Little League World Series title. Indeed, few argue that winning means absolutely nothing—but one worries about the cost/benefit ratio.

Parents, like coaches, are more zealous around Little League majors—that is, the ones who do not simply treat it like free child care. Some have invested much time, money, and their own self-worth in Johnny becoming an all-star, and now the clock is ticking down the weeks left in his Little League career. They're not afraid to let a coach know what they think is best for their son (e.g., pitching every other game and playing shortstop the rest of the time).

Many cling to the fence at Liberty and yell batting instructions to their kid as he steps to the plate, contradicting everything the manager might have just told him in the dugout. I've seen managers walk the kid right into the batter's box to make sure *they* get the final say. Some fathers openly berate their sons for some failure, real or perceived. This is what they always say if a coach or another parent suggests they back off: "My kid can take it." And clearly, he will have to. Marty Schupak once told me that 40 percent of parents think their kid is better than he actually is, 40 percent underrate him, and only 20 percent are "realistic."

Here's how my wife describes the spectator section at Liberty during games: *Men standing around with their arms crossed.* The mothers generally stay seated, but they often join in the heckling and hectoring. At least Little League "keeps the parents off the street," as Yogi Berra pointed out.

Most baseball fans remember Rob Dibble, a fireballing relief pitcher for the Cincinnati Reds, now a network sports analyst. Dibble's temper was even more fearsome than his 99 mph heater, and he was frequently suspended for such antics as heaving baseballs out of stadiums when he got angry. Probably no one will be shocked to learn that Rob's folks were once voted the "Worst Little League Parents in History" by their league back in Hartford, Connecticut. What's surprising is that Rob's mother was the protagonist, needling his coaches, even storming into the dugout on occasion.

Years later, when her son's temper got the best of him in the big leagues, she wrote a moving letter to Rob, admitting that she was the reason "why you're like this. I pushed you too hard." She explained to a reporter that she'd never said to him, "Better luck next time," but rather, "Rob, how come you played so bad?"

Little League seasons may seem peaceful in the chill of April, but tempers fray by the time June rolls around. Conspiracy theories proliferate. Playoff and all-star games often turn ugly.

Brian Thomas, our league president and a former Marine, once told me that he buys a lottery ticket every week, and if he wins the big prize he's going to build a domed Little League stadium "and not let anyone over the age of sixteen inside." A couple years ago he umped a Little League all-star game where several players on one team crowded the plate trying to work out a walk. A parent of a kid on the other team kept shouting out to the pitcher, "Throw the ball at their fucking heads, that will get them off the plate." Brian walked over and asked the parent to cut it out or take a hike. When the fellow said, "Make me," Brian said, "I can't, but perhaps a call to 911 will get the job done."

Last year, in a local championship game, tensions between parents from two Rockland towns erupted, with one group of fans retreating to their cars to retrieve weapons—baseball bats and hockey sticks. At that point the police arrived and the game was suspended. So there was no telling what might happen when I umped my game at Liberty.

It didn't take long for me to wonder if I should drop out of Little League after this season, and take Andy with me. In the second inning, someone hit a line drive to right and the runner dashed home. The relay throw came in like a bullet right at the runner's head as he crossed the plate. The catcher, luckily, reached up and snagged the ball just before it blasted the kid—who had failed to slide—into oblivion. Okay, no tag, kid scores, play's over. But I seemed to recall a Little League rule that a runner *must* slide if there's a play on him at home, to prevent him from getting beaned and to protect catchers from getting bowled over. So, as the runner trotted back to the dugout, I called him out.

Naturally, his manager came out to question it. I'd expected that. Then he started arguing, saying there was no such rule regarding sliding into home. Okay, maybe I was mistaken. But then he started pointing his finger in my face, brushing against my chest, calling me names, and charging that I was a lousy ump. The last I could live with—who said I was an ump anyway?—but the rest was way out of line. Then he protested the game and called for a halt in play, perhaps on the verge of challenging me to meet him in the parking lot after the game. By now, the parents, male and female, were on me pretty good, too.

Fortunately, the manager of the other team came out and saved my hide, quietly informing me that, probably, the other guy was right, this did not quite warrant an out call, and it was okay with him if I reversed the decision. Which I did—as quickly as humanly possible. But if this was a crucial playoff game, would that Good Samaritan have taken me off the hook?

It could have been worse. Much worse. In East St. Louis, Illinois, a coach, angered by a call on a close play at the plate, rushed the ump with a bat and threatened to kill him, according to police reports. When other coaches intervened, he stormed off and returned with a handgun, stood about ten feet from the ump, and squeezed off a few rounds. Fortunately, all of the shots missed. The gunman was arrested.

The ump was sixteen years old.

Next up for the Aliens were the Yankees, whom we'd barely tied the first time around. I liked playing them, though, because their manager, Glenn Meyerson, was a good guy, whom I 'd known for a few years around the ball field. Glenn had served as league trea-surer for a couple years (one of only two Nyackers on that panel). He is tall, amiable, with dark curly hair, and works as an execu-tive recruiter for technology companies.

Born on Long Island, he moved up here at about the age of six. Like me, Glenn never played Little League and was a San Francisco Giants fan who had to search long and hard to pick up their games on the radio from Philly, Cincy, Pittsburgh, and St. Loo. Glenn has managed his son Ben's teams all the way up the Little League ladder, but has also coached CYO basketball and his daughter's soccer teams. He says he just loves working with kids. Perhaps a deeper explanation is, "Deep down I wish I'd become a schoolteacher." I suspect this is true of many managers, present company included.

As he's coached older kids in successive years, Glenn enjoys it somewhat less. He liked the teaching atmosphere of the lower leagues more than the competition that surrounds the upper levels. Glenn was still seething about a recent incident. Visiting an opposing team's bench before a game, he observed a mother arrive with her kid, a part-time player. They'd driven all the way up from Long Island just for the game, after being told that the team might be short of players with a forfeit in the offing. The mother meekly asked a coach if her son could start for a change, given the long trip. The coach could have blown her off with a "perhaps" or even "sorry, no." Instead, he thundered, "He doesn't deserve to start, ever," then walked over to the manager and suggested he tell the mother she should pack up the kid's equipment and quit the team if she was so unhappy. (Which meant the team now had nine other players on hand and didn't need this kid anymore.) Glenn didn't know what happened next; he was so disgusted he fled the scene .

Several years on the board have shown Glenn that some parents also behave terribly, setting a poor example by heckling umpires and opposing teams. It's nastier and more intense in Little League than in soccer and basketball, he reports, for there seem to be more fathers trying to realize their childhood fantasies through their sons. So beware of today's young soccer and basketball players— when *they* have kids.

Concerned about Andy's pitching, and helmet tossing, I decided to start Matt against Glenn's team. It would reward him for his great effort in the previous game. Well, as they say, no good deed shall go unpunished. Matt yielded five runs in the third, walking every other batter. His mother stood at the fence behind home, muttering to Donna Albert, "This is killing me," not for the first (or, alas, last) time this season. We trailed 7–1 before I could get Matt out of there.

Then in the fourth inning, *their* pitcher couldn't find the plate, and we tallied seven runs, with the Kippster striking the key blow. The Yanks got a run off Andy in the fifth to knot the score at 8–8, and it remained that way until the last of the sixth. Another nail-biter. Ian led off with a walk, and Kipp and Amos followed with singles. Our best contact hitter, Little Stevie Wonder, struck out, leaving it up to Robby again—and he smacked a hard single to right for the victory. The Cardiac Kids had done it one more time. A spontaneous chant of "RBI Keiser" arose from the parents' section, and soon the kids picked up on it, so now it was here to stay. Next up: round three with the Tigers.

Andy's erratic pitching troubled me, and I didn't have a clue how to set him straight, so I set up a private lesson with the pitching pro out at the sports center. He's a former Mets farmhand named Tommy Rowe, whose nickname, naturally, is "Skid." I suppose if he still threw smoke they'd call him "Tobacco." As a Dylan freak, I'd prefer "Desolation" Rowe.

The notion of private tutors for Little Leaguers is not new, it's just exploded in recent years. Experts attribute it to several factors. Childhood has become hideously competitive all along the line, from the classroom to the clothing stores. Many parents apparently feel they can put kids on an "athletic track"—or they treat them like a growth stock. Others smell college scholarship money (for girls as well as boys, if not more so) or a million dollar pro contract—the so-called "greed factor." Some parents want their kids to reflect glory back on them; it's no longer enough to do your best, you have to be the best.

A sociologist at Northwestern, Bernard Beck, observes that years ago, parents were younger and went into child rearing without much of a plan, a little foolhardy and a little courageous. But today's parents are far more serious. Many delay having children to pursue a career. "And having had success in their careers, they use the same goal-oriented principles when it comes to raising their kids," Beck explains. "They study what's needed for success. They look at the competition. It's a very rational, very market-oriented approach."

And so more and more kids see private coaches, go away to sports camps, or join "traveling" soccer, hockey, or baseball teams for games that take them far from home—before they're even out of elementary school. Baseball tutors seem more like pediatricians, treating kids for "tournamentitis." On Monday morning they get calls from frantic parents begging for an appointment because Junior struck out twice on Saturday night and needs to get well right away.

One worthy by-product of this trend: It separates feuding sons and fathers. A Chicago-area dad who spends more than $100 a week on instruction for his two kids told a reporter that tutoring prevents "confrontations" between father and son. His kid explained: "You don't really listen to your dad. He sometimes yells. And sometimes, he doesn't know what he's talking about." Sometimes, however, a dad drags his kid to his lesson, literally kicking and screaming. Often the most important thing an instructor does is rebuild the child's confidence after it's been shattered by a critical father. Some of them like to put the dad in the batting cage and let *him* take a few swings, just to show that any lack of skill on the kid's part is probably an inherited trait.

Since Andy was never thrilled about extra training, and we couldn't afford it anyway, we barely contributed to this trend. We'd visited Skid Rowe the previous year for a single session, a mid-course correction, and left dissatisfied, though now I couldn't recall why. That half hour had seemed to fly by, and at $30 this was a rather costly lesson—in obsession. But I didn't know where else to turn for expert advice and so I'd made another appointment with Skid. Andy was not thrilled, but didn't fight it, as deep down he wanted to be the best pitcher in the league, or so he said.

This time there was no battle with my wife over extra pitching help, perhaps because she didn't know about it. What she didn't know wouldn't hurt us. If I'm going to have someone "on the sly," would she prefer a mistress or a pitching coach?

Skid seemed to be in his mid-thirties, over six feet, with a moustache, still a physical presence. While they warmed up, he noted that Andy didn't rotate his front shoulder all the way in throwing, which I'd been working with him on for, oh, two or three years. Then Andy threw a few pitches from the indoor plastic mound. Skid had him work on one mechanical thing, the "glove tuck," the kind of small but significant adjustment Andy normally needs months to master (and he was trying to make him do it in fifteen minutes). When it was clear Andy wasn't getting it, Skid finally said, "Well, work on it, you'll be okay."

But the half hour was not a complete waste. Skid earned his pay at the end by saying, "For ten years old, he has a great arm, he should go far."

"Really?" I replied, figuring he was just flattering us to earn another lesson—or a tip. I really had no perspective on this, and I'd always thought Andy had a rather ordinary arm with above-average "moxie" on the mound.

"Yeah, he throws pretty hard, he has a 'live' arm," Skid explained. That's a popular if vague term used by coaches today. A live arm. Certainly preferable to a dead one. But reason enough, for now, to keep Andy on a pitching track.

Thunderstorms rumbled, but this time I wasn't rooting for a rain-out as we prepared to battle the Tigers, even though they remained unbeaten. Rocco had now gotten on base twenty-eight times in thirty appearances, with his only two failures coming against our pitching. I'd planned to start Andy, but Matt looked better in warm-ups with a new full windup I'd been urging, so he got the nod. I loved Matt, but he was Mr. Erratic. He often brought to mind Robert Frost's notion that poets are like baseball pitchers: "Both have their moments. The intervals are the tough things."

With thunderclouds brewing Matt had a great first stanza, striking out Rocco after he'd fouled off five pitches. Then we scored a couple runs on walks and steals. After our recent comebacks we looked frisky and happy, while the Tigers looked scared—of us!—and drained from excessive practice in 100 percent humidity. But then the sky turned black, and thunder sounded just across the river. No rain fell, but it was clear that it was dangerous to stand around out there, so we ran to get our equipment and pack up. "Okay, if your parents are here, go sit in your car for a while," I instructed. "It will probably rain, then pass over, and we'll resume the game." Up 2–0, what do you expect me to say?

One of our younger players was having none of this, however. "Let's get out of here!" he screamed to his mother as they dashed to their van parked out in left field. He heard his teammates yelling for him to stick around until the game was called, but he said to his mother, "Ignore them, let's go!" And they went, the vehicle peeling out and heading for home. Later I learned that he was terrified of big boomers. It was evacuate the ship and every kid for himself.

A few minutes later the ump called the game. Thrilled with her boy's one-inning performance after some rocky times, Vicky Scimeca took Matt out to Pizza Hut to celebrate. He'd actually struck out the Mighty Rocco! It was kind of tragic, in a way—for that special K ultimately didn't count. But even though the game got wiped out, it boosted everyone's confidence (even mine) to new heights. Now, if we fell, it might actually hurt.

If they now respected us, the Tigers still played with a swagger against the rest of the league. After our rain-shortened contest they won their next three games 17–0, 16–0, and 15–4.

On the last Saturday of May, we faced the Rockies again at Memorial, as the temperature approached 90 degrees. I'd been working with Andy all week on a new batting stance, trying to get him more relaxed and swinging level. His policy of looking for a walk had resulted in many free passes, keeping several rallies going. In fact, he led the team in runs scored. Still, it was time to get the bat going; he was one of our bigger kids and we needed a few hits from him, badly.

"You gotta swing the bat," I told him.

"Oh, I thought it came with batteries," he replied. He'd learned at least one thing this year in school—sarcasm. (Or did he get it from me?)

As I often did, time permitting, I threw a few tennis balls to Andy out front in Mudville before we left for the game. He complained about the new stance and hit poorly. Then when we got to the park he pitched dreadfully in warm-ups, perhaps because he'd been running around the field chasing Big Joe, against my wishes, and now looked exhausted, so we bickered some more. Perhaps I was just mad at myself for blowing thirty bucks on his pitching lesson. Afraid he would embarrass himself, I made a late switch to Matt as starting pitcher.

The pitching switch backfired, as Matt yielded four runs in the first. One ball fell in front of Kipp in center. He was still playing every batter too deep, unable to forget the one ball Rocco hit over his head back in game number three. No one else in the league had done that since, or seemed capable of it, so there was every reason to play shallow, but we had to constantly wave Kipp in. I think he liked to play back because it was so peaceful out there and he could do some deep thinking.

Out in right field, also too deep, John Marley kept up his usual chatter with Kipp when their paths crossed: "I am *beyond* worrying about the next batter" or maybe, "Why do they call it a 'squeeze play'?" From the bench we had to constantly wave John in or out, left or right. This went on game after game. Often he'd just wave back.

Down 5–2 in the third, it looked bleak. From the bench we overheard a conversation between the Rockies' first and second basemen.

"We're beating the A's!"

"Yeah, but they're famous for coming back, so watch out."

Famous, I loved that. Had we made *The New York Times* or what? Jay Leno would be calling any day. In any case, the comeback kids lived up to their legend rallying for six runs, with Matt the Bat stroking his second double of the game and Andy (with his new stance) rapping a key single. Then Andy came on to pitch and we coasted to a 13–5 win. After a rocky start to the day, he had responded gloriously, making me wonder if maybe he needed to get benched—or visit "Desolation" Rowe—a little more often.

Pat Jarden probably appreciated the comebacks more than anyone. Somehow, she made it to almost every game, despite undergoing surgery, then chemotherapy, for cancer. Pat could endure only about an hour outside, but now she knew enough about the Aliens to come late, not early—and she'd hardly miss a thing.

The Aliens, and their skipper, could sure use an easy game, and it looked like we'd get one, with the Pirates on deck. Then we heard news that suggested this might not be true at all. "Dad, you're not going to believe this," Andy said, after getting off the bus, running down the hill, and rushing into the house after school. "The Pirates beat the Tigers!"

"Oh, come on," I said. "Sounds like a rumor. Surely, not the Pirates. . . ."

"It's true, Jack told me." Well, that was a pretty good source, since Jack was Eddie Badger's son. Unless he was trying to trick us.

"What was the score?"

"Something like 5–4."

"Wow."

"So . . . we're tied for first?"

"Well, technically . . . I guess so." We'd caught the Tigers. "Gosh."

I could barely wait to call Richards.

"Eddie must be out of his mind," Richards said dryly. "Maybe Rocco was sick or something."

"No idea, but it counts." Then it occurred to me. "But *we* have to play the Pirates tomorrow, and the day after that, and it sounds like they've gotten tough." Pirates and Tigers and A's—oh my!

13

Arriving for our next game in Nyack on Friday night, I enjoyed telling the Aliens that they were now a first place team. I should have stopped there, instead of uttering pathetic baseball clichés such as "Destiny is now in our own hands," meaning that all we had to do was win the rest of our games and we'd finish first. At least my wife wasn't in the dugout to hear that. Barbara loves to give me a hard time about baseball psychobabble. She cracks up every time she hears an athlete say he's trying to *stay within* himself. "What are the other options?" she'll tease. "An out-of-body experience? Or staying within *someone else?*"

While our teams warmed up, I found Pirates' manager John Miller in a jolly mood over at their bench. I thanked him for helping us out by taming the Tigers. "Fine," he replied, shaking my hand, "but we plan on winning tonight, too."

"Fair enough, but how'd you manage to beat the Tigers?"

"Danny Stroud," he answered. The diminutive nine-year-old had turned into quite a pitcher since the season began. True, Rocco reached base three times, but Danny pitched out of jams and the Pirates got away with a few trick plays on the bases—delayed steals and the like, driving the Tigers nuts. "I told my guys we were better than our .500 record," John said, chuckling, "and they believed me."

Of all the minor league managers, John was the only one who had a real ballplayer for a father and, not coincidentally, he'd excelled as a youth player himself back in Baltimore County. He's such an Orioles fan he goes to Yankee Stadium to root for them and refuses to step foot in Shea, still stinging from the Mets triumph over the O's in the World Series—thirty years ago. His father, a former semipro pitcher and first baseman, coached John through six years of youth ball. Dad was ambidextrous and threw a lot of curveballs, so John had the unique experience of growing up "trying to hit off a guy who threw junk from both sides." As a coach, Mr. Miller focused on learning to do things correctly, but also having fun.

When he started coaching his son Danny's teams, John applied what he'd learned as a boy from his father, emphasizing fundamentals. This year he'd drafted the youngest and smallest team, but that was okay with him. He knew they had potential—and he'd just have to stress speed-related things, such as bunting and stealing.

We were scheduled to play the Pirates the next evening as well, creating another pitching dilemma. We still hadn't developed a fourth pitcher, and our lack of pitching depth was beginning to catch up with us. I decided to start Andy tonight and hope for a one-sided game, maybe a four-inning affair, and then use Steve and Matt tomorrow.

That strategy appeared sound, as Andy pitched brilliantly for four frames, and Matt the Bat continued his hot streak with a couple of singles, but we were only up 3–1. And since Andy had reached his six-inning limit for the week I had to yank him, and bring in Steve. Delighted, Jon Albert turned to his parents, who had never seen their grandson play, and said, "Steve will close them out." He'd done well in this spot all year, and this should be no different.

But for some reason, this wasn't his night. Maybe the ump wasn't giving him the corners, or perhaps he was trying too hard with his grandparents there. For whatever reason, he gave up a single, walk, and double, and then two more walks. Just as bad, the Pirates were running wild on the bases, with delayed steals, encouraging us to throw the ball around and wait for the inevitable bobble. One of our parents rushed up and yelled out to me, "This isn't baseball—they're cheating with all that baserunning stuff—this is just Little League." I was sympathetic to this view, but I had to admit that the puny Pirates were well-drilled, making the most of what they had, and that I had not prepared my guys sufficiently for these tactics. So I knashed my teeth and waited for Steve to pitch out of the jam and keep the game close.

This looked unlikely. Steve was growing agitated on the mound, so I raced out to try to calm him. More than our other pitchers, he seemed shaken by fielding miscues behind him, and we'd made a bundle. He responded by striking out the batter, and tagging out another runner at the plate. Then he walked two more and we were down 7–3. Now he started to sniffle out there, which couldn't help his pitching, and I went out to talk to him again. (Steve was acting his age, which was nine.) Weeping slightly, he quietly suggested, "Take me out."

I didn't know what to do. Or rather, I knew what to do but didn't do it. If we had another pitcher to put in, Stephen would already be history. I was tempted to bring in Matt and worry about tomorrow later—recalling Leo Durocher's sage advice. But even if Matt shut them down we might not rally tonight, and we'd likely lose tomorrow, too, with *no* experienced pitchers left. I should have figured this just wasn't our night, taken a beating with Ian or another inexperienced pitcher, and moved on, but we'd struggled all year to catch the Tigers, and now we had, and everyone was pumped up about it (kids, parents, and coaches alike), and we were on the verge of relinquishing first place before we even tasted it.

So I did exactly the wrong thing. Despite Steve's request, I left him in.

"Steve," I told him, "I still have confidence in you, you can get these guys out, you know I can't bring anyone in right now, you have to get through this, their worst hitter is up, just get him." He shook his head okay and tried to regain his composure, slamming the ball into his glove a few times. As I trudged back to our bench I heard chilly silence from the direction of our coaches and parents. Steve's tears were all too apparent, and no one knew about our lack of pitching options, or would care if they did know. To them it seemed clear—get someone, anyone, in there.

Okay, Steve, bail me out here, I thought. Strike out this shrimp. End the nightmare. Naturally he walked the kid and now it was 8–3. Only then did I remember that Steve's grandparents were witnessing all this. What might they be thinking? (Later, I learned that Grandpa said to Jon Albert, "You sure you haven't pushed Stephen too fast?")

Finally, Steve got an out, and walked off the field straight to where his parents and grandparents were sitting, usually a no-no, and I was afraid he'd never re-emerge. Unfortunately, he was scheduled to bat second in this inning and I had no pinch-hitters. I saw Dan Wolff go over and confer with the Alberts, probably apologizing for me or expressing his own disapproval. Then Stephen took a little stroll with his mother. Meanwhile, some of the other moms deputized my wife to walk over and express their concern.

"Is Steve coming out *now*?" Barbara asked.

"Could be," I replied. "I'll ask him what he wants to do."

When Steve walked back to the bench, I expected him to say that his mother had a message for me: Take your job and shove it.

Instead, she'd merely suggested he might be cold and gave him a long-sleeved shirt to put on under his uniform. She also told him to try to get through one more inning and leave it to our hitters to come back, as they always did. I couldn't have said it better myself. Mothers!

Steve seemed eager to get back in the game. I said I was sorry about what happened, but now we needed him to concentrate on hitting, hoping for a miracle that might soothe Steve's feelings and salvage my reputation.

With a shudder, I realized that once again I'd forgotten to make them rub the Alien's head at the start of the game. The only other time I'd overlooked that we'd lost to the Tigers. The Alien was our Don Zimmer, a positive presence on the bench while never appearing to move, breathe, or say a thing. Belatedly, I picked up the Alien and made them give its bald pate a good buffing. I'd read that Derek Jeter actually rubs the real Zimmer's head for good luck.

"Get me five runs," I begged.

Which is exactly what they did. (I should have asked for ten.) Amos and Steve walked, Robby and Matt singled, Andy struck out—so much for the new stance—but Ian Rocker came through big-time, clearing the bases with a double, and we were tied at 8. These Aliens were truly out of this world.

The problem was, we still had a sixth inning to get through, and who would pitch? Pumped up by our rally, Steve volunteered to give it a go, and he didn't pitch half bad. But with two outs and one on, he walked two more guys and two scored—no tears this time—so we were down again, but only 10–8. We had them right where we wanted them. That kind of comeback was child's play for us.

When Kipp led off with a triple and one out later Steve singled—what a trooper—it seemed inevitable we'd at least tie the score, as we had RBI Keiser at the plate. And, as usual, he hit a hard shot to right. But the little Bucco second sacker lowered his butt, grabbed the grounder, tagged Steve running to second, and then flipped to first to get Robby for a game-ending double play! I blinked in disbelief.

Thank god for the Kippster. As the guys milled around the bench with their heads down, kicking the ground and then the fence, angry that we'd tossed away first place, he shouted, mock-serious, "Now they got us mad! Let's get ten runs in the first inning tomorrow!" Nearly everyone greeted this with eloquent cries of, "Yeah!" Little John, as usual, said something funny but not quite fathomable: "Let's whip them going west all the way from here to Hawaii."

When I got home, B.B. informed me that the mother of one of our players had announced late in the game, "Greg could be charged with child abuse." Or maybe she said "should be." Or even worse, "might be."

"And what did the other mothers say?" I asked, timorously.

"Well, no one backed her up," she said, "but then again, no one took issue with the idea, either." Oh great.

"And what about Steve's folks?"

"They just sort of kept to themselves and looked, uh, concerned . . . and the grandparents looked stricken."

"And you?" A long pause ensued.

"Why didn't you take him out?"

Pro football coach Mike Ditka once spoke revealingly about what he learned in his Little League baseball days back in Aliquippa, Pennsylvania. "Winning is everything to a kid," he declared. "You can't pick up competitiveness in later years if you don't practice it when you're young." Winning is everything? *Practice* competitiveness? For want of a better phrase, I would call that a "football mentality," which I always thought I lacked, especially since I'm not a football fan. Now I was finding that it's hard to balance trying to win and playing for the fun of it. What I was trying to do was play to win . . . for the fun of it, but perhaps that was impossible.

I thought I'd better call the Alberts, after letting a few more minutes pass. When I did, Jon Albert answered the phone.

"I want you to know," I began, shakily, "I'm sorry about what happened. I made a mistake leaving Steve in there."

"Oh, that's okay, Steve's taking it pretty well, he was just embarrassed in front of his grandparents."

"That's bad enough."

"But really, he hung in there—he's got to learn to do that, what do they call it, character building?"

"He's only nine, and his character seemed okay the way it was. But I was proud of him."

"Me too. My father was upset, but I told him he just happened to see Steve's worst game ever. I told Dan Wolff it gave Steve a chance to overcome adversity. The best thing was, no one on the team got on Steve. Donna took him for a walk and told him to take a couple of deep breaths and reminded him that the team still stood behind him. We're not high-pressure parents, but we do want him to learn that you can't give up when things go wrong—just concentrate on the next hitter and try to hold the score down. Really, it's okay."

"Not really, but thanks for saying so. Won't happen again. Give Steve my best and tell him he'll get plenty more chances to pitch." After that I felt a little better—no lawsuit seemed in the offing—but still I feared I'd blown it with the other parents and coaches for good.

In pre-game practice the next night at Liberty, the Aliens did seem a little feistier than usual and ready for revenge. Ian had left for his family's weekend house, but I'd learned my lesson and asked a bunch of kids to audition as pitchers. Robby had been asking for a chance for a while. He had never pitched before—but now, I was taking all volunteers. And, in fact, in warm-ups he looked best of all, with little speed but good control. He'd put the ball in play at least.

"Hey, there's a first for you," Big Enrique pointed out. "A one-eyed ump." Sure enough, the umpire wore a patch over his right eye. I tried to calculate whether that meant he'd have trouble calling the inside or outside strike, but gave up. Our players, of course, nicknamed him "Cy."

Along the bench I warned our guys to watch for the sacrifice bunt from these Pirates. Little John informed me that he understood what *sacrifice* meant, but why do they call it a *bunt*?

"One dollar for anyone who can explain it," I announced.

Kipp, always a clever one, explained, "It's a combination of *bat* and *don't*. It used to be called a *bont*, but it's easier to say *bunt*." The kids fell for it. Here's your dollar, Kipp, anything to end this discussion. Then it bothered me the rest of the night. Why DO they call it a bunt?

The Kippster had promised a ten-run explosion, and by now I took seriously every Alien vow. And sure enough, we went out there mad as hell and not willing to take it anymore. Amos cracked a single to right and the rout was on. Bang bang bang and then Big Joe hit a shot to the wall that went for a "home run" (double and two errors), and we ended up with nine runs, only one less than the promised ten-spot.

It reminded me of my favorite Bible joke—that the first words of Genesis are actually, "In the big inning, God created the heavens and the earth. . . ."

Eventually we went up 13–0, and now the Pirates' tricky baserunning would do them little good. Everything was going our way. Andy muffed a pop-up at shortstop with two on—and we got a double play out of it because one of the Pirates didn't know about the infield fly rule and was out trying to advance.

"Matt's pitching well," I told his mom, who was resting comfortably in a lawn chair, sitting on a big lead instead of standing near the fence, fidgeting.

"Yeah, there's a girl he likes who's here," she said, shaking her head in wonderment.

But then the Pirates rallied for four runs in the third. Someone hit a rope to right, and Matt slumped on the mound. Nothing unnerved him like a long hit off a good pitch. He couldn't get over the unfairness of it—there was no justice in this world. So he proceeded to walk the next five guys in a row, usually on 3–2 pitches. I figured the one-eyed ump was having trouble seeing the low outside corner, which was the only part of the plate Matt's pitches normally crossed. Admittedly, with deeper pitching, Matt would have been out of there, but we still had a big lead, they weren't hitting him at all, and he was not bursting out in tears—so far. Still, I feared a repeat of the previous night, so I told Robby to go out to the bullpen and warm up.

We scored one more in the fourth, so we had exactly a ten-run lead with a chance to close it out this inning. To our parents, this was a cakewalk. But to me, we were on the brink of disaster. Matt had thrown so many pitches he couldn't last more than an inning (if that), and we had nothing but inexperienced pitchers behind him. If the Pirates scored even once, we'd have to play a fifth and possibly sixth inning, and they had more depth in their bullpen. If a weary Matt could not hold them scoreless this frame, the Aliens would likely collapse, completing a Lost Weekend.

True to script, Matt walked the leadoff hitter, and after getting an out, walked Danny Stroud. Then he walked the next guy. Bases jammed, one out, no way in the world they don't score—and good-bye ten-run rule. I strolled out to the mound to inform Matt and Enrique that they simply *had* to keep the runner on third from scoring, and to act like the *winning* run for the Pirates was sitting out there, even though we led 14–4. They looked at me like I was nuts, of course, but swore they'd prevent any wild pitches or passed balls.

By the time I returned to the dugout, Matt had already bounced a ball way past the plate. But then the hand of providence or some other Alien intelligence reached down again and reversed our fortunes. The wild pitch plunked off the wooden backstop and bounced right to Enrique as he rumbled to the rear. He grabbed it and made a perfect underhand toss to Matt covering home. Matt reached back and tagged the runner and we held our breaths as the one-eyed ump hollered "OUT."

Wow! Where did that come from? We hadn't executed that play more than twice all year. And now it had saved our ass. Except that the runners had moved up, and now Danny Stroud was at third, and still quite likely to score, although two were out. Okay, Matt, concentrate on the batter and get ready to cover home again.

He threw a strike this time and, perhaps surprised, Enrique lobbed a rainbow back to him. Seeing the ball floating back to an exhausted pitcher, Danny Stroud decided to steal home. As one, everyone along our bench, screamed out, like Meat Loaf, "Throw home!" On the mound, Matt flinched at the sudden noise, but he snagged the ball and fired to Enrique, and we watched the slide, the tag, and the ump bringing his right fist up, again signaling *out!*

Oh, doctor! I fairly leaped in the air, and then rushed out to hug Enrique, still in his catching gear. He had his mask off and wore the biggest grin, his braces, decorated with multicolored bands, dancing, and I felt good for him, since he'd watched Amos take away half of his job without complaint. All right, Pudge! Then I smacked Matt on his big old back, while most of the fans, and perhaps many of the Pirates, looked on, wondering why we acted as if we'd just won the title. But for those in the know, it was the most suspenseful one-sided contest since Reagan–Carter—or was it Ali-Liston?

. . .

Out in the parking lot, Matt and his father lingered for a while, savoring the win and Matt's heroics. Matt had certainly had his ups and downs this season. His mother, who commutes to Westchester for her job as a bank vice president, claims that her son burns to be a pitcher because he likes to be the center of attention. Still, she believes it's better to be overconfident than underconfident—"my problem," she confesses.

"Matt, I appreciate your guts out there tonight," I said, "and you know, you probably pitched a no-hitter—that's something."

"I just walked a few," he said, looking on the bright side, as usual, with a sweet grin. "On three and two."

I was desperate for an easy win, but apparently the Aliens felt, *what fun is that?*

14

We needed a breather and the not so amazing Mets were next. It was a beautiful day for a night game, warm and crystal clear. During my pre-game pep talk I begged the Aliens for a four-inning win, for I had to leave at exactly 7:30 to attend a meeting at Andy's school. We hadn't finished a game in ninety minutes all year, but I figured with this crew, what the hell, it didn't hurt to ask.

Emotionally spent after the Pirates weekend, we simply could not hit against Dennis O'Neill's team. The softer the Mets' pitcher threw, the weaker we swung. We had to supply our own power, but admittedly we were a little short in that department, and the ball didn't carry off our bats. Perhaps the bats were the problem! Maybe it was time to get a new, more expensive one, even that $220 pressurized gas model. To raise the money we could apply for a grant, or mortgage our house.

Back on the mound after his meltdown five days earlier: Little Stevie Wonder. Tonight, as he'd completed his warm-ups, his father said, "We worked on some things in the backyard yester-day, fixing his mechanics, and he's got his confidence back." My jaw dropped and I replied, "You know he's not supposed to throw the day before the game!" This was one of my few cardinal rules, to avoid tired or damaged arms.

"Relax, you'll see," he said, laughing. Then Steve started twirling a masterpiece. For once, I just sat down and tried to enjoy a well-played game. The Mets made several sparkling plays in the field and so did we, the coaches joked with their players and each other—this was what youth baseball ought to be like all the time. Still, a win for us wouldn't exactly spoil the fun, especially if we wanted to stay just a game behind the Tigers, but we went to the top of the fourth leading just 1−0.

RBI Keiser had told me he'd come late, after a school function, and he arrived in the second inning, ready to enter the game the next inning. I decided to wait for a key spot to use him as a pinch-hitter. Our bench players had done well all year, drawing walks and getting the occasional hit, but we'd never had a batter like Robby available in the pinch and I wanted to have some fun with it. (Hey, managers are supposed to have fun, too.)

"Rob, you sure you can handle the pressure?" I asked, teasing him as he cleaned his glasses.

"Sure thing, bring it on." He looked like he meant it.

So he sat out the third and the start of the fourth. But then Andy walked with two outs and alertly raced to second when the catcher took a snooze as ball four rolled to the screen. We needed a single to go up 2−0 and John Marley was due, so I called for Robby. John already had his helmet on and didn't appreciate getting lifted for a pinch hitter, but I told him, "It's RBI time—you understand?" He nodded yes.

"Did you pinch Robby already?" he wondered, recalling our earlier colloquy.

"In the butt."

Making me look like a genius, Robby smashed a double on the first pitch, Andy scored, and we had an insurance run. Then Stevie set the Mets down in order again. "You see," Jon Albert said, referring to their controversial workout the day before, "Father knows best!" But I figured four innings was enough for him, so I brought on Andy, and he wrapped up a thoroughly delightful 3−1 victory, a no-hitter for our hurlers, no less.

GREG MITCHELL

I looked at my watch and it read 7:29. The Aliens had made my
7:30 deadline for departing, and played the whole six innings to
boot. They got a bigger kick out of beating the clock than beating
the Mets. Like I always said, winning isn't everything.

That week I got my first flattering, if slightly rattling, phone call
from Keith Borge. Keith managed a team in the majors, one of his
players had quit for the year, and he needed to call someone up
from the minors. He was short on the mound and could really use
an experienced pitcher, and another manager had mentioned Andy
as one of the best available.

"Probably Eddie Badger," I told him.

"Huh?"

"I presume it was Eddie who suggested Andy. That would lock
up the title for him, that's for sure."

"No, actually, it was someone else. Eddie's the only one who
won't return my calls!"

"I'm sure he knows Rocco's at the top of your list."

"He should have been in the majors from the start this year."

"Eddie will never let him go. He won't even talk to you, I bet.
But I don't want Andy to go up either. I'll talk to him about it,
though."

Of course, I hated the idea. It would blow a hole in our team,
change the chemistry, and divide my attention, as I'd want to keep
an eye on what Andy was doing up in the majors. It went against
everything I'd worked for all year, to mold a team that would play
as a family and have fun and wind up in a fairly happy place—
together. On the other hand, it was quite a compliment to Andy—
it was like Tim Robbins getting summoned to "the show" near the
end of Bull Durham. So I'd present it to him neutrally, and see what
he said. This was dangerous, because if he chose to make the jump
I'd either have to let him do it or stand in his path—painful either
way.

190

With relief I heard Andy say, "No way, Dad, we can't break up the Aliens, we're going to win it all! But can I tell everyone they WANTED to call me up?"

That seemed like a perfect compromise, but I wondered if he simply didn't want to leave the comfort of home—playing for his own father. I'm sure leaving the nest was a frightening prospect for him, as it was for me. It might take months to prepare him (us) for next year. It was too much to expect him (us) to adapt to the idea overnight.

It was now mid-June and that meant minor league baseball had returned to our local ballpark, an hour up the Hudson in Fishkill, New York. And a lovely little ballpark it is, Dutchess Stadium, home of the Hudson Valley Renegades of the Class A New York-Penn league. We'd never caught a game there, but it was a hell of a lot closer (and cheaper) than another Mets game.

Andy had a ball. Although we got mediocre seats, they were better than almost anything at Shea (except when you get to sit with the manager's wife). The food was fine and the lines short. They had cool merchandise. You could actually hang out with the mascot (a raccoon, or maybe it was a beaver?), and Andy even asked it for an autograph. Between innings they stage corn-eating contests and sack races, and fire gifts into the crowd with giant slingshots. Who won the game? Who cares? I'm not sure we even knew who the locals were playing.

It was something new for Andy, but minor league ball brought back a lot of memories for me. As Roger Angell has observed, baseball is indeed a game of recollections and recapturings.

Since I grew up far from a major league park, I was fortunate to have a Triple A team less than an hour away. Buffalo had the most redundant team name in all of sports—the Bisons. Their chief radio announcer was Bill Mazer, a loquacious, balding fellow who (with a red hairpiece) went on to a radio and TV career in New

York City. Every so often I'd go to a game in Buffalo to watch washed-up former big leaguers such as Luke Easter, Max Surkont, and the immortal Duke Carmel play their final innings.

Then, one day, when I was in college, a miracle occurred. Race riots swept many cities during the summer of 1967, and some of the looting and burning took place near decrepit War Memorial Stadium in Buffalo. Few fans would venture to a Bisons game now. The team had to relocate for the rest of the season, but where to go? One July morning I woke up to find the Bisons scheduled to play the rest of their home games at Hyde Park Stadium—four blocks straight up Whitney Avenue from my home. From my street you could see the lights of the stadium at night.

And this wasn't just any Bisons team. It featured the hottest prospect to hit baseball in years—the nineteen-year-old catcher from Oklahoma, Johnny Bench. Hyde Park Stadium was basically a football and track field for Niagara Falls High. My friend Paul had played his Babe Ruth games there, and that felt about right. It was a brick and concrete structure with benches for spectators behind the plate, no seats along the infield at all. There was no outfield fence, so they put up a storm fence. (I imagine most of the AAA players flashed back to . . . Little League.) Fully packed, the stands might seat two thousand people, and indeed the team played to nearly full crowds at the start, attracted by the novelty.

It was a blast to see broken-down vets (like Ernie Broglio) and promising young players pass through. I watched the Bisons lose a doubleheader to the Mets' farm team by identical 1–0 scores, losing to pitchers named Seaver and Koosman. After games, teenage girls, and some older women, our local Baseball Annies, would crowd around Bench as he left the locker room, but he seemed to be an aw-shucks Okie. I'd loiter there too—he was exactly my age, right down to the same birthday—and just say hello, and he came to recognize me and smile.

Now that the Bisons were our hometown team, the local newspaper where I worked as a summer reporter increased its coverage.
When our chief sportswriter went on vacation, I covered the team
for a three-game home stand. What could be better than that,
except perhaps doing play-by-play with Bill Mazer? I sat in the
press box and even acted as official scorer one game, flicking the
big *H* and *E* on the scoreboard. I also got to go into the locker room
after the game and interview the players. They seemed big,
sweaty, and brusque, with a big league attitude almost laughable
in this humble context.

The true highlight of the year arrived later in the summer.
Minor league teams operated with restricted rosters, so injuries
and call-ups could leave a team shorthanded. The team's manager
(often a former big leaguer) might activate himself for a game or
two, praying he could still cut the mustard without pulling a
muscle. In previous years I'd seen managers Hector Lopez and
Wayne "Twig" Terwilliger suit up for some games. Now the
super-sub would be ancient thirty-seven-year-old Don "Zip"
Zimmer.

This was before he became a lovable, puffy-cheeked baseball
icon as manager of the Red Sox (Bill Lee called him "the
Gerbil"), coach of the Yankees, and, of course, role model for the
Alien. But in 1967 he was already famed as a former Dodgers
infielder. I happened to be in the park for his comeback game and,
wouldn't you know it, Zip comes up with the bases loaded and
clocks one out of the park! The place went wild and he enjoyed
himself rounding the bases—and it took a while, as Zip (it was a
misnomer) had already turned rather rotund. After the game, he
deactivated himself, perhaps wanting to go out with that dinger,
like Ted Williams.

End of story? Not quite. Fifteen years later I was in Miami for
spring training to write a magazine profile of Earl Weaver, manager of the Baltimore Orioles. Weaver and I strolled down the

left field foul line at training camp and he talked my head off, as he was wont to do. Looking to connect with him personally, I told him that I hailed from Niagara Falls and saw him manage the Rochester Red Wings. "Yeah, I was battling with Jimmy Palmer [his star pitcher] even back then," Weaver gasped, a little bitterly.

"You know," I said, trying to impress him, "in Niagara Falls, I saw Don Zimmer's last home run!"

I expected him to chortle and ask for details, but instead he replied, in that famous gravelly voice, "So did I!" Turns out Zimmer's dinger had come against Weaver's Red Wings. And then he added: "You know who he hit it off, don't you?" Before I could guess, he boomed out: "Palmer!" I cracked up. The pitcher was probably in Triple A on one of his many injury rehabs. "And I'd just gone out to the mound and told him not to throw that old guy a curve, and he still did it. Palmer!"

After chatting with Weaver, I survived a brief career as a free-lance baseball journalist for national magazines and *The New York Times*. With John Cheever, I agreed that "the task of an American writer is not to describe the misgivings of a woman taken in adultery as she looks out of a window at the rain but to describe four hundred people under the lights reaching for a foul ball."

What amazed me was how much the people I interviewed lived up to their public image. You know, Earl Weaver was actually an irascible blowhard; Ozzie Smith was a nice guy, Garry Templeton a wise guy; Eddie Murray was sullen and Steve Garvey eager to please; Jim Palmer was pure ego in or out of jockey shorts. I could have skipped meeting them and written the profiles from my home with a few contrived quotes. But then I would have missed Dick Williams spitting sunflower seeds all over my pants as we chatted behind the batting cage at the Murph in San Diego—and Gene

Tenace threatening me with a bat in the clubhouse for asking one too many questions.

As a Yankee fan with a deep interest in Japanese culture it was a thrill to fly to Vero Beach to interview Roy White. The longtime Yank left fielder had completed a year playing for the Yomiuri Giants in Tokyo, and they were spending a couple of weeks at spring training with the Dodgers. Roy had some entertaining stories about adapting to Japanese customs (bowing to the umpire, and all that). It was an even bigger pleasure to chat, through an interpreter, with world home run king Sadaharu Oh, the manager of the Giants. "Mr. Oh" was rather average in size, but what a handshake.

A few years later I went to Japan and attended a game in, of all places, Hiroshima, later writing about it for *The New York Times*. Amazingly, the stadium had been built almost directly on ground zero about five years after the atomic blast. I had to wonder, while watching the Hiroshima Carp, and inhaling some sushi, whether the fans were thinking about anything other than baseball as they watched their local heroes playing America's game. It was not the fact of baseball in Hiroshima that was unnerving, it was the place where it was played—once a killing field, now a ball field. It is often said that the ghosts of Babe Ruth and Lou Gehrig haunt Yankee Stadium. One does not want to reflect too deeply (especially at a ballgame) about the apparition potential at Hiroshima Stadium.

Sitting with two other Americans right behind home plate, I felt horribly self-conscious. Hiroshima does not attract many foreign visitors except around August 6, for the annual commemoration of the atomic bombing, so it is rare to see American faces at Carp games. Out of uneasiness we found ourselves cheering loudly for the home team. When the Carp second baseman, an American named Ken Macha, came to bat, I yelled out that classic bit of baseball chatter, "Show 'em where ya live!" He doubled over with laughter in the batter's box. It was the last thing he expected to hear . . . here.

. . .

Not taking no for an answer, Keith Borge called again and asked if I'd changed my mind about Andy's call-up. He hadn't been able to identify another likely suspect and Fast Eddie still hadn't called him back about Rocco. Hey, this pennant race in the minors was pretty hot stuff, I told him, and no one wanted to miss it, even for a little glory in the majors.

We'd face the Rockies next, and the timing couldn't have been better with the Tigers on deck. The Rockies were struggling, which was a shame, since manager Tommy Gannon was such a swell guy. By now he knew he'd committed a fatal blunder in the draft. His first couple picks had missed half their games because of soccer conflicts—Mysterious Mark times two.

"Hey, Greg, we saw you at the Beach Boys concert last night," Tommy said by way of greeting, referring to a nearby gig.

"No way, wasn't there," I replied. I had a reputation to uphold. "The Beach Boys?"

"Yes, you were. Up on stage. My son saw the lead singer up there with a blond beard and green cap and he said, 'Isn't that the A's manager?' " Of course, he was referring to Mike Love, who does look a bit like me, I suppose, though he's a few years older and just a bit wealthier.

"Well, at least it wasn't David Crosby," I observed.

Gannon had endured a tough season with dignity, but he was ticked off about an incident in their previous game, sparked by his team pulling off its first double play of the season. With two runners on, the Rockies' shortstop fielded a grounder, touched second for a force, and then threw to third, nailing the runner easily. But the unorthodox play caught the home plate umpire by surprise and he missed the play at third. He asked the third base coach to make the call. "I didn't see it," the coach said, absurdly, so the ump ruled the runner safe.

Apparently Tommy went nuts over that. His team was getting

murdered in the game, so it wasn't about winning or losing. He just wanted his kids to have the satisfaction of pulling off a head's-up play. And more than that, he thought the coach's blatant disregard for fairness set a horrible example for kids on both teams.

Gannon has served as head groundskeeper for the league for a few years and he's done much to upgrade the ball fields. He's a paper hanger by trade (though his income mysteriously plummets every spring). More than anyone I've met he seems to truly believe in—and not just pay lip service to—making Little League fun "for the kids." Part of that is making sure the fields they play on are safe and yield good hops and, just as important, look like the real thing, with chalk lines and a working scoreboard. Tom jokes about going out to the field and "doing a few lines," but he's serious about his duties. He vividly recalls opening day a few years ago when the kids came to Liberty Field and discovered the new dugouts, and they all went "wow." That makes it all worthwhile, he told me, "that's what it's all about, a great moment for me."

At the same time, Tom has managed his son, Craig, up the ladder. Coaches, he says, always claim they want to win "for the kids," but many are mainly out for themselves. He recalls a recent game where the two managers refused to shake hands at the beginning of the game. A few minutes later someone hit a prodigious home run and players on the other team, ignoring their manager's wishes, congratulated the kid as he rounded the bases. Five minutes after a game ends, kids fraternize with the enemy around the snack bar, while the coaches, he observes, are out in the parking lot, "slamming the steering wheel."

Managers, of course, are role models for kids. Perhaps Ben Christensen once played for one of those win-at-all-costs coaches. He's the all-American pitcher from Wichita State who got mad one evening recently when an Evansville batter took a few swings near the batter's box while he was completing his warm-up tosses between innings. Ben thought the hitter was trying to time his pitches. He got mad—and his next warm-up pitch headed right for the batter's face.

It's hard enough to get out of the way of a pitch during a game, but at least you're paying attention. On this occasion the unwary batter took the ball right in the cheekbone, opening a deep cut and causing severe eye damage. After performing retinal surgery, doctors doubted his eyesight would ever return to normal. The young man's father readied a lawsuit against the pitcher, while local prosecutors considered pressing criminal charges. Almost as disturbing was the reaction from the Wichita side. Christensen claimed it was an accident, which seemed preposterous. His coach said, "We're the ones who got hurt in the deal," because his pitcher was banned for the rest of the season. The team's pitching coach was also suspended when he admitted that he taught pitchers to "brush back" any batters straying too close to the plate during warm-ups.

A few weeks later the Chicago Cubs selected Ben Christensen in the first round of the college draft—and offered him a lucrative signing bonus.

Facing Tommy Gannon's team, Andy kept things under control on the mound, and then we broke out with nine runs in the last two innings. Kipp lashed four hits, but even more impressive was the performance of Cool Taddy Bell. I'd decided that he was so fast we needed to get him on base more often. So the day before, I'd taken him out and taught him to bunt, tossing about a hundred pitches until he got it down pretty well. Now my prize pupil made me proud with a pair of bunt singles—and several stolen bases, leading to two runs. We had a new secret weapon.

All of us came alive when Tad batted. We loved watching him run in his distinctive elbows-out fashion, and shouted his name when he got on base. He ran like a bunny with his tail on fire, as Red Barber might have said. Even the smaller Aliens treated him like a kid brother. He was our sparkplug, our good luck charm, the team pet. Some of the parents called him "Mr. Charisma."

Jeremy, Little John, and Enrique had also singled, and Big Joe made a nice play at third base, so it was a real family affair, my favorite kind of game. Apparently John and Taddy, the two third-graders, were waging a friendly competition over who would end up with more hits for the season.

"I got a hit," one of them would brag.

"No, it was an error," the other one would argue, uselessly, since our official scorer didn't know the meaning of the word.

Earlier in the game I had another little run-in with Andy. Considering that he was the manager's son, and often at the center of the action, I felt he had behaved well for the most part this season, rarely taking advantage of his holy position. But in this game, back in the second inning, he had acted goofy during his warm-up pitches and I'd shouted out that the Rockies might make him pay for it. Sure enough, they quickly scored a run, and I couldn't resist reminding him from the sidelines that I'd warned him. Andy yelled to me from the mound, "You're . . . not . . . helping!" I felt like shouting back, but decided to hold my tongue with so many eyes and ears trained our way.

Of course, I shouldn't have said anything to start with, and instead waited until he returned to the dugout. To his credit, he hung in there and got the third out. Then, rather uncharacteristically, when he came off the field, he walked straight over to me and, *sotto voce,* said he was sorry for talking back. "All I meant," he explained, "was that it was not helpful for you to criticize me at that point." Which was undeniably true. I apologized, too, and we embraced briefly. Maybe we'd both grown up a bit this year, but both of us had a ways to go yet.

We were now 11–2, with two ties, and the once-beaten Tigers loomed in the final game of the regular season. With a victory we could claim half the title. Or perhaps more than that. Was it true the Tigers had lost again—this time by forfeit?

15

The rumors had floated from classroom to classroom and then home from school. Andy had heard from Ben, who'd heard from Casey, that the Tigers had forfeited the night before against the Rockies because they didn't have enough players to take the field one inning. Also, a Tiger player had gotten kicked—or kicked out of the game—or something. Was all or any of this true, and if so, what did it mean?

I wanted to play it cool and let the facts emerge—if the truth was out there—but this was important stuff, for if the Tigers lost it would mean we were now tied for first and could win the title outright with a victory the next night. Or, if the Tigers deserved to lose by forfeit but Fast Eddie had talked his way out of it, perhaps there was someone to appeal to? Or was that none of my damn business?

In any event, it promised to be a good story, so I called Tommy Gannon, manager of the Rockies. He laughed when he recognized my voice, knowing exactly why I was calling.

"So you heard about it, huh?" he asked, innocently.

"I heard something—about ejections, kicking and/or screaming, cars fleeing the scene. Just another night at a youth baseball field, huh? It can't all be true, right?"

Well, it seems for most of the game it was a typical Tigers blowout. They were up 11–0 after three innings with Rocco mashing a pair of doubles. A kid I'll call Trouble was slated to lead off the fourth for the Tigers but refused to bat. He was a tall, sullen-looking kid, and in one of our games with the Tigers this year, when he was playing first base, he nearly reduced one of our players to tears by taunting him about his looks. On another occasion he spit in his hand for the postgame handshakes. That kind of kid.

Anyway, Trouble for some reason had refused to go to the plate opening the fourth inning. Maybe he'd just had a rough night. He'd singled in the first inning, but got thrown out at home, surely embarrassing for a "tough" kid. Then, probably still sulking, he struck out in the second inning, a rare Tiger failure. All Tommy knew was, he refused to come off the bench in the fourth.

Normally, no problem. Eddie could simply send up a pinch-hitter. But Eddie only had nine players for this game, and if he lost one he'd have to forfeit; Little League rules do not give you the option of playing with eight. Poetic justice, I figured. When Eddie, as I'd predicted, lost Del Campo in spring training, he never filled that roster spot. Why add a weak player he'd have to play every game? So he'd played the season with thirteen, while everyone else used fourteen, and had gotten away with it, until now.

"So the kid didn't bat?"

"Never batted, but you know, I didn't care. We were losing 11–0, but the real reason was . . . there was a really bad scene . . . his father kicked him."

"*Kicked* him?"

"Yeah, he took him down the right field line and argued with him, shouted at him, trying to get him to bat, and finally kicked him."

"In front of everyone?"

"Well, like I said, it was down the line, but we could see it all, you couldn't miss it. One of *our* parents went down the line and told the father to stop, and the dad turned around and spoke that immortal line, 'It's my kid.'"

"And he still didn't go back in the game?"

"Still didn't bat. Went out to the car or something."

"What are you going to do?" Remember, Tommy was a member of the board.

"The kid's father is not an official coach, but helps out on their bench a lot. I'm going to take this up at the next board meeting."

Apparently the Tigers batted around that fateful inning, and Trouble had failed to hit a *second* time. They just skipped him in the order. Then they took the field in the fourth with only eight players. But Tommy Gannon was so upset by the kicking incident, his team was down 16–1, and the skies were darkening, so he didn't feel like demanding a forfeit, which could have been declared on multiple grounds, including humanitarian. When lightning flashed, the ump called the game—but since the Rockies didn't finish batting, it was not an official contest. So at the minimum it didn't yet count as a Tiger win, and could be declared a loss.

Tommy didn't feel like pursuing the forfeit, but rather investigating the physical attack he'd witnessed. He had his priorities straight, and if we beat the Tigers in the final game we'd have strong grounds to call ourselves the regular season champs anyway.

Our motivation for beating the Tigers was higher than ever, but my expectations remained modest. In my heart I still believed they had the better team, and they practiced a hell of a lot more than we did, too. Basically, the teams were well-matched, but they had Rocco—it was as simple as that. He'd only made out three times all year, meaning he'd reached base something like forty-seven times in fifty at bats—a ludicrous .940 on base percentage.

Yet the kid *still* didn't have his own Web page.

Also, I had other concerns surrounding this game. Andy's beloved grandfather, John Bedway, his Aunt Marcia, and his Uncle Tom were flying in from Ohio for the game. None of them had ever seen Andy play in a game and now they were coming for the Big One. Logic, and a desire to win, dictated that Andy start on the mound, against Rocco, no doubt. How could the normally casual Andy stay calm through all of that? He'd coined a nickname for our hurlers, calling them PUPs—"pitchers under pressure." I accepted the fact that Rocco would probably outpitch him, but I was afraid Andy would fall flat on his face in front of his Ohio family. I knew I was supposed to aim for the top, and the title, but right then I probably would have settled for a tight, respectable 5–3 defeat.

It's true that B.B.'s father compared baseball to paint drying, but he admits that this was not an original insight. He heard it from an old friend, a Reds fan, who also used to say, "That game was so slow I watched guys in the outfield putting on weight."

John Bedway is a football guy. When he played college ball as a University of Cincinnati Bearcat in the late 1930s, with his friend and fellow lineman Nick Skorich, they were known as the "gold dust twins," and gained some national attention. John served in Europe during World War II, taught school, and co-founded a successful coal business in southeastern Ohio. With his wife, Janet, he raised three fine daughters (of which B.B. is the youngest) and two fine sons.

Growing up in the coal town of Adena, Ohio, the son of first-generation Lebanese grocers, just before and during the Great Depression, John loved all sports but did not attend a major league baseball game until college, when he saw Ernie "the Schnozz" Lombardi play for the Reds. Still, he got to see some extraordinary things. Each of the union locals fielded a ball team, and the hard-fought battles were well attended. One family had nine sons and one day for fun they took the field as an entire team. Some of the players hoped to attract pro scouts and use baseball as a ticket out of the coal mines (the way many inner city kids view basketball today).

Occasionally the famous Negro League team from Pittsburgh, the Homestead Grays, would come around for an exhibition game against an all-star coal squad. John thinks he may have seen Satchel Paige pitch, and at one game, a Grays batter—possibly Josh Gibson?—hit a ball so far in left field "it cleared the switching yards," as he recalls.

But John suffered from one handicap: He had poor vision, his family could not afford eyeglasses, and so he had trouble hitting or catching a fast-moving ball. This was no problem in football and basketball, at which he excelled despite being rather short of stature. But when he played his first sandlot baseball game, not wearing a glove, the first grounder that came his way dislocated the middle finger on his left hand. He splinted the finger using two popsicle sticks, so it's no wonder the digit remains bent today. He couldn't track pop-ups either, so his baseball days were short-lived.

His mother didn't want John to play contact sports, and when she found out he was secretly playing football, she attended a game and then asked him, "Why do you always run to where others can jump on you?"

After World War II, he coached sports at Adena High School, but the kids on the baseball team "knew more about it than I did," he admits. It was about this time that local boy Bill Mazeroski (the future Pirates star) started playing ball in one of the mining camps. John stayed close to football and attended a lot of Cleveland Browns games when his buddy Nick was coach, and he (and B.B.) got to have dinner with Leroy Kelly and some of the other star players of that era. He followed baseball only at World Series time, and his sons never played Little League, although one of them, Tom, remains a huge football and basketball fan.

But lately, "Jiddi," as he is known to Andy (the Arabic word for grandfather), has followed his grandson's baseball career closely. With my own father deceased, he holds an especially hallowed place in my heart. After every game I e-mailed him updates on the latest exploits of "Big Train" Mitchell on the mound, but he hadn't made it to a game in Nyack . . . until now.

Barbara's father and sister arrived Friday afternoon before the game and retired to the Holiday Inn over the hill to rest. Uncle Tom could not get a flight until later and would miss the contest, unfortunately. Andy seemed psyched about the game when he came home from school, but not especially on edge. He was happy to start on the mound and seemed confident about pitching well. As usual, he appeared to have fewer butterflies than his skipper.

"Hey, if we lose, we can still beat them in the playoffs," he announced matter-of-factly on the way to Memorial. It was a balmy June evening at Memorial Park, the still-bright sun glinting off the sailboat-flecked Hudson. Soon, all of the Aliens had landed except Mysterious Mark. He had hurt his back at a soccer practice, and now he was out for the year, I informed the Aliens.

"Hey, coach," Kipp asked, "can you be *out* . . . if you've never been *in*?"

"Good question, my boy, we'll have to consult Nietzsche on that one, or Freud, or perhaps Uecker." I was thinking, however, that maybe Shakespeare was more apt ("What, not one hit?").

Our guys acted relaxed and just pleased to be playing a game, at this time of the season, that actually meant something—in fact, almost everything. Eddie, as usual, was hogging the field, but his team looked so tense I decided to let them stay out there a while longer and get more tired and uptight. Andy seemed pretty sharp in warm-ups and got to chat with his Jiddi and Aunt Marcia for a few minutes before the game.

I noticed that Trouble was in the starting lineup and his dad was hanging out along the bench.

As Rocco warmed up on the mound, the Bedways took their seats in lawn chairs right behind the plate, sitting with some of our mothers, and I could tell everyone was pleased to meet them and vice versa. Suddenly we heard a shout from the center of the diamond, and saw Rocco lying on the mound with his arms covering his head. The third baseman, making a practice throw to first, had conked him right on the noggin, and he'd gone down in a heap. (Apparently no one had told the third sacker—don't knock the Rock.) Someone rushed out with an ice pack, and then Rocco's father escorted him to the bench, as Eddie sent another pitcher to the mound.

"All that practice," Dan Wolff commented, slyly, "and the third baseman still can't throw to first without beaning his own pitcher?"

But then the substitute pitcher retreated to shortstop and Rocco trotted back to the mound, to applause all around. Okay, we wanted to beat their best, which looked unlikely when he struck out the side in the first and looked blazing fast. When Andy took the hill I hoped he'd get off to a good start. If he collapsed later on, okay, but I wanted him to show Jiddi his stuff for at least a couple of innings.

Fortunately, he seemed on, striking out the first two batters, and getting the third on a fine play—racing in to seize a swinging bunt and throwing the batter out at first. This might be the high point of the game, so I walked over between innings to see what Jiddi thought of it, and he was, naturally, fairly shining with joy, with a big grin on his round face. He couldn't get over how Andy could throw strikes under pressure. At least in football the quarterback gets to hand the ball off half the time.

We took the lead in the second, as Matt singled and moved

around to score, helped by a patented Andy walk. In the bottom of the inning, when Andy got two strikes on Rocco, I thought we might actually win this game, but then the Rock rallied with a single, and soon it was 1–1.

At about this point, the Game of the Year suddenly turned into America's Funniest Home Videos. A dog scampered on the field, and play stopped for five minutes while kids and coaches tried to chase him out. Then a juggler appeared in the gazebo beyond center field, distracting the batters. A coach had to run out and ask him to take his act elsewhere. Two batters later, a child riding a bike in back of home crashed into a pole and toppled to the ground, in pain. The heat was apparently making everyone— man, child, beast—crazy. Hey, let's play two!

Then Big Joe Reynolds summoned me to the bench, grimacing, and announced that he'd just gotten a splinter in his thigh. You had to laugh—if you got the joke. One of the oldest insults in baseball concerns players who get into games so rarely they "pick up splinters sitting on the bench." But who ever heard of that actually happening to anyone? It was a cliché come to life.

A quick inspection revealed that the sliver, which had pierced Joe's uniform pants, was the size of a toothpick, the skin around the puncture was turning blue, and this was worthy of a trip to the emergency room at Nyack Hospital. This was our first serious injury of the regular season and it happened to a player sitting on the bench.

Finally, sanity prevailed (maybe the sun dipped behind the trees), and play resumed. It was up to Andy to hold them down, and he did, striking out the side. He and the Aliens had already exceeded my expectations for this game, so now—let's win! But Rocco breezed again in the fourth, giving him a perfect 12 K's for the game so far. I considered lifting Andy before he faltered, assuring him and the Bedways a nearly perfect memory, but I knew he was our best hope to win, so he went out for another inning—and promptly walked the leadoff hitter.

Then Rocco hit a little grounder that died in short right field. Little John rushed in and picked it up as the Tiger base runner rounded second. Instead of quickly firing it to second to hold the runner, John cocked his arm and then pumped it a couple of times. I couldn't figure out what was going on, but then it dawned on me: John was *daring the base runner* to take the extra base on him.

Typical John! No doubt he had seen some hotdog right fielder do this in a game on TV, and now he was aping him. It was great theater—until the base runner took him up on the dare and headed for third. Shocked that he would run on *his* arm, John did a double take, then uncorked a near-perfect throw! But our third sacker bobbled the ball, and the tag was late.

Still, you had to smile. Funny kid!

Then Andy walked two weak hitters at the bottom of the order, and suddenly we were trailing. We went to the sixth needing two runs to keep the season going. Rocco, by now, was laboring, pushing instead of throwing the ball, sweat staining his uniform—and it made me worry about that lump on his head.

Leading off, Andy drew a walk, and soon we had bases loaded, two outs, Rocco reeling, way over his pitch count! The stage was set with our hottest hitter, Little Stevie, at bat. It looked like another Alien miracle, and on the first pitch, Stevie stroked a hard grounder down the first base line. But the first sacker grabbed it and beat him to the bag—and we had sewn up second place.

A discouraged bunch of Aliens trudged to the sidelines following the last out. ("It breaks your heart," Bart Giamatti once said about baseball. "It is designed to break your heart.") As the kids hit the bench, slamming bats and gloves around, I told them they'd played splendidly and should hold their heads high, and who cared about the regular season anyway? The only thing anyone would remember after June were the playoffs (this was actually true).

"No one gets a trophy for winning the regular season crown," I reminded them, "it only goes to the playoff winner." We'd achieved what we set out for—a bye in the first round of the playoffs. And we'd proven we could play tough with the Tigers and, perhaps, even win.

This seemed to assuage the Aliens and they rose with some fire in their eyes. "Take a few days off," I instructed. "Enjoy your bye."

I saw John Marley raise his hand, but this time I made a preemptive strike. "No, John, I do NOT know why they call it a bye."

"But it's a good . . . bye . . . right?" Kipp asked.

There was no need to pep up the Bedways. Our play needed no excuse. They'd seen a great game with an exciting finish. Andy had pitched well and got on base twice via walks. Jiddi was his usual positive self, still raving about Andy's play on that bunt way back in the first inning. And he was amazed how hard Andy and Rocco threw—and how anyone had the courage to stand in there and swing against them, and sometimes actually hit the ball. It looked almost like pro ball to him, and it wasn't even the Little League majors.

"Forget about what I said about paint drying," he instructed us. What a breakthrough. First Barbara, then Jiddi—belated baseball fans. If only my father were still around to see his grandson, and son, in Little League. We'd just lost the pennant, but the Mitchells and Bedways remained on a kind of high all weekend walking around downtown Nyack.

As it happens, I was about to visit our town's only baseball Hall of Famer, who is precisely Jiddi's age, and something of an expert on the care and feeding of young ballplayers. Bob Wolff moved to

Nyack in 1976 with his wife, Jane, and, now in his seventies, still commutes several nights a week to Long Island to anchor an evening sportscast. He's vigorous, bright, and he played the ukulele during his Hall of Fame induction ceremony. "I'm completely blessed," he told me in his sunny Nyack apartment down by the river, about a quarter mile from Memorial Park, "I've gotten every break. A great deal of my pleasure was watching my boys play baseball."

Well, he's seen a lot of other baseball, too. Bob starred in high school on Long Island, then played outfield at Duke until he broke his ankle in his sophomore year. He went to work for a radio station in Washington, D.C., after emerging from the Navy at the end of World War II. Soon he was calling Washington Senators games on radio, and became a pioneer in announcing big league games on that new invention, television. He was "Mr. Baseball" in Washington for nearly fifteen years, and also announced national contests, including Don Larsen's perfect game in the '56 World Series.

When his first son was born, Bob broadcast the opening game of a doubleheader, went to the hospital between games, and got back to the park in time to call the end of game two. Both of his sons proved to be good little players but, on the road most of the time during the spring and summer, he missed their games. He got much more involved with them when they hit high school and he served as the voice of the New York Knicks and New York Rangers—winter teams. Because of baseball, "our common bond," Bob remained close to his boys, talking strategy and mechanics into the night, and throwing them thousands of batting-practice pitches.

His elder son, also named Bob, became an all-American pitcher at Princeton. His other son, Rick, an infielder, played with Harvard and got drafted by the Detroit Tigers. Playing in the minors, Rick told his dad that he "must be the lowest-paid gradu-

ate of Harvard." Recognizing that he probably would not make it
to the bigs, Rick retired and wrote a book called *What's a Nice
Harvard Boy Like You Doing in the Bushes?* He has stayed with baseball in a variety of capacities: as a columnist for *Sports Illustrated,*
author of many books, and sports psychologist with the
Cleveland Indians. Today he's a book editor and hosts a weekly
show on New York's all-sports radio station WFAN, on youth
athletics.

His father was inducted into the broadcast wing at the baseball
Hall of Fame in 1995. Bob can spin hundreds of anecdotes, such as
how he ended up with a sore arm in the booth after calling the
Larsen no-hitter, "because I pitched the last inning with him"; or
describe how he spent a month learning how to pour beer on live
TV with either hand, thus becoming the first "switch pourer" in
baseball history. (He titled his recent autobiography *It's Not Who
Won or Lost the Game—It's How You Sold the Beer.*) But, gamely, I
tried to stick to the subject of Little League.

Like his son Rick, "the real expert," Bob believes that Little
League should be strictly noncompetitive—don't even keep
score—until the kids are at least ten years old. Then the kids can
really learn the game in peace, and no one would sit on the bench
most of the time. "You never know who might turn out to be a big
star later," he explains. Drafts should be held by picking names
out of a hat. He believes that society has "intruded" too much on
youth sports; kids use adult behavior as a model, and so you see all
this "posturing" and "trash talk," and pitchers glaring at infielders when they miss a grounder.

Still, he enjoys attending games to watch some of his nine
grandkids play. "All that fun," he says, chuckling, "and just
think, no beer commercials!"

On Monday evening, Steve Wanamaker summoned all of the managers to the concession stand/office at Liberty to discuss the play-

offs. Everyone except Badger showed up, perhaps fearing that the discussion would turn to the Trouble incident. My advice to all Little League managers: Don't ever be the one who doesn't show up at a meeting. Little League coaches and officials are quicker with gossip and sarcasm than almost anyone, and if you're not there—beware.

After we took our seats in the cramped office—about the size of a dugout—Wanamaker announced that, if we didn't object, the playoffs would be "double elimination." You keep playing until you lose twice. That sounded okay, especially with our bye, but as he released the schedule it became apparent that it would take at least ten days to play the games, running into early July, well after the end of the school year. I'd asked the parents of my players to put off vacations for a week after the regular season ended, but they were free to do what they wanted after that. Now it became clear that if we went deep into the playoffs—and obviously we hoped to get to the final round—we'd be playing a few days after that deadline.

Also, I knew that at least one of our players, RBI Keiser (gulp), would definitely be away that second week, and if we suffered a rain-out or two, so would Andy and I. We usually fled to Ohio right after school let out, and B.B. was already unhappy that this trip had been delayed. But now, if the playoffs dragged on, we might have to miss the final game—or sacrifice our nonrefundable airline tickets (and risk serious marital discord, too).

There was another reason to favor a fast, single-elimination tourney: We had no pitching depth, and if we had to play a lot of games in short order, we'd likely sputter. Double elimination was a great equalizer—after a couple of games *everyone's* pitching would be shot so anyone could win. Of course, I didn't mention any of that when I asked Steve if we could go back to single-elimination. I claimed there was a lot of rain in the extended forecast (true), and I was sure no one wanted to play almost up to July 4.

As it turned out, everyone did want to play until then. "Hey, the more games the better," John Miller said. Of course, the Pirates had eight pitchers.

"I'm sure we'll all lose a player or two who has to go away, but the idea is to play, so let's play," Glenn Meyerson chipped in. "What's wrong," he asked me, joshing, "you short on pitching?" I just grinned, in defeat. Then the meeting broke up, with good spirits all around and everyone looking forward to the playoffs, which would start in two days.

16

As expected, the Pirates and Yankees won their first playoff games, earning the right to take on the two "bye" teams, the Aliens and the Tigers, in the second round of the playoffs. We drew the Pirates, who had just scored twenty-one runs against the Mets and would no doubt pitch tough little Danny Stroud against us. I could handle losing the playoffs, but didn't want to blow the first game and face quick elimination after all we'd been through.

Andy, meanwhile, had made the majors, though not in the way we imagined. League officials had chosen a ten-year-old all-star team, which plays in tourneys up to the state level; but with only nine kids that age in the majors they had to select three from the minors to fill out the squad. And they picked Andy, along with Rocco and Danny (no relation) Mitchell. I was surprised and delighted, and couldn't wait to tell Andy. His goal all season was simply to make the *minors* all-star team.

Naturally, he was thrilled and eager to tell friends. He seemed a little reserved about it, though, and I sensed that he knew exactly what it meant—not only facing tougher competition he might not be ready for, but playing in games where his father, for the first time, would be (as we say) "outside the fence."

"Don't worry," I told him, laughing, "it probably will be as rough for me as it will be for you."

"I know, but can I think about it?" I could almost hear his heart sputtering. "And let's not tell the Aliens."

"Why's that?"

"I'm an Alien first, an all-star second."

On Monday, the day before the Pirates game, I got a call from Eddie Badger. Always wonderful to hear his voice. "We need to reschedule our game with you on Friday," he announced. "When can you play?"

"What do you mean our game Friday? We don't have a game with you on Friday yet. We still have to beat the Pirates and you have to beat the Yankees to get there."

Eddie assured me this was a foregone conclusion.

"Well, I'm not so sure," I said, "and anyway, why can't you play Friday?" Eddie reminded me that Friday was moving-up day for the fifth-graders at Upper Nyack elementary, as they would head off for middle school next year. There was always a party that afternoon on school grounds, with hot dogs and games. I knew all this, since Andy was one of those fifth-graders, but I hadn't considered it a threat to a playoff game that night. Most of the kids in our league don't even go to that school, many who do are not in fifth grade, and only about half the school's fifth-graders attend the party anyway. Besides, the party would end by game time, and there was no reason a player couldn't leave a few minutes early—assuming he went to the party to begin with.

"I don't even know if we'll be in that game," I repeated. "Second, the party shouldn't interfere. Third, we're on a tight schedule as it is, and if we start postponing games now, none of us will be able to field a team by the time it's over."

Eddie nearly had a coronary. "We CAN not play and we WILL not play," he spat out. "I'll talk to Wanamaker about this," he vowed. This threat rang a bit hollow, since I knew Wanamaker would stand firm and had other bones to pick with Eddie.

"Fine," I replied, laughing at the absurdity. "Good luck postponing a game you're not even in yet."

Still, I wondered if I was being too much of a hard-ass just because it was Eddie, so I called Richards Jarden. "Forget it," he told me. "Just ask yourself—if it was reversed, would Badger postpone the game if you asked?" Well, that seemed to settle the matter once and for all, or so I thought.

Then I went out and screwed up the Pirates game right from the start, arriving at Memorial without our scorebook. For some reason, possibly nerves, I got mental about it, and drove home to get it. I could have ripped a couple of pages out of John Miller's scorebook but that didn't occur to me. By the time I got back, we were halfway through batting practice and I had to rush warming up our pitchers. I was sweating from running around, and not displaying the usual calm that helped get us to this point. Instead, I was Mr. Frazzle. Perhaps worst of all, I didn't have time to fill the ditch in front of the pitching rubber, as I usually did.

At least I'd finally settled on a starting pitcher. Andy was now our best bet, but I wanted to hold him back, if I could, for the (unscheduled) Tigers game on Friday. This was risky, for if we lost game one, we'd have to go unbeaten the rest of the playoffs. But Matt had pitched well in his one inning against the Tigers last week, and Steve had tossed a partial no-hitter recently, so I had confidence they could hold off the pesky Pirates.

"Let's show them why we're the Incredible A's," Little John boomed, making a muscle. But he'd already confided to his family that he didn't think we'd ever beat the Tigers. Amos seemed particularly up for this game, but I was hoping he wasn't feeling *too* chipper. He was among the team leaders in hits but tended to get

three in one game and barely make contact the next. His explanation: When he did well he'd get overconfident and swing at
everything the next game.

John Miller had flown off to Puerto Rico again on business. Jim
Mitchell, Danny's dad, would skipper in his place, and he would
take John's spot directing traffic at third base. Only half-joking,
John had told him, "You've got a cell phone—call me when we
get some base runners!"

Looking out of sync, Matt walked two of the first three hitters and
a run scored. Now, how would we do against Danny Stroud? It
looked like he was popping the ball, but he walked Steve, then
gave up singles to Amos and Robby and walked Andy, and soon
we had three runs. Matt fell apart in the second, however, walking
a batter, hitting another, and giving up a ringing triple to Stroud.
Vicky Scimeca noticed Matt's knees buckling after that and knew
he was shook up.

It got worse in the third. Matt walked the first two batters, and
they later scored. After that, I briefly pondered bringing in Andy,
figuring I'd worry about the next game when it arrived, but I
brought on Steve instead. He got one out, then forced the next hitter to hit a high fly in back of short—my worst nightmare, since
Andy still wasn't retreating well on pops. He made a good effort,
and even got his glove on the ball, but it ticked away, and our
years of reluctance to practice that play had come back to haunt us,
at the worst possible time. Soon we were down 7–3.

After four innings we trailed 9–5. Steve managed to escape the
fifth without giving up a run, but now it really looked bleak: The
game had dragged on so long, it was approaching eight o'clock,
and rain clouds were moving in. A few drops fell. For certain the
game would be cut short after this inning, so this would be our last
ups.

It was gather-round-the-Alien time. I told the guys they'd rallied before and would no doubt do it again and begged them to "go out and get four runs NOW." By request, Amos smacked a hit to right, Robby walked, throw in a couple of wild pitches, and it was 9–7. Then Andy walked, and when ball four got away, he rounded first and headed for second—and when the catcher fired the ball into center field he came all the way around to score. A "home run" on a walk. Only in Little League! That made it 9–8.

Then Taddy, utilizing *his* specialty, beat out a bunt, stole second and third, and came home on a passed ball. Miraculously, we were tied! Four runs on two hits and some head's-up baserunning of our own—literally stealing a page from the Pirates. Our bench exploded, and Andy hoisted Taddy off the ground (not a difficult thing), as the Bucs finally recorded the third out.

But now what? The ump, Mario Bonanno, invited me to home plate. (He has two all-star sons, known as the super Mario brothers.) Obviously, he wanted to discuss calling the game at this point, with twilight approaching. Did I want that? Or should we go for the win, now that we had the Pirates on the run? During my stroll to the plate what I felt was simply *relief*—to have dodged the bullet and gained a second life. I wanted to celebrate the comeback with Andy and the team, go home, savor it over a beer, and look forward to finishing the game tomorrow. That seemed like fun. And isn't fun what it's all about?

"It's up to you guys," Mario said.

"Let's play," Jim Mitchell said. I waited a moment, mulling it over.

"I'd say no," I responded. "I mean, it's not so dark now, but by the time we get up again, it may be impossible to see the ball at all."

"Like I said, up to you," Mario said. We weren't getting anywhere. Then I remembered something.

"You guys ever hear about that lawsuit?"

"What lawsuit?" Mario asked, very interested.

"Brian Thomas got sued for ten million dollars. He was assign-ing umps in another league and some kid got hurt when it started to get dark—because the ump let the game go on."

"Okay, let's call it, it's okay with me," Jim said.

"Oh, yes," Mario agreed readily. Suddenly everyone was on the same page. I didn't tell them that the lawsuit had been dis-missed years ago. We all shook hands and said we could finish the next evening. Then I went back to the bench.

"We will not be denied!" Kipp shouted, and it seemed, maybe, true.

"Alien Resurrection!" screamed Andy, the sci-fi movie fan.

"You guys are making my hair fall out," I added. "You can start rubbing *my* head for good luck next game."

A little later that night, two Pirates tracked down John Miller in Puerto Rico. One of them said into the phone, "You won't believe this, coach, it was dark and rainy and they *tied it up*."

Completion of the suspended game was set for six o'clock the fol-lowing evening at Memorial. For once, there was little strategy to ponder. I had no choice but to put Andy in as pitcher, a stroke of fortune or brilliant foresight, take your pick. He was tanned, rested, and ready to go, while the Pirates could not come back with their ace, Danny Stroud, since he'd already pitched in this game.

This time I made sure I packed our trusty scorebook. I even packed a spare, but another crisis loomed. When I checked my trunk, the Alien was nowhere to be seen. I realized that in all the excitement the previous night our mascot must have gone home in Richards's car. And I knew Richards had to spend most of the day in Manhattan, doing an installation at Bloomingdale's or some-thing, and might arrive late for the game.

Fortunately, just before six, I saw him striding toward our bench, Alien in hand.

"Great to see you," I said, "and you, too, Richards."

"I have to warn you about something," he said gravely.

"What's that?"

"The Alien went to New York City today, and you know how it is . . . he came back with an *attitude*."

Just what we needed—a mascot acting like a *Seinfeld* character. Yoda, Yoda, Yoda.

It was a beautiful late-June evening down by the river as I assembled the Aliens on the bench and reminded them this likely would be a one-inning game and so they had to bear down from the start, on every pitch. One miscue could be fatal.

Continuing where we'd left off the previous night, the Pirates had the top of their order due, and the batter led off with a hard single to right field. He stole second and third, and now it seemed inevitable that he would score, by hook or by crook. But Andy whiffed the next two batters, and even more amazing, did not throw a wild pitch.

Up stepped a tough out, Cory Hunt, and under unbearable pressure, Andy finally threw a ball in the dirt, low and outside, destined to skip back to the screen, with a run scoring easily. But Amos, like a cat, dove, got a piece of it, kept it in front of him, and stared the runner back to third. Whew. Letting out a deep sigh, Andy went back to work and fanned the batter, stranding the potential winning run at third. Where'd he get that ice water in his veins? Not from me, that's for sure.

The old Amos 'n' Andy battery had come through again.

"Okay, let's end it NOW," I begged the Aliens as they returned to the bench, smacking Andy on the back as he passed. As Amos unstrapped his gear, I went over and poked him on the chest protector. "You saved the season right there," I told him. "Just like hitting a game-winning home run."

Again, we did not score, and I wasn't sure I could survive another inning. The Aliens were abducting a year off my life every night. Andy had no such doubts, and went out and struck out the side. But we did nothing in our half, and we went to the eighth inning of the game—possibly a record for local Little League minors. Andy set them down one-two-three again. Swell, but the more innings he pitched tonight, the fewer he could hurl later in the week if we ever managed to score a frickin' run and face the Tigers on Friday.

Okay. Bottom of the eighth. Danny Mitchell seemed to sag, walking Stevie on four pitches. Then Amos got his fourth hit of the game, and we had first and third and none out. We couldn't possibly not score *now,* right? But if RBI Keiser didn't deliver again, the notoriously erratic Matt and Andy followed.

Robby stood at the plate. He may not have looked like Mike Piazza up there, but then he never did—thin, striking a kind of lazy stance. Yet his concentration on the pitcher was complete. "Look at that *focus,*" his father whispered to me, almost in astonishment, finally figuring out the secret to his son's success.

With a stroke of mercy, RBI pounded a line drive to right and Steve trotted home. The bench rushed out to smother Robby (making Steve wonder why teams always mob the guy who knocked in the winning run but not the fella who scored it). The Aliens had won one of the greatest games in history, or so it seemed to us, and advanced to round two of the playoffs—and yet another showdown with the Tigers.

When we got home, the phone rang, and I figured it was a kid or parent wanting to rehash the game, which I was all too eager to do. No such luck. It was Eddie Badger.

"So how'd you make out?" he demanded to know.

"We won. And you, against the Yanks?"

"Won 23–5." Ouch. I found out later they'd led 16–0 after two innings.

"Congratulations," I offered half-heartedly.

"I still want Friday's game postponed. We can't play."

"You mean you won't play. Listen, take it up with Wanamaker." Then I hung up and went over and gave Andy a big hug.

Now fateful Friday approached. Andy would leave elementary school behind in the morning and encounter the Tigers that evening in game two of the playoffs. What a graduation gift. Wanamaker had indeed refused to postpone the game. Fast Eddie had fanned the flames of our rivalry, and now the weatherman was predicting temperatures in the mid-90s. It was hard to decide which blast of hot air was more frightening.

Parents had already started calling, wondering if there was a league rule against scheduling a game during an ozone alert. Like most kids today, mothers have no experience of playing baseball for hours and hours on hot summer days. (Some of the dads do recall those moments, fondly, so we raise far fewer objections.) One mother hinted broadly that she might not let her boy play if she thought he'd turn to toast.

"The game's not going to start until six o'clock," I assured her. "The field's right next to the river, so we can always go for a swim if it's too hot." What's a little chemical contamination when you need to cool off?

Record heat or not, play must go on, and I'd come to believe that the hot spell might be a blessing in disguise. I'd told my guys to arrive at the field barely fifteen minutes before game time to conserve energy (and appease their parents). Perhaps Eddie Badger would self-destruct by refusing to trim his hour-long warm-up, or maybe his ace pitcher, Rocco, would melt in the heat. Whoever won this game would need just one more victory to take the title, but I kept my hopes in check. The Tigers had beaten us all season and probably would again; they had the better team, even if we had more fun and more character (or was it characters?). Beating the Pirates in extra innings was thrill enough for me, and I figured the Aliens would be satisfied with that as well. Or was I underestimating them, with possibly tragic consequences?

17

orning dawned, hot as forecast, as we grabbed a
camera, along with three paper fans I'd brought
back from Japan, and headed to school for the graduation ceremony. Andy wore a plain white polo
shirt and khaki shorts. The black boys all wore coats and ties.
"They're used to dressing up," Andy explained, "they go to
church more than white kids." I'd barely stepped in the door to
the gym when a parent, a longtime friend of ours, accosted me.

"Why are you making the kids play that game today?" she
asked, smiling but dead serious. She had a son on the Tigers, of
course.

"What do you mean, I'm making them play? You must have
been talking to Badger."

"Well, yes."

"It's the league's decision. And anyway, why not play?"

"The heat . . . the class party."

"It will be just as hot all weekend, and the game isn't until six,
when it cools off and the party ends."

"Eddie said five."

"No, that's when he wants his players there . . . for excessive
batting practice."

"Oh." And she walked away.

Then my former colleague Bob Giacobbe approached and,
rather sheepishly, said he was carrying a message from another

Tiger parent. The same message. I gave him the same response. "Tell Eddie to talk to me himself instead of letting you do the dirty work," I said, trying to maintain a grin. The nerve of that guy to spoil the graduation ceremony for me. But Eddie just sat in his chair across the room and never said a word.

Fortunately, the pageant began on time. One by one, each fifth-grader stepped forward, and the rich diversity of Nyack's many races and cultures was striking. Among the kids was Dekey from Tibet, her broad face framed by shining dark hair. Her mother had fled Tibet on foot over the Himalayas. She sat next to Andy's friend Peter, a charming Korean boy adopted as an infant. When their teacher, Ms. Humphrey, originally from Barbados, called out Andy's name and he rose to retrieve his diploma (and a hug), it was clear that he was the tallest in the class except for one other boy and quite a few girls— the gender growth curves wouldn't cross for another year or two.

This height promised to help his baseball career but reminded us that he had grown up way too fast. He already had some of the 'tude of a teenager and now he nearly had the physique, as well. "Everything has changed," I whispered to my wife, "except his voice." Afterward, at a mercifully brief reception under the hot sun, Andy made the rounds, hugging favorite teachers good-bye, then we jumped in our car and drove to a local pizza joint for lunch and some celebratory air-conditioning.

Back home, Andy chilled in front of a fan while I worried over a starting lineup. Since Andy had hurled three innings against the Pirates, he could only pitch three more innings this week. Should I start Andy on the mound and hope he kept us close (for a while)? Or hold him in reserve for the second half of the game? Counting on Eddie to be his own worst enemy, I decided to risk everything on the burnout factor. When Badger's team collapsed in the heat, Andy would come on late in the game to close the deal. If Andy could handle the pressure. Which his own father was foisting on him.

• • •

Andy had little interest in the fifth-grade party, but I was curious to see how many members of Eddie's team actually showed up. As it turned out, attendance was light, and only a handful of Tigers appeared. After complaining so loudly that I would wreck the party for his kids, Eddie led the Tigers out of the school a full ninety minutes before game time!

Ironically, Andy and I stayed a little longer, then rushed home to take showers, change into our game clothes, and perspire some more. I chose my green Rock 'n' Roll Museum shirt to match my A's cap. (I've always tried to follow fashion—at a safe distance.) My cynical-about-baseball wife volunteered to clean her son's muddy cleats. Andy, as usual, seemed even-keeled, more impatient than nervous. We performed our usual Kabuki routine in the car on the way to the park. "Andy, I just want to remind you about two things." "Two things, Dad, TWO things." God help me if I thought of a third.

We got to the field about half an hour before game time to find the Tigers in the middle of batting practice and already parched. It was still nearly 90 degrees under a hazy sun. Beyond the outfield a few lonely sailboats bobbed on the Hudson in the dank summer air. Slowly our players drifted in, strolling across the outfield chugging water, as if all we had to do was show up, stay hydrated, and victory would be ours. "The Tigers look bushed already," Kipp said, with a mischievous grin.

Badger barked orders from the sideline. We were perspiring just watching him. Trouble's father, still near the bench after kicking his own son, was already hassling the umpire about something. It was hot, and on a night like this who knew what might happen? Just that week a forty-six-year-old Little League coach in Sturgeon Bay, Wisconsin, had cursed an elderly umpire in front of his players, then followed him into the equipment room, where he sucker-punched him. The umpire's sin?

He had failed to call a balk on an opposing pitcher. The ump needed four stitches in the jaw; the coach now faced felony assault charges. Afterward, the team's manager—a town alderman—stuck up for his coach, claiming he was "extremely good with kids . . . he still believes the pitcher was balking." That league, like ours, does not require background checks, and so no one knew that in 1986 this manager had been convicted of reckless endangerment after nearly striking his pregnant former wife with his pickup truck.

On the bench before the game, I told the Aliens they'd already accomplished more than anyone could have hoped for, so they should just go out there and have fun.

We failed to score in the first off the fireballing Rocco, and then Matt hauled his large, yet fragile, ego to the mound. He immediately walked four Tigers, leading to four runs (are we having fun yet?). It looked like an instant replay of the Pirates game—which was okay, if it ended the same way, though this seemed unlikely. In the second inning, Andy drew a walk but then made the final out on a misguided steal of home.

Between innings, ump Ray Westbrook, normally a genial fellow, angrily ripped off his mask and went over to tell Fast Eddie to stop making ball and strike calls from the bench. Perhaps we needed that to get us going, for in the third inning Kipp and Stevie singled in runs, meaning we were back in the game at 4–2. Eddie was getting even more tense, yelling at his players for mental and physical lapses. Was Rocco, inevitably, tiring? It didn't seem to matter, as the Tigers scored three more to take a seemingly insurmountable 7–2 lead.

Then, it happened, as if bound to happen, or in any case as it always seemed to happen, for the Aliens. Andy walked to lead off the fourth, and so did the next three batters as Rocco faltered, sweat rolling down his broad cheeks. That brought up the

Kippster. I had a lot of faith in him. Nervous at the start of every game, he always settled down and proved tough in the clutch. Last year in the playoffs he had ripped a triple off one of the best pitchers in the league, which gave him confidence against other hard throwers. So he felt no fear standing in against Rocco.

Still, it was a shock when he crushed a triple to left center. And the game was tied! The Miracle A's had done it again, and I still had my ace (pitcher) in the hole.

In the bottom of the fourth inning, the first two Tiger batters reached base and now Andy came on to try to save the day. Sure enough, he struck out the first hitter, but the next one stroked a single that scored two and the Tigers were back on top 9–7. The game had taken a bad turn, and I suddenly realized that it was approaching eight o'clock and no inning at Memorial can start after that. We would not get a chance to play the sixth and final inning, meaning we only had one more shot at tying the score. It was, indeed, a reprise of the previous game against the Pirates.

Before we batted, I called everyone to the bench. "Okay, guys, we've only got one more ups, not two," I said, fairly calmly. "Nearly every time I've asked you to perform the impossible you've done it, but I have to ask one more time! Sorry, but we need two runs to tie, *right now*," I pleaded. "So go out and do it! Win one for the . . . Kippster!" It wasn't exactly Rockne, or even Reagan, but it was the best I could do. Then we all rubbed the mascot's sticky skull, screamed, "Go Aliens!" and got ready for some excitement. Jon Albert yelled toward the kids, "I smell a rally coming!"

Apparently I looked so focused and intense coaching at third base it caused Jim Marley to turn to his wife and say, "You can practically see Greg's endorphins popping." He'd noticed that a few times this year and felt the kids picked up on it, got serious, and played better—"played baseball for real," as he put it.

There was just one problem. We had the bottom half of our

order up, not exactly murderers' row. Matt the Bat grounded out, but Andy walked. It suddenly dawned on me that something funny was happening in back of the screen toward the Tiger bench. Someone seemed to be shouting out to our batters as they stood at the plate—with Rocco's pitches heading their way. I couldn't quite identify what was happening, as Little John swung and missed the first two deliveries. Then I figured it out: Eddie was standing at the fence, and as the pitch came in, he instructed our batters to "swing" if the pitch looked bad and "take" if it looked good!

There, he did it again—and John had struck out on a pitch over his head.

Before I could bolt from the coaching box and run down the line to protest, I saw Arlene Keiser spring from her seat, walk up to the screen, and shout something to the ump. He turned around, took off his mask, shook his head as if in agreement, then shouted over and told Eddie to cut it out right away. Too late, for now we were down to our last out, with our number eight batter due up.

Enrique would have to keep the game, and probably our season, alive. He'd never conquered his upper cut but often could work out a walk. Over on the sidelines his father said to himself, *Oh, please, don't let my kid make the final out.* I knew how he felt. With Andy up I often wished for nothing more than a base on balls, or a gentle hit by pitch. So I grabbed Enrique as he headed to the plate and offered the usual confounding advice. "Don't be afraid to swing but we'll take a walk," I said.

"I'll go for the walk," he replied. "Rocco's wiped." Well, that made things simple.

With two strikes on him, Enrique still looked for a walk, and got it, putting the tying run on first. I turned around and saw Big Enrique burst into a giant grin—spared. Little Enrique was wearing the same smile over at first. (Like father like son.) Rocco was so tired he'd started shotputting the ball to the catcher. Still, Badger would not take him out. Big Enrique said to John Albert, "If they take out Rocco and put in anyone else, we're dead—we got a buncha free swingers!" But Rocco stayed on the mound.

Then, with Jeremy up, our runner on third made a mad dash for the plate on a wild pitch—ignoring my cry of "Stop!"—and was tagged out, ending the game.

The base runner was Andy. My own kid was the goat.

But wait—*the catcher dropped the ball.* The umpire signaled safe, Badger had a fit, and we were still alive! "Good going," I whispered to Andy as he sheepishly ran back to the bench. Now we trailed 9–8.

Enrique had managed to lumber all the way to third on the play. Determined to get a piece of the ball, Jeremy fouled off a couple of pitches and then walked, the ball got away, and Enrique rumbled home—beating the tag by inches! We'd knotted the score again. "I can't believe you guys," I shouted as the joyful Aliens returned to the bench, "scoring exactly two runs. You always give me precisely what I ask for—so I'd better be careful what I ask for!"

Still, to secure a tie and live to play another day, we had to shut down the Tigers in the bottom of the inning, with the top of their order facing a less-than-awesome Andy.

The leadoff hitter grounded out, but the next batter singled, stole second, and went to third on the overthrow. Winning run on third, one out—almost a given in Little League that he'd score, if not on a hit then on a ground ball, a fly ball, maybe even a foul pop, or a straight steal, delayed steal, wild pitch, passed ball, safety squeeze, suicide squeeze . . . the possibilities were almost endless. Hell, runners had scored from third against us while our pitcher was daydreaming on the mound.

Somehow, Andy remained focused—good old tunnel vision—

and struck out the next batter for the second out. Yet that only post-poned the inevitable, as Rocco, the best hitter in the league, if not the universe, sauntered to the plate. Even if he just made contact and hit a little grounder—in this heat, was anyone on my team capable of fielding a ball cleanly and making an accurate throw to first? Time seemed to stop as he started to dig in. No stranger in the crowd could doubt 'twas Rocco at the bat.

But then a lifetime of listening to ballgames on the radio, watch-ing them on TV, playing baseball board games ("You Be the Manager"), and studying managerial strategy in newspapers, books, and magazines—all those thousands of seemingly wasted hours—finally paid off. A voice, first faint, then practically screaming, echoed in my head. "*Walk him . . . walk him . . . WALK HIM, YOU KNUCKLEHEAD.*"

I turned to my coaches and said quietly: "We're going to walk him." As usual, Richards smiled benignly, and then asked, sensi-bly, "Is it *allowed?*" Others voiced shock or dismay. After all, none of us had ever witnessed an intentional walk in Little League.

"I have a good feeling about pitching to him," Bob Keiser said. "Rocco is due to make out."

"Due!" I replied, laughing. "The kid has made out three times in the past three months. I'd say there was a pattern there!"

Then I dashed onto the field and frantically signaled the ump for time as Andy was about to deliver the first pitch. "What's Greg going out there for?" Jon Albert asked his wife. His son, at first base, had precisely the same thought. Meanwhile, back behind the screen, Jim Marley said to his wife, Betsy, "This man really wants to win this game." Maybe this strategy was bizarre for Little League, but it was a no-brainer in professional ball. There was a runner on third, but first base was "open," and Rocco sure couldn't do any damage down there. Also, with a runner on first, we might get a force play at second—a shorter throw for my weary infielders.

There was one more astonishing detail, making this move especially sweet or potentially painful. The next hitter, naturally, would be Badger's son, Jack. (This was turning into Hollywood on Hudson.) But first we had to execute the intentional walk. In the big leagues the pitcher actually has to throw four wide pitches, but I had no idea how to do it in Little League. Apparently no one did. For when I told the ump what I wanted to do, he asked *me* how it was done. "I have no idea," I said, trying to recall some mention in the official rule book, which of course no one was carrying, or had even read. Then I said, tentatively, "I think you just signal him to take first?" That was true in some leagues, though perhaps not ours.

Right or wrong, Westbrook pointed to first and told Rocco to mosey on down. The look on Rocco's face was priceless as he stared back in disbelief. "Ultimate respect, Rock, ultimate respect," I chanted, to make him feel better (it was even the truth). Then he dropped his bat and trotted down the line—perhaps imagining he had achieved mythic status like Mickey Mantle (maybe he had). His father, understandably, looked confused. "What are they *doing*?" he shouted out to the ump.

This was Enrique's reaction: "*Wha?*" But he kept his opinion to himself.

As I headed back to the bench I heard a smattering of applause and murmurs from the parents on our side, and then Andy in his sweetest singsong voice, not at all embarrassed, called after me: "Thank . . . you . . . Dad." Doesn't a father always try to shield his children from harm—protect them in times of danger?

"What did you just DO?" Famous Amos asked me from third base.

"Probably screwed up the whole season," I replied.

"You know," Dan Wolff said, "I *thought* I saw a lightbulb going on over your head."

Big Enrique turned to Jon Albert and yelled: "I love it! Real baseball!"

Now all Andy had to do was strike out Jack. My own son could make me look very smart or very stupid in front of dozens of people, including some of my best friends. How often does a kid get to do that to his dad? I'd kept my emotions pretty much in check throughout the game, even during our comebacks, but now the butterflies in my stomach started fluttering. Andy, improbably, acted as if it was just another day at the office.

Jack appeared to be up there looking for a walk, or a wild pitch. Andy fired the first pitch and the batter jumped back as if about to get hit by a cannonball, but the ump called it a strike, right down the middle (nice try, kid). Jack playacted on the next pitch as well, a genuinely inside pitch that he claimed hit him—first announcing that it had struck his elbow, then his shoulder. "Well, which one is it?" the ump responded, amused.

Then Andy threw another ball: two and one. Then he threw a wicked fastball that Jack actually swung at—and missed. Two and two.

By now it was getting gray, if not dark. The game was two hours old, an eternity. A cool breeze blew off the river, finally. Coaches, players, and parents on both sides shouted encouragement but in a deeply respectful way, as if the moment spoke for itself. The confrontation was classic. It could have been Ralph Branca vs. Bobby Thomson, Ralph Terry vs. Willie McCovey, Mike Torrez vs. Bucky Dent. As Andy went into the windup there was a collective gasp. . . .

Strike three called! Andy leaped in the air and the Aliens exploded off the bench. "YES!" the manager shouted, and hugged the nearest player, Enrique, who hugged back. It was as if we had already won the game, not simply tied it.

Jack slammed down his bat. Eddie angrily informed the umpire that he was protesting the game because of the intentional walk. Was it legal in Little League, he wondered? And if so, didn't the pitcher have to actually throw the four pitches? (He was a sore loser and he hadn't even lost yet.) The ump promised to head out to Liberty to see what a league official might say.

Parents rushed out to hail my strategy, calling it pure genius— but what if it had backfired? Andy thanked me again for taking Rocco off his hands. I hugged him and blathered that he had saved my butt by striking out Jack. Gathering the loopy Aliens around me, I promised to call their parents in a couple hours to let them know when we'd finish the game the next day. Whatever the hour, we were sure to win, I declared. I almost believed it.

What I didn't tell them was that Andy could only pitch one more inning, and none of our other regular hurlers could pitch at all. We'd have to win immediately or face almost certain defeat. So I'd have to ask the Aliens to perform another miracle tomorrow: One inning, sudden death, for a clear shot at the championship.

"Okay, see you at ten tomorrow morning," a wild-eyed Badger said after I trotted over to his bench, no doubt with a shit-eating grin on my face.

"How's that?" I replied.

"You know, the home team gets to decide," he answered authoritatively. Of course, he was the home team.

"Oh, come off it, Eddie, you can steamroll others but not me!" I replied, laughing. "The league says we have to mutually agree. I'll call you later."

As I stuffed various bats, balls, and gloves back into our equipment bag, Andy celebrated with a Sno-cone the color of nothing previously observed on this planet. Fit for an Alien.

After a few phone calls to and from the league office, the conclusion of our epic duel with the Tigers was set for 5:30 the next afternoon. As it turned out, intentional walks were indeed legal in Little League. True, you have to actually *throw* the four pitches— but Wanamaker had ruled that unworthy of sustaining a protest.

The following morning I felt like I was in suspended animation, beyond rumination. We'd send the guys out there and hope for the best, like when we played sudden death against the Pirates. Surely no team around here had ever played two suspended, tie games three days apart. It was *déjà vu* all over again, but we were getting used to it.

Then, around midday, I realized that I should be panicking. Andy would pick up where he left off and face the Tigers in the first (and perhaps last) extra inning. Normally, I wouldn't pitch him two days in a row, and in fact league rules prohibited it— except in the case of suspended games. He'd only pitched two innings the night before, and I figured it was safe to throw him one more today. But that meant he'd max out at six innings for the week, so that was it for him.

Then who would I bring in? Couldn't summon Matt or Steve because they'd already appeared in the game. That left Ian, who had pitched once all year; Big Joe, who hadn't pitched at all and had just gotten a two-inch sliver removed from his leg; and Robby, who also had never pitched. Well, we'd just have to win in one frame, and if not, I'd go with my "experienced" right-hander— Ian.

About 3 P.M., I got a call from Ian's mother. Due to some kind of child care problem he wouldn't be able to make it to the game at all. Great.

"Andy," I said, "we've got to get a run and then you'll just have to shut them out in the bottom of the inning."

"No prob, Dad. We'll rock that joint." Then he went back to listening to Chumbawumba on his tape player. I hoped the lyrics from their anthem, "Tubthumping," rang true today: *I get knocked down/but I get up again/nobody gonna keep me down.*

Then Andy confessed that the previous evening he was so sure Rocco would smack a game-winning hit in the final frame that he actually thought about hitting him with the first pitch.

"No way!" I exclaimed.

"Way."

"You're kidding."

"Not hard, you know just brush him with a change-up. That would have put him on first without doing any damage. Just like the intentional walk, right?"

"It might have worked," I responded, shaking my head, "but you should never try to hit anyone, even gently. But I guess it's true what they say."

"What's that?"

"Great minds think alike. At least when they're desperate."

When we got down to Memorial at five o'clock we found the Tigers sweating out on the field, as usual. Matt rushed up, having left his own fifth-grade graduation party to make the game. "My brother thinks we're nuts," his mother reported. Enrique said he was bone tired, but would still catch. Big Joe arrived, but he was not in his uniform, and he was limping. He'd played in some kind of Big Brother softball game that afternoon and pulled a groin muscle and couldn't play. Scratch another relief pitcher. Well, I knew that Robby was at least a good *hitting* pitcher.

We expected to face Rocco for one frame, which would also bring him to the six-inning limit for the week. But his team had a couple of other decent relievers to draw on. Imagine our surprise when the Tigers took the field—and Rocco trotted out to first base! Another kid took the mound, to our relief. "Great!" Stevie shouted, happy he wouldn't have to face the Rock.

"Wow, wonder what's up?" I said to Richards.

"Maybe he's still pissed off because of the intentional walk."

"Possibly," I replied. "Or maybe his father told Eddie he pitched so long last night he didn't want to risk hurting his arm today."

In any case, the substitute hurler clearly was not ready for prime time. He flung several of his warm-up pitches to the screen, and Little Stevie decided to wait him out for a walk. And indeed he did take the first pitch—òn his leg—and dashed down to first. Then Amos walked on four pitches. That brought up RBI Keiser, but could he deliver yet again?

The first pitch to Robby sailed back to the screen, and the runners moved up. Coaching at third, I told Stevie to be careful—there were no outs, so he should play it conservative for now. Robby was a good contact hitter so he'd likely get him home somehow. Getting tossed out at the plate on another wild pitch would be a disaster.

Naturally, when the first pitch got away from the catcher, Steve headed for home. The ball plunked off the screen, back toward the catcher. I screamed at Steve to stop. He then had two reasonable options—keep going (he had a fair chance of making it) or retreat to third (better safe than sorry). Instead he did the worst thing possible. He paused. Then he continued home. Perhaps he recalled that his parents had told him to get the game over in a hurry because they had dinner plans.

The throw from catcher to pitcher had him beat as he slid, and the ump screamed, "OUT." Steve popped up and started walking back to the bench with his head down. I took off my hat and was getting ready to slam it against my thigh, when I saw Stevie waving his arms excitedly. What the hell was he doing, I wondered, brushing the dust off his uniform? Then I saw the ball on the ground, and the ump signaling *safe*.

For the second time in two nights, a sure out at home had turned into a run. What was going on here? Forget about angels in the outfield. They seemed to be hovering around home plate, kicking balls out of gloves for us.

Pandemonium on the bench. Eddie out of the opposing dugout to argue. Us up 10–9. Jon Albert whispering in my ear, "Thank

God." Another wild pitch a moment later and we were up 11−9. Now, could Andy hold them?

He looked strong in his warm-ups. Of course, pitching with a two-run lead didn't hurt. I looked for my wife behind the screen and, as usual, with Andy on the mound, she alternated between clenching her fists, clutching the arm of the mother next to her, and closing her eyes as if in prayer.

Jeff Tangredi, a pretty decent hitter, led off. Andy got a quick strike and then Jeff fouled one back, high, toward the screen. Strike two, although Enrique gave it chase. Enrique hadn't caught a foul pop all year. I'm not sure he even saw one all season. Our pitchers tended to strike out or walk everyone, with little in between. But there he was, flipping off his mask and giving it a good effort, perhaps for the novelty of it, or figuring he might as well get some running in.

Then, either a gust of wind came up, or I'd misjudged it from the beginning, but gosh, it now looked like the ball might come down in front of the screen.

"Catch that—in the air!" Big Enrique ordered his son.

Suddenly, Enrique stopped just in front of the screen, stuck out his glove—and the ball landed in it! Like he'd done it a hundred times before. I turned around and saw Big Enrique smiling from ear to ear, his right fist high in the air, in a victory salute, and Jon Albert pounding him on the back. That image was worth every hour I'd spent on every ball field all year.

As he reached over to pick up his mask, Enrique wore a big smile himself. I felt so good for him, after an in-and-out year. Now he was Mr. Clutch. He'd remember this the rest of his life. So would I. But this was what Enrique, behind the mask again, told himself: "Lucky!"

Now there was no way we could lose. Andy struck out the next batter without much fuss. Then he faced his friend Owen, a lefty hitter who often made contact. Feeling no mercy, Andy got two strikes on him, and then his friend hit the ball and it looked like it was headed on the ground into center. But it died in the high grass. Andy picked it up barehanded, paused a moment, and then flipped it to first. Stevie was so excited he started doing a victory dance before the ball reached him, but remembered to catch the ball, and hold on, and then everyone was boogeying.

When he got to the bench, Steve rushed over to hand the ball to his dad. "I want the game ball for *this* game," Steve announced. Well, it should be divided twelve ways, I figured, but possession is nine-tenths of the law (especially when it comes to baseballs), and I'd never felt sentimental about game balls—just the games themselves.

Enrique went over to shake hands with Jeff Tangredi, one of his best friends, the kid who had hit that foul pop back to the screen. "Why'd you catch it?" Jeff asked good-naturedly. "I just stuck out my glove!" Enrique replied modestly. "Was hoping it would go over the screen!"

After a year of threats and disputes, blowouts and near misses, we'd finally beaten the Tigers. And at the best possible moment. Now they were on the brink of elimination while we needed just one more win to take home the crown.

"You're in the driver's seat now!" Steve Wanamaker told us. He'd come by to watch the deciding frame and, already scouting for the majors next year, wanted to know who our catcher was. I told him, tough luck, Enrique was already twelve and ineligible for future play in this age group. Wanamaker also had his eye on Andy for next year and asked to meet him. I was glad he had a chance to see him pitch a fine inning and make a nice play to end it.

When his mother came around, Kipp told her he'd had the most fun ever this season. "See, you didn't miss anything not being in the majors this year," she replied.

The Aliens lingered around the bench. I'd never seen a happier bunch in my life. They'd been waiting all year for this moment, and I felt ashamed that I'd ever doubted they could top the Tigers. "I didn't want to pitch anyway," Robby confessed. That got a good laugh from everyone. A nervous one from me. The playoffs weren't over yet.

18

S uddenly, we were the talk of the town, or at least pock-
ets of it. The Aliens had overachieved all year and now
we were "peaking at the right time," according to our
admirers. Rivals accused us of merely getting lucky, or
playing over our heads (which was possibly true), or complained
that we had God, fate, or most significantly, the umpires on our
side. We didn't care what anyone said. Back in February, at our
first team meeting, with snow still heaped along the Hudson, I had
declared, with evident sincerity, that I'd be delighted if we could
win half our games and not embarrass ourselves in the playoffs.
Now we were one victory away from taking home all the marbles.

The only question was, who would we play next? The Pirates
had fought off the Rockies and Yankees to earn a shot at the Tigers
and a chance to battle us for the championship. We expected the
Tigers to win, but Danny Stroud was ready for them, and they
might be dispirited after their shocking loss to the Aliens. To beat
Stroud the Tigers would probably have to start Rocco—meaning
he might not be available to face us if they did win.

One major obstacle stood in our path: RBI Keiser had just
played his last game as an Alien. He was about to fly off to his
grandparents in Michigan, where he would ride a horse, a big
Belgian, in a Fourth of July parade—or something like that. Who
knew he could even ride a horse? He felt sick about it, and I kept
hoping the once-in-a-lifetime opportunity to walk off a baseball

diamond as a champion would force a change in plans, but it didn't appear likely. And then Robby was gone. The next day I learned that Ian was leaving for vacation, too. So there went our only "experienced" pitcher past our Big Three.

I had my own travel worries. B.B. had generously rescheduled our departure for Ohio, taking the nonrefundable penalty, and it was now set for Wednesday (July 1). This had seemed like a safe date, beyond the end of the playoffs, but now it threatened to wreak havoc on our season, and perhaps even our marriage. The Tigers were scheduled to play the Pirates on Sunday, then we'd play the winner on Monday. If we won, it was all over. If we lost that game, we'd get another shot to end it on Tuesday, celebrate that night, and fly off happily to Ohio the next morning. But one more rain-out could threaten that scenario.

Naturally, it rained over the weekend, and the Tigers-Pirates battle was pushed back to Monday. Now we'd *have* to win that game Tuesday or risk playing Wednesday without manager and son (unless we canceled our vacation outright).

Monday, thankfully, bloomed sunny and pleasant, and I really looked forward to the Tigers-Pirates elimination contest, even though it meant passing up a Lucinda Williams concert in New York. (She would come around again, but a season like this, never.) What a pleasure to attend a meaningful game and not worry about setting the lineup, changing pitchers, and worrying about how your own kid was doing—and what parents think about all this.

Commuting to New York on the train that day, Jon Albert ran into the father of one of the Tigers. "See you in the championship game," the man said. John thought to himself, *Don't count on it, buddy, the Pirates are tough now.*

Andy and I drove down to Memorial Park, bantering happily in the car—a far cry from our usual tense exchanges on Alien game nights. Andy wore his A's cap, for obvious reasons. We parked in the lot by the river a little late for the start of the game. It was nice not having to off-load several pounds of equipment and an Alien mask. Instead, I just grabbed a water bottle, and we set off for the Pirates' side of the field. It was more shady over there, anyway, and I saw Richards and Kipp, and Donna and Steve Albert, standing along the fence and waving to me.

"Hey, guys," I said, "what's the score?"

"Not so fast," Richards said. "Take a look."

I turned around and noticed that the game apparently hadn't even started. Badger was standing at home plate hitting grounders to his infield, and there was no one on the mound getting ready to pitch to the Pirates. Damn Eddie, I thought, he'd hogged the field all year, but this was too much!

"Might be a forfeit," Stephen announced. "Eddie only has eight players."

"What?" I exclaimed.

"He's got eight guys and they're giving him five more minutes to field a team," Richards added. Somehow this was fitting. Eddie had left a roster spot open all year, and now it had come back to haunt him. And we'd rather face the Pirates, even with Danny Stroud pitching, than the Tigers.

Another five minutes passed, and Eddie marched his team off the field. John Miller went over to confer with the ump and then came back to his bench, and told the kids, "Okay, we'll play it tomorrow night."

"Whoa!" I exhaled. "John, take the forfeit, you know they deserve it."

"I know, I know, but it's for the kids, they should play."

"But it sets the next game back, and the playoffs should already be over."

"I know, but what the hell."

This was the worst possible scenario. Now we couldn't play

until Wednesday at the earliest—with our top hitter gone, and ace pitcher and manager slated to leave town. When I got home, I had to march upstairs and plead for mercy from my wife. Because she knew this was Eddie's fault, not mine—and that Andy's grandfather in Ohio would not want him to miss the finish—B.B. agreed to put off the trip indefinitely. Baseball might be like watching paint dry, but even Barbara wanted to see how this canvas turned out.

The next day, after some soul-searching, Andy decided to accept the invitation to join a majors' all-star team, to be managed by Marty Schupak.

"It's okay that I won't be there to coach?" I asked.

"I have a feeling you'll be around. I want to pitch, but what's the worst thing Mr. Schupak can do to me? Put me in right field or on the bench?"

"And if he does that?"

"I'll still be an all-star." Maybe he was ready to leave the nest after all.

That night, we repeated our visit to Memorial for the Tigers-Pirates game, arriving in the third inning. The Pirates were up 2–1, with Danny Stroud pitching well and knocking in the go-ahead run with a single. Again, we stood by the Pirates bench and the players seemed happy to see Andy, whom they recognized as a friendly rival. Unfortunately, we seemed to bring the Tigers luck, as they quickly regained the lead, 3–2, though Stroud managed to strike out Rocco with ducks on the pond.

When the Pirates batted in the fourth, I noticed that Rocco was not pitching. "When did you knock Rocco out?" I asked John Miller.

"Didn't," he answered, chuckling. "Hasn't pitched. Guess they're saving him for you—taking us lightly. But guess what: They won't be playing tomorrow, we're beating them tonight." I appreciated Eddie's apparent respect for us, but was amazed he was so certain he could crush the Pirates, especially since they'd beaten him last time they played with the same pitcher on the mound.

With Rocco watching from first base, the Pirates knotted the score in the fourth, then took the lead in the fifth. Finally, Eddie brought Rocco in to pitch, but he'd waited too long to play his ace. And even if the Tigers rallied and won, he wouldn't be able to use him against us the following night.

But it was academic now. The Pirates scored a couple more runs and Stroud set the Tigers down in order in the fifth. By now, rain threatened and it was getting dark, and when it started pouring, the umpires called the game, denying the Tigers their last ups and a chance to rally. A tough break for Eddie, but he only argued half-heartedly, already whipped.

Later that evening I learned that we'd face the Pirates at Liberty Field. We'd been playing so well at Memorial, our "home" field, I'd hoped to finish the season there. It's often said that every player has one ballpark where he feels uncomfortable. Unfortunately, for Andy, that ballpark was Liberty. But, hey, we'd take it. Give us Liberty or give us death! Everything pointed to a championship. A week ago we'd scheduled a team party for Wednesday night, figuring the playoffs would be long gone. John Marley's family would host it. Now, as it turned out, it could be a postgame victory party. Perfect.

This only added to the pressure, however. The problem was: Andy had to pitch a complete game, so I could use Steve and Matt the next night, if need be. If one of them appeared in game one, and we lost, then the other would have to hurl a complete game tomorrow, or I'd have to bring on someone who'd never pitched before. So Andy had to throw six innings—win or lose—and he'd never pitched more than four in a game all year.

Despite the tension, I remained fairly calm during the day. The noontime mail brought a note from Robby out in Michigan to his teammates in Nyack. It read:

Dear The Aliens—I'm sorry I couldn't be at the championship. I'm just typing this to wish you guys luck. If you don't win, I will have to hurt all of you! So, play your best and win that championship. GO ALIENS.
                                                        —R.B.I. Keiser

With Robby providing my pre-game pep talk, I felt even more confident about the outcome. I did make one lineup change, after Kipp informed me that he felt uncomfortable leading off. This made me laugh, as he had led off all year and batted about .500. But it was true, he often opened the game by swinging wildly at the first pitch, or even the first three pitches. You couldn't get him out after that. So, on a whim, I decided to bat Stephen leadoff and drop Kipp to second.

I toyed with starting Amos at catcher. I knew the Pirates would be running the bases and bunting like crazy, but I couldn't forget Enrique's game-saving catch against the Tigers and I really thought he deserved to be in there. Also, he was more vocal than Amos, and Andy liked it when he shouted out something like, "Top of the order, throw faster!" So he'd catch and Amos would play third. Taddy, meanwhile, would play second with Robby away, his first start there all year, but he'd been playing well, and I knew he'd give us a good effort. He was small but no smaller than most of the Pirates.

For early July, it was a pleasant, cool evening, a good break for us. The sun threw shadows halfway across the outfield at Liberty Field. No way Andy pitches a complete game on a hot night. Jim Marley informed me that the Question Man might act a little sleepy out there. Excited, he'd barely slept the night before and told his parents he felt like he was in a movie. I'd hate to guess what movie that was. *Quiz Show?*

B.B. arrived at the game a little earlier than usual. A lot of other parents were already there, sitting in the bleachers behind our dugout in back of first. Everyone was in the mood to celebrate, but B.B. was tense, as usual. Vicky Scimeca confessed she was glad Matt wasn't starting on the mound. "I'm glad *you* have to go through this tonight," she told my wife, "*you* can probably handle it!" Barbara wasn't so sure of that.

The Aliens' confidence seemed a bit off, too, which perhaps was a good thing, considering that cockiness might have undone the Tigers. A couple of kids moaned that Robby was missing. I was worried myself. It was at Liberty a few weeks ago that Andy had lost his composure on the mound after a few bad calls, and it would be devastating if it happened again. Just before the game, I called the team to the dugout, read RBI Keiser's inspirational message ("win or I'll hurt you"), and delivered what I hoped would be my final speech of the season.

"Look, guys, you've given me, your parents, and yourselves everything I've asked for all year," I said quietly. "Now you have to do it one more time. Get three or four runs the first couple innings and there's no way they can stop us. Now give the Alien a rub—hell, give him a big kiss—and let's go!"

Soon after they took the field I sensed something was wrong. In his warm-ups, Andy threw strikes but didn't seem to have a lot on the ball, which was strange, since he hadn't pitched in five days. Maybe I'd overpitched him last week?

He fanned the leadoff hitter anyway, but the next batter singled, and then Matt bobbled a routine grounder to short. That brought up their cleanup hitter. He, too, hit a grounder to shortstop, but Matt wouldn't settle for just a force at second base. He fielded the ball, leaned forward to tag the runner, then tossed to

Taddy alertly covering second—and Tad caught it and held on. A double play to end the threat! The gust as I exhaled almost blew Cool Taddy Bell out to center field.

Now we were surely on our way, and the flip-flop at the top of our order immediately paid dividends, as Stevie and Kipp both singled. Amos struck out, but Matt singled in a run and we broke on top.

The next frame opened with a grounder to Taddy, who made a good play tossing the Pirate out at first. The next batter did the same thing, except this time Taddy slipped on the grass and couldn't make a throw. Tad enjoyed the play so much, he re-enacted it between batters, running in and deliberately slipping and landing on his butt. Ten-year-olds!

John Miller, coaching at third, flashed a signal, and the batter laid down a nice bunt up the first base line. Enrique, who knew the Pirates liked to bunt, jumped out, grabbed it, and made a strong throw to first—where Little Stevie Wonder stretched to haul it in while keeping his toes on the bag. The next batter grounded out, ending the inning, but Andy seemed very hit-table—he'd struck out only one so far. Matt came over between innings and said, "Something's wrong with Andy. Guys who can't hit are hitting."

"I couldn't have said it better, big guy. Now, what are we going to do about it?"

"Score some runs?"

"Once again, you took the words right out of my mouth." I'd decided to not tinker with Andy's delivery since we were winning and he was throwing strikes.

It looked like it might not matter, when we exploded for three runs in our half of the inning. Taddy faked a bunt, walked, and immediately stole second. Little John cracked a hard single to right, scoring our second run. Steve beat out an infield hit, Kipp struck out, but then Amos blooped a ball to short right. It fell in and Steve beat the throw home and we were up 4–zip. I hugged Little John as he came back to the bench and our guys started high-fiving, sensing that we were now unstoppable. Kipp, in perhaps his final Little League game, was jumping around like a grasshopper.

In the third, Andy recorded a couple of K's, but everyone was at least hitting hard fouls off him. Enrique threw out another batter trying to bunt, looking more and more like that other Pudge—Rodriguez. I'd finally identified the flaw in Andy's delivery: He was "short-arming," not bringing the ball far behind him before delivering, thus reducing his velocity. But his control was impeccable, so he was getting away with it against the less-than-imposing Pirates.

Then things really got fun. Andy led off with a single, and various walks and hits plated four more runs. We were up 8–0, and I was thinking we might end it in four innings under the ten-run rule. But, with the Aliens, it would not, could not, end that easily.

Danny Mitchell led off the fourth for the Pirates with a single. Andy struck out the next batter but then Danny Stroud scorched a triple to right center. That made it 8–1 but Andy was tiring. Then the ump was waving his arms, John Miller was arguing, Danny Stroud was walking off the field—and out number two was going up on the scoreboard. It seems that Stroud had thrown his bat while hitting the triple, something he'd been warned about earlier. So the ump, Larry Hahn, called him out. (He was the league's umpire-in-chief.) What a break.

Which looked even bigger when Andy gave up two more hits and it was 8–2 before he restored order. Still, no sweat, if Andy settled down.

As the next frame began, we saw Larry Hahn approaching the Pirates' spectator section and yelling angrily. And someone was screaming back. It was an African-American man, and given the state of affairs in the league, it was rather easy to guess that it had to be one of the Pirates' fathers. We couldn't imagine what he was yelling about. His son wasn't even in the game at the time and hadn't been called out on strikes or involved in a controversial play, but his father was yelling about "race" this and "racist" that.

Larry Hahn clearly didn't take kindly to that and he walked over to John Miller and offered a few heated words. Then John stepped in front of the bleachers and said that if the outburst continued the Pirates would likely forfeit, which would be a shame, so please quiet down and "let the kids play . . . we're here for the kids, remember?" That ended it, and I finally approached the ump to ask what the hell was going on. The father, he said, had accused him of making calls against the Pirates (notably, the thrown bat incident) because they had a black player and we did not. Someone had finally played the race card—in perhaps the final game of the year.

Okay. Play ball.

We could still invoke the ten-run rule if we tallied four times, but the Pirates brought in a new hurler, and we did nothing. Then they took another shot at Andy. He had entered uncharted territory, never having pitched into the fifth inning, ever. But our whole team seemed to sag. Someone misplayed a pop-up. Someone else botched a grounder. Andy gave up a single and finally walked a batter. Suddenly it was 8–4, two on and two out. I walked out toward the mound and called Andy over. He gave me a brutal look—thinking I was about to lift him. In fact, I was thinking of doing just that, depending on what he told me.

"DON'T take me out. I'm fine. Two errors."

"And a hit and a walk. How do you feel?"

"*Fine.* Not tired at all."

"Okay then, listen, the next batter could hit a home run and we'd still be up, 8–7. So relax." Of course, *then* I'd probably take him out, but I didn't say that.

"I'm already relaxed. You relax. Don't worry about it, I'm fine." Okay, I thought as I headed to the bench, if he gets hammered, there's always tomorrow. Oh ye of little faith. Andy fanned the next batter, making a fist as he trotted off, just like Dennis Eckersley. One inning to go.

We did nothing in our half of the inning, barely giving Andy a rest before he had to come out for the final frame. I asked him how he felt, and again he said, "Fine." Later I learned that he told Matt, between innings, that he was tired and should come out, but "I started the game and I should finish it." (A macho little Roger Clemens.) Or, more likely, he simply wanted to be in the middle of the diamond for the victory celebration, and who could blame him?

So this was it, and the infield was suddenly alive with chatter. All of them, even the Aliens in the outfield, nervously swung their arms or rocked back and forth—sensing the likely ending and wanting to fast-forward to it and not have to endure the next three outs.

His velocity back—fueled by adrenaline, no doubt—Andy struck out the first batter, then yielded a weak single. Two more base runners and the tying run would come to the plate. But Andy struck out the next batter and now he was one out away.

That brought up Sammy Speer—not Jackie Gleason's bandleader, but pretty good with the stick. After a called strike, Andy turned around, and Matt at shortstop grinned and shouted something. But Andy was all business out there. He tugged his soiled A's cap down over his eyes and threw again. Ball. Then another ball and a swinging strike. Two and two.

Now the chatter was almost deafening—on the field, among the coaches, and in the parents' section. And everyone saying the same thing: "Come on, Andy, you . . . can . . . do . . . it." Nine months of play, and work, for this.

Down at first, Stevie wasn't thinking of a trophy. "C'mon, Andy, get this guy," he shouted, "I want to go party at the Marleys'!" Out in right field, John Marley windmilled his arms and began feeling sorry for the Pirates, who now slumped in the dugout, nearly defeated.

Andy rocked and dealt and the pitch sailed a little high. But with two strikes on him, Sammy Speer could not lay off, and tried to make contact, but failed, utterly. And then, just like in the big leagues, the pitcher, my son, raised his arms over his head, the catcher ran out to hug him, the right fielder threw his cap in the air, and the other fielders and coaches converged on the center of the diamond.

It was like the end of any World Series in New York, except there were no mounted policemen patrolling the field, and no drunken fans rushing out to pull up some sod or take home a chunk of the outfield wall.

Over in the bleachers the parents stood and applauded and cheered, shook hands, embraced, acted almost like . . . kids. They didn't throw anything in the air, however.

I clipped Richards on the shoulder, and gave him a hug—one of the few times I've ever embraced an adult male beyond my imme-diate family and closest friends. I learned that Richards somehow can hug while holding on to a scorebook and pencil. From an empty-handed B.B. I got a kiss. She was positively glowing with pride, and relief.

Then the kids started bashing each other happily with their caps and gloves (if they still had them). Thank goodness the bats were still in the dugout.

"Victory lap! Victory lap!" Enrique shouted. This had become quite the thing ever since Cal Ripken ran around the outfield after shattering Lou Gehrig's games-played streak. The Aliens dashed off for their victory lap, but Enrique didn't bother to shed his catching equipment, so he clunked around the outfield like a Robo Cop. Jeremy had the presence of mind to grab the Alien head and carry it with him, knowing that our mascot, who had contributed so much, and endured such physical abuse without complaint, deserved some of the glory, too.

Fortunately no one asked me to join in. I was still mentally exhausted from six innings with Andy on the mound, and pleased to accept a few words of appreciation from the parents, who were now spilling onto the field next to the dugout, murmuring happily. Who said a "Nyack team" couldn't win it all?

I hadn't managed a single private moment with Andy yet. It would have meant a lot to me—I'd never won anything like this before, neither had he, and we certainly had never won anything together. But it was even more enjoyable watching him surrounded by joyous teammates, acting like, and apparently being treated like, he was just one of the gang. Perhaps that was his, and my, greatest achievement of the season.

When the kids completed their second lap, they joined our throng along the first base line, but they just wanted to get the heck out of there and party—there was a rumor that the Marleys had a trampoline in their backyard. But a couple of the parents made them line up or crouch for photos. John Marley would not stop running around the bases until his mother, Betsy, threatened to tackle him. Good break for me; maybe he'd be too tired to ask any more questions. Ever.

One of the kids called a time-out to retrieve the Alien and get him in the photo. At first no one said anything about including the manager. Perhaps, as the saying goes, he was liked, but not well-liked? But then Enrique yelled out, "C'mon, coach, get in here," and the picture was complete.

I don't remember much about the party. I know the Marleys were real troupers, as they had guests from overseas arriving later that evening and Jim had to rush to the airport to pick them up. Mainly what I recall are kids bobbing up and down on that trampoline after playing six tough innings—especially Taddy, who not only could run faster but jump higher than anyone. It was a particularly big night for him and his parents. His brother's team had won the title in the majors, but that was expected. Now the Bells had book-ends, partly due to Tad's fine effort in his first start at second base—emerging from his brother's shadow at last.

It was great to see the kids having a ball, everyone joining in equally, with no bench, no substitutions, or anyone (coach, parent, or player) concerned about "playing time." They were all playing now.

Someone tossed them the Alien head and the kids on the trampoline batted it like a beach ball trying to keep it in the air. I shouted that he might fly right up to the stars twinkling overhead, returning home. But now that the Alien had seen Manhattan, and played a crucial role with a championship team, that seemed unlikely.

While the kids celebrated and released months of tension, we parents sat at outdoor tables chatting quietly, a bit drained, excited, but happy it was finally over. Vicky Scimeca seemed particularly relieved. "There's no need for Matt to pitch tomorrow!" she observed, smiling broadly. "Now I can look forward to a few free evenings without a knot in my stomach."

After about an hour of this, we finally got the kids off the trampoline and the Marleys presented me with a few gifts from the players, including a green and gold A's shirt professionally relabeled "the Aliens." I managed some kind of acceptance speech, thanking coaches and parents and especially players, but I'm afraid I didn't rise to the occasion with profundity or eloquence. Quiet satisfaction would have to suffice, and it did. All I could add was to quote Yogi Berra, our Will Rogers, when he said, after receiving some prestigious honor, "Thank you for making this day necessary."

"Good job, Dad," Andy said, giving me a big hug. I wasn't sure exactly what he meant. Was he referring to managing the team, coaching him, or just the speech? Or all three?

"You too, Andy." I wasn't sure what I meant either, but it was heartfelt, and abounding.

Mark Twain once said that every boy deserves one great summer. Andy had already had one, and he still had several summers of boyhood remaining.

As we drove home after the party, Andy and I sat in the front seat of our Honda oddly quiet, jazzed out or self-satisfied—or both. We usually fought over the radio, but this time I let him punch in a Sugar Ray tune. Was that the name of the group, or the name of the lead singer? I'm not sure even Andy knew. Crazy rock 'n' roll band names—at least back in the days of Sam the Sham & the Pharaohs you knew who the front man was. Anyway, this reminded me of something.

"Well, Andy, after tonight, there's one thing for certain."

"What's that, Dad?" he said, turning down the music, for a change.

"We . . . Don't . . . Suck," I declared. He laughed, giggled really, but barely missed a beat before responding.

"And no one can say—'Yes, you do!'"